ANNA & MICHAEL OLSON
COOK AT HOME

ANNA & MICHAEL OLSON
COOK AT HOME

recipes for every day and every occasion

whitecap

Visit our website at www.whitecap.ca

Edited by Alison Maclean
Copy-edited by Ben D'Andrea
Proofread by Lesley Cameron
Cover and interior design by MURPHYWOODS
Photography by Michael Mahovlich

Printed and bound in Canada by Friesens

LIBRARY AND ARCHIVES CANADA CATALOGUING IN PUBLICATION
Olson, Anna, 1968–
    Anna and Michael Olson cook at home: recipes for every day and every occasion.

Includes index.
ISBN 1-55285-702-6

    1. Cookery. I. Olson, Michael, 1964– II. Title.

TX714.O48 2005   641.5   C2005-903043-7

The publisher acknowledges the financial support of the Government of Canada through the Book Publishing Industry Development Program for our publishing activities.

CONTENTS

INTRODUCTION

We fell in love in the kitchen.

HOW WE MET

ANNA Our first encounter almost didn't happen. I was on my way to a line cook's job in a busy restaurant in the heart of the French Quarter of New Orleans, but was taking a quick visit with my folks before I left. On a trip back from Niagara Falls, New York, to visit my aunt, my mom and I stopped at Inn on the Twenty for lunch. I had scheduled a casual meeting with Michael, just to get the inside scoop on the Toronto and area restaurant scene. A while earlier I had applied for a job at this winery restaurant, and Michael had been courteous enough to respond in writing that he had no opportunities at that time, but to keep in touch.

My mom and I enjoyed a leisurely lunch and waited for a bit for Michael to appear. About 15 minutes after our scheduled appointment, we decided to leave and sauntered off to the parking lot. Behind us came a gentle voice, "Anna? Are you Anna?" My mom swears a shiver went down her spine as I turned and answered, "Yes, it's me."

But the happily ever after didn't really start there. I went off to New Orleans and it wasn't until months later that synchronicity came into play. The very day I had decided that I'd had enough of New Orleans, Michael called with a job offer I couldn't refuse. A week later I was working in Jordan, Ontario, and then the rest became history.

MICHAEL I clearly remember the first time I met Anna. She had applied to work in the kitchen of Inn on the Twenty, where I was chef, and I had suggested that she drive to Niagara for a visit and casual interview. It turned out that the only day she was available was my only day off so I agreed to meet her at the restaurant at 2 pm. I thought this would give her an opportunity to drive around the area to check out housing, the local villages and so on. I got to the restaurant just at 2 pm and held the door open for two ladies who were exiting and smiled. It dawned on me that the younger lady might be the one I was to meet so I called after them.

As it turned out, Anna and I had a great discussion on her training and expectations of the business. I thought it would be great to add to the "fabric" of the kitchen team someone who had recently lived and worked in the U.S. — she could bring new ideas and techniques, but I had no positions available at the time. It wasn't until months later when a spot did become available that I thought of Anna and called her.

We fell in love in a noisy kitchen with salt on our fingertips and white uniforms on our backs, and as our personal relationship grew, so did our professional one.

Our differing stories about how we first met bring to our attention how we all have varied perspectives. The recipes in this book are shared collaborations, yet we each have our own opinions, thoughts and tips about why a recipe is special for each of us.

THE KITCHEN DANCE

ANNA When cooks work "on the line," it is an adrenalin-charged, fast-paced environment, yet there is a sense of grace within the clatter of pans and sizzle of ingredients. As cooks, we learn each other's movements and patterns — one cook knows to lift their arm higher as they reach for the salt while another leans below to open the oven to check on a roasting lamb rack. In the midst of the chaos, this dance yields beautiful plates of food that glide out to the dining room on the fingertips of servers.

At home, Michael and I share the same dance. When we plan a dinner, whether for a crowd or just ourselves, we implicitly know who will prepare each dish or part. Michael is always in charge of meats, roasting, grilling and braising. I've always been the "starch girl" — my Eastern European heritage at play, I suppose. I love making salads, while Michael can whip up a soup in no time. The stereo sings and a bottle of wine is poured into tumblers as we move about the kitchen — it's fun!

We appreciate that not every household has two cooks in its kitchen, but the dance can still be beautiful. Whether it's with a couple, a parent and child, or even better, with a grandparent and child, the dance is joyous and memorable, even if it's just at the dish sink at the end of a meal, catching up on the day's event or the conversations shared over an evening of entertaining.

MICHAEL Professional cooking involves learned skill, motivation and the ability to get a lot accomplished working as a team. You spend a great deal of energy getting the food initially prepared and the "service" is the crunch time where each dish is cooked to order as quickly as possible. In order to coordinate a number of dishes to be completed at exactly the same time there are verbal cues and a sort of "dance" that cooks have, developed through working together and anticipating each other's movements. A kitchen staff that knows and respects each other moves through a meal service fluidly.

Anna and I can work together on a meal easily because we know each other's strengths and tendencies. We don't typically cook at home at breakneck speed like restaurant service, but I have to admit that we can throw together a dinner party for 8 or 10 people in less time than it takes for a pizza to be delivered. We cook together as a way of communicating — we talk, laugh, joke around and play music while we cook. Someone always takes the lead in the kitchen and there are many occasions where one of us will look after the other as a simple show of affection.

We take pleasure in sharing the formulas and patterns that we've learned as professional cooks and that make the kitchen dance effortless.

COOKING AT HOME

ANNA We don't eat restaurant-style food at home. Yes, the lobster or foie gras may make an appearance on special occasions, but a Monday night supper in our house is made up of the same ingredients you have in your fridge and pantry. However, we do eat well — both nutritiously and tastily. Generally we start with a salad or soup followed by a nice entrée and maybe a piece of cheese or a little something sweet later in the evening. We tend to eat late, usually around 8 pm, just because we like to wrap up our evening chores before we sit down to eat. To us, time spent in the kitchen cooking and eating represents our "down time." It's funny how, even when we spend all day in the kitchen at work, cooking at home feels completely different and, in fact, it's quite grounding. We're refueling, both physically and mentally.

MICHAEL Home is so much more than a house or an apartment — it's the refuge that we develop which offers comfort (mental and physical), safety and nourishment. Just consider how many of both our childhood and adult happy memories are centered around a meal.

Anna and I generally prepare simple meals that reflect the season at hand. We like to eat what the local farmers' markets offer in warm weather and dare to dream in the winter months.

While cooking at home is like good design, part function and part fashion, the memories that stem from your concoctions are truly original — there are no imitations.

MOTIVATIONS

ANNA So many things inspire us to cook the way we do at home, and this is why we have created menus around the topics that motivate our choices. These themes are also very fluid and dynamic. We hope you will feel free to mix and match recipes within our topics and play with your favorite flavors, or introduce yourself to new ones.

Our goal is for you to create meals that allow you to recharge, learn and celebrate all that is so wonderful about cooking at home.

MICHAEL Every meal is justified by the activities around it. Sometimes we are in such a rush that we can't find the time or energy to cook and on other occasions we like to make a big effort and revel in the celebration!

We hope our themes will inspire you to cook for those around you. We continue to be influenced by travel, holidays, special events and even new kitchen gadgets! Get in the kitchen and make something delicious. Don't just eat to live — live to eat!

We hope every moment you spend in the kitchen is a delicious one!

PEOPLE

>We hesitate to hum along with Barbra Streisand: "People … people who need people … are the luckiest people …" (Now that song will be stuck in your head all day.) But it's so true! How we prepare our meals depends on the people in our lives. FAMILY suppers are occasions to regroup before we return to our individual schedules. Meals shared with FRIENDS give us a chance to open our doors to those whose support we value. NEW GUESTS will also have a place at our table — invited by us or others. Our hope is to make them feel welcome and comfortable. While socializing is a big part of our lives, COCOONING meals — that is, time spent alone — provide ample time to recharge our batteries. And certainly not least, although youngest, on this list, are KIDS, who need special care and attention.
>We've worked hard to create menus that are balanced in taste, texture and nutrition. Bear in mind that we aim to have you enjoy the cooking process as much as the final product.

FAMILY

>It may seem redundant to devote a whole cookbook section to those you cook for every day, but isn't family the most important category of all? Our menus and topics assume that your family will be there — big gatherings, holidays and even quiet evenings.
>Whenever possible, cooking for family — between skating lessons, late meetings and TV time — should mean an opportunity to sit at the table together, talk and enjoy one another's company. Our menus are designed to give you ample time to cook together and, more importantly, to leave you with enough time to dine together.

SUNDAY SUPPER

This is our favorite meal of the week. Whether we've worked all weekend (as people in our line of work tend to do) or have enjoyed some much-needed down-time, there's a blissfully relaxed pace to preparing Sunday supper. We tend to cook and serve the meal an hour or two earlier than our suppers during the rest of the week, just so we can savor the smell of roasting chicken in the late afternoon and not feel rushed to clean up and get ready for the workday to follow.

Soupe au Pistou

Perfect Lemon Roasted Chicken

Sweet Potato Stuffing

Tarragon Green Beans

Plum Almond Cake

SOUPE AU PISTOU

This French version of pesto soup will get everyone eating their vegetables without even noticing.

FOR SOUP

1 Tbsp	15 mL	extra virgin olive oil
3/4 cup	175 mL	diced onion
1/2 cup	125 mL	diced celery
1 cup	250 mL	diced red bell pepper
3/4 cup	175 mL	green beans, cut on the bias
2 cloves	2 cloves	garlic, minced
2 sprigs	2 sprigs	fresh thyme
4 cups	1 L	chicken or vegetable stock
1/2 cup	125 mL	diced yellow zucchini
1/2 cup	125 mL	diced green zucchini
1 cup	250 mL	fresh baby spinach
		coarse salt and ground black pepper

FOR PISTOU

2 cups	500 mL	fresh basil leaves
2 cloves	2 cloves	garlic, chopped
1 tsp	5 mL	coarse salt
1/2 cup	125 mL	extra virgin olive oil
1 tsp	5 mL	finely grated lemon zest
1/2 cup	125 mL	Parmesan cheese shavings

For soup, heat oil in a saucepot over medium heat and add onions and celery. Sweat vegetables until translucent, but don't brown, about 5 minutes. Add pepper and green beans and sweat another 3 minutes. Add garlic and thyme sprigs and stir. Flood vegetables with stock, bring to a simmer and cook, uncovered, for 10 minutes. Add yellow and green zucchini and simmer another 10 minutes. Remove thyme sprigs, stir in spinach and season to taste.

For pistou, pulse basil, garlic and salt in a food processor or grind to a paste with a mortar and pestle. Add olive oil and lemon zest while mixing. Pistou can prepared up to a day in advance and chilled.

To serve, ladle soup into bowls, dollop with pistou and sprinkle with Parmesan shavings.

SERVES 6

ANNA The vegetables in this soup are in season and available at the market at the same time, which is why they make sense in a soup together. Of course, feel free to omit a veggie that may not be your top pick, or add one that is.

MICHAEL I like this soup because it's one of those comfy, homey soups that may be different each time you make it until you add the pistou, which brings all those different flavors together.

PERFECT LEMON ROASTED CHICKEN

The fragrance of rosemary and lemons, backed by hints of onion and garlic, is such an inviting combination, sure to draw even the most reluctant diners down from their room for Sunday supper. Serving this roast chicken with a vinaigrette instead of gravy makes this a seasonless supper. Only a few spoonfuls of sauce are required for a burst of flavor.

FOR CHICKEN

1	|	1	4 lb (2 kg) roasting chicken (air chilled, preferably)
1	|	1	onion, sliced
2	|	2	lemons, sliced
6 cloves	|	6 cloves	garlic, peeled
4 sprigs	|	4 sprigs	fresh rosemary
			extra virgin olive oil, for basting
			coarse salt and ground black pepper

FOR VINAIGRETTE

2 Tbsp	|	25 mL	fresh lemon juice
1/2 tsp	|	2 mL	Dijon mustard
1 tsp	|	5 mL	finely chopped fresh rosemary
4 Tbsp	|	50 mL	extra virgin olive oil

For chicken, preheat oven to 350°F (180°C). Arrange half of the onion slices, lemon slices and 3 cloves of garlic in a roasting pan just a few inches larger than the chicken. Place the chicken on top of the vegetables and fill its cavity with the remaining onion, lemon and garlic. Insert rosemary sprigs into cavity. Baste chicken with olive oil and sprinkle generously with salt and pepper.

Cover pan and roast for 20 minutes. Remove cover, baste chicken with juices from the bottom of the pan and continue roasting until an internal temperature of 175°F (80°C) is reached, basting 3 or 4 times during roasting. Remove pan from oven and let chicken rest for 10 minutes before removing and carving.

While roast chicken is resting, prepare vinaigrette. Strain onion, lemon and garlic from bottom of pan, saving juices to return to pan (discard vegetables). Place pan over medium heat and add lemon juice, stirring to pull up any caramelized bits. Stir in Dijon mustard and rosemary and remove from heat. Whisk in olive oil slowly and season to taste.

To serve, carve chicken and spoon vinaigrette over chicken.

SERVES 6
SEE PHOTO ON PAGE 16

ANNA I find that a roasting pan just a little larger than the size of the chicken helps keep flavors and juices in. By covering the chicken initially during cooking, you encourage the extraction of flavor, then uncovering it allows for dry heat cooking and caramelization. Mmmm — crispy skin!

MICHAEL Roast chicken should be designated the official "chef's day off" meal because it does away with fancy techniques and exotic, elaborate flavor combinations. In one short step, dinner's in the oven.

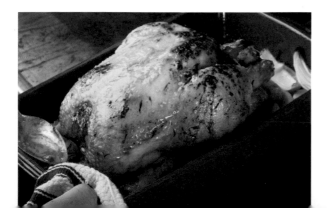

SWEET POTATO STUFFING

This stuffing is like a savory bread pudding and makes a perfect accompaniment to any type of roast. The puréed sweet potato adds a brilliant color to your dinner plate.

1/2 lb	250 g	sweet potato
4 cups	1 L	cubed white Italian bread
1 Tbsp	15 mL	unsalted butter
2	2	shallots, minced
1 clove	1 clove	garlic, minced
1 Tbsp +1 1/2 tsp	22 mL	chopped lovage
1 1/2 cups	375 mL	2% milk or half-and-half cream
5	5	large eggs
1 Tbsp	15 mL	Dijon mustard
1 tsp	5 mL	fine salt
3/4 tsp	4 mL	ground black pepper
1/4 cup	50 mL	grated Parmesan cheese

Peel and dice sweet potato and boil, uncovered, in salted water until tender, about 12 minutes. Drain well, purée and cool.

For best results, be sure to use day-old bread or gently dry bread cubes in a 200°F (95°C) oven for about 20 minutes.

Preheat oven to 350°F (180°C). Heat butter in a small pan over medium heat and sweat shallots and garlic for 3 minutes. Stir in lovage. In a bowl, whisk sweet potato purée, milk (for a richer pudding, use half-and-half cream), eggs, mustard, salt and pepper. Whisk in shallot mixture and pour over bread cubes. Allow to sit for 10 minutes, stirring occasionally. Pour into a greased 6-cup (1.5-L) baking dish and top with grated Parmesan. Place in a larger pan with a 2-inch (5-cm) lip. Place pan in oven and fill around stuffing dish with an inch (2.5 cm) of boiling water. Bake for 35 to 45 minutes, until stuffing springs back when touched in the center.

Sweet Potato Stuffing can be made up to 2 days in advance and reheated, covered, in a 300°F (150°C) oven for 25 minutes.

SERVES 6

ANNA I like to serve this stuffing in a nice casserole dish for a rustic Sunday supper, when plates and platters are passed around the table, family-style. If I'm upgrading a bit, I bake the stuffing in ramekins and turn them out for a plated presentation. Try this dish with scrambled eggs for brunch — spectacular!

MICHAEL Lovage is an herb that grows like a weed (even in our gardening-challenged yard we can grow this) and has a pungent celery flavor that is an aromatic addition to soups and sauces. If you can't locate lovage, use chopped celery leaves but double the quantity in the recipe.

<PERFECT LEMON ROASTED CHICKEN, PAGE 15

TARRAGON GREEN BEANS

The addition of a simple herb can transform an everyday vegetable into a work of art.

4 Tbsp	50 mL	unsalted butter at room temperature
1 Tbsp	15 mL	chopped fresh chives
1 Tbsp	15 mL	chopped fresh tarragon
½ tsp	2 mL	fine salt, plus salt for pot
1 lb	500 g	fresh green beans, trimmed

Beat butter with chives, tarragon and salt until evenly blended and chill until ready to serve.

Bring a pot of water to the boil and add salt. Add green beans and boil, uncovered, until tender (test by tasting). Drain well. Place beans in a serving dish, top with a few spoonfuls of chilled herb butter and serve immediately.

SERVES 6

ANNA Tarragon is an herb that was overused in the '80s and then disappeared from menus in the '90s. I'm glad to see it back in fashion — but in moderate amounts.

When salting water for cooking vegetables, there should be enough salt in the pot to make the water taste like the sea.

MICHAEL A compound butter consists of flavor (herbs) or texture (ground nuts) added to softened butter, which is then piped or shaped and chilled. It can be used to add a kick to veggies, to baste meats or to finish sauces.

PLUM ALMOND CAKE

This moist, fruity cake makes great snacks through the week.

½ cup	125 mL	yogurt or sour cream (full fat)
½ cup	125 mL	vegetable oil
¼ cup	50 mL	orange juice
1 Tbsp	15 mL	orange zest
1	1	egg
½ tsp	2 mL	almond extract
1 cup	250 mL	sugar
1¼ cups	300 mL	all-purpose flour
¼ cup	50 mL	ground almonds
2 tsp	10 mL	baking powder
¼ tsp	1 mL	salt
4	4	red plums, halved and pitted
2 Tbsp	25 mL	dark brown sugar

Preheat oven to 400°F (200°C). Line an 8-inch (20-cm) springform pan with parchment paper.

Whisk together yogurt, oil, orange juice, orange zest, egg and almond extract. Whisk in sugar.
In a separate bowl, sift flour, ground almonds, baking powder and salt. Stir into wet mixture until just blended. Scrape batter into prepared pan and arrange plum halves on top, flesh side facing upward. Sprinkle plums with brown sugar and bake for 30 to 35 minutes, until a tester inserted in the center of the cake comes out clean. Cool in pan for 15 minutes, then remove from pan to cool completely.

MAKES ONE 8-INCH (20-CM) CAKE
SERVES 10 TO 12

ANNA This is one of those great cake recipes that can double as a coffee cake for breakfast the next morning. If plums aren't in season, apricots, raspberries or even prunes make delectable substitutes.

MICHAEL When I moved to Niagara, I was overwhelmed by the bounty of produce for purchase for the restaurant. In my enthusiasm, I bought a ton (literally) of plums. My delight in this find matched the dismay of the kitchen staff who spent days pitting and preserving plums.

FRIDAY NIGHT CATCH-UP

You've had a busy week, and everyone has been pulled in different directions. Friday night is like a sigh of relief. The weekend lies ahead, and tonight's dinner is a great opportunity to relax, enjoy some fun food and talk to each other. There's no need to rush — open a bottle of red wine or make a large pitcher of iced tea, and let everyone create their own pizzas. Make them one at a time and invent your own combinations.

Design-Your-Own Pizza
Iceberg Blue Cheese Salad
Raspberry Cream Cheese Brownies

ANNA This dinner is a regular Friday occurrence for us. We stand around the kitchen while the pizzas are baking, chat, laugh and catch up on the week's news and gossip. Because it's such a low-key meal, the pizza dough, too, is low-maintenance. It can't be underworked or overworked (I like to make it by hand to save on cleaning up the mixer). The dough doesn't require a specific rising time — just enough time for it to relax and stretch easily — kind of like us. After all, it's Friday!

MICHAEL When I feel we're frazzled and pushing ourselves too hard, this time spent cooking together is rejuvenating and, on this rare occasion for two chefs, the food isn't the center of attention — we are. It's our time to reconnect and recharge.

DESIGN-YOUR-OWN PIZZA

We like the casual approach of this pizza night. A simple yeast dough takes less time to make than you might think and with this design-it-yourself toppings method everyone gets what they want.

FOR DOUGH

1⅓ cups	325 mL	tepid water (100°F/40°C)
2 tsp	10 mL	instant yeast
2 cups	500 mL	all-purpose flour
½ cup	125 mL	pastry flour
1 Tbsp	15 mL	coarse salt
2 Tbsp	25 mL	extra virgin olive oil
		cornmeal or olive oil for pan

IDEAS FOR TOPPINGS

RAW	COOKED	MEATS	CHEESES
Cherry Tomatoes	Asparagus	Bacon	Ricotta
Sundried Tomatoes	Eggplant	Peameal Bacon	Bocconcini
Kalamata Olives	Zucchini	Pepperoni	Mozzarella
Fresh Basil and Oregano	Mushrooms	Prosciutto	Cheddar or Gouda
Sliced Red Onion	Roasted Garlic	Salad Shrimp	Parmesan
Sliced Red and Green		Crabmeat	Asiago
Bell Pepper		Hard-Boiled Eggs	
Fresh Garlic		Smoked Salmon	

For dough, combine water and yeast and stir to dissolve. Add remaining ingredients and stir with a wooden spoon until very stiff, then turn dough onto a lightly floured surface and knead for 5 minutes. Place dough into an oiled bowl and cover with plastic wrap. Let sit for 30 minutes while preparing toppings.

The choice of toppings is yours. Being the end of the week, it might be a good opportunity to clean the fridge a little and get creative (that leftover roast chicken from 2 nights ago would make a great topping!). Just arrange, chop and grate as needed.

To assemble pizzas, preheat oven to 500°F (260°C) and sprinkle a baking sheet with cornmeal (or rub with olive oil). On a lightly floured surface, turn out dough and cut into 8 pieces. Cover all but 1 piece of dough with a tea towel. Press this piece of dough flat with your hands and start pulling and shaping it into a thin disk, less than ¼ inch (5 mm) thick. If dough starts to spring back, just let it rest 5 minutes, then resume stretching. Place flattened dough onto prepared pan and top with desired ingredients. Bake pizza for 10 to 15 minutes, until toppings are cooked to your liking and crust is browned. Let cool 2 minutes before slicing and eating.

While waiting for the first pizza to cook, you (or whoever is next in line) can be building a pizza.

SERVES 4

ICEBERG BLUE CHEESE SALAD

Salad heaven! This melding of crisp, creamy, salty and sweet makes this absolutely satisfying to our sense of taste. The addition of garlic powder to the salad dressing is a little out of our culinary personality, but there's something about it that just fits!

FOR DRESSING

4 oz	125 g	blue cheese
2 Tbsp	25 mL	mayonnaise
2 Tbsp	25 mL	sour cream
½ tsp	2 mL	garlic powder
¼ tsp	1 mL	ground black pepper

FOR SALAD

½ head	½ head	iceberg lettuce, cut into 4 wedges
½ cup	125 mL	thinly sliced sweet onion, such as Vidalia or red
4 Tbsp	50 mL	sunflower seeds or shelled pumpkin seeds (pepitos)
8	8	prunes
		extra virgin olive oil, for drizzling

For dressing, beat blue cheese to soften. Stir in remaining ingredients until evenly blended and chill until ready to serve.

To assemble salad, place a lettuce wedge on each plate. Dollop blue cheese dressing around and over lettuce and sprinkle with onion slices, sunflower seeds and prunes. Drizzle with olive oil and serve.

SERVES 4

ANNA For a warm-weather refreshment, place the iceberg wedges in the freezer for 10 minutes before serving. The salad will be like a drink of cool water!

MICHAEL We've enjoyed this salad at home on Friday pizza nights, but we've also served it as a course for a fine-dining meal. There's something ultimately gratifying about this combination, whether it's followed by pizza and chicken wings or cinnamon-cured duck with blackberry sauce.

RASPBERRY CREAM CHEESE BROWNIES

What better way to end the evening and start the weekend than with brownies? Cream cheese adds depth of flavor, but its tang also cuts the sweetness of the chocolate a little. A little bit of cheesecake meets brownie — and what a happy introduction it is!

FOR BROWNIES

3½ oz	105 g	unsweetened chocolate, chopped
⅓ cup	75 mL	unsalted butter, cut into pieces
½ cup	125 mL	cream cheese at room temperature
1 cup	250 mL	sugar
1 tsp	5 mL	vanilla
¼ tsp	1 mL	almond extract
2	2	large eggs at room temperature
¾ cup	175 mL	all-purpose flour
½ tsp	2 mL	baking powder
½ tsp	2 mL	fine salt
½ cup	125 mL	raspberry jam

FOR ICING

4 oz	125 g	cream cheese at room temperature
¼ cup	50 mL	unsalted butter at room temperature
1½ cups	375 mL	icing sugar, sifted
1½ tsp	7 mL	vanilla

Preheat oven to 350°F (180°C). Butter and flour a 9-inch (23-cm) square baking pan, knocking out excess flour.

In a small, heavy-bottomed saucepot melt chocolate and butter over low heat, stirring until smooth. Remove from heat and allow to cool while starting next step.

In a mixing bowl, beat cream cheese until soft. Add sugar, and cream until smooth. Beat in vanilla, almond extract and eggs, adding one at a time until evenly blended. Stir in chocolate mixture. In a separate bowl, sift together flour, baking powder and salt and add to chocolate mixture, beating just until batter is combined.

Spread half of batter evenly in pan. Drop raspberry jam by spoonfuls onto batter and spread carefully to form an even layer. Drop remaining brownie batter by spoonfuls onto jam and spread carefully to form an even top layer. Bake for 25 to 30 minutes, or until a tester comes out clean. Allow brownies to cool.

To prepare icing, beat cream cheese with butter. Beat in icing sugar until smooth and stir in vanilla. Spread over brownies and chill for an hour before slicing.

MAKES ONE 9-INCH (23-CM) PAN

ANNA Of course, any jam or marmalade would do well in this recipe — strawberry, apricot, orange, even grape.

MICHAEL I like these brownies right after dinner, but I've been known to sneak a sliver for a late-night snack.

FRIENDS

>Do you find that with true friends, no matter how long since you last visited, you can pick up your conversation right where you left off with barely a "Hi, how're ya doin'?" Those are friends to treasure, and when we do get a chance to get together with friends, we like to make it a relaxed and tasty meal.

>Good friends are probably very comfortable starting their visit in the kitchen. Don't worry about having the kitchen perfectly tidy. After all, you've been working hard — let it show! Stand around the kitchen with glasses of wine and get chatting — and put your friends to work, chopping, stirring or tossing.

SPRINGTIME GET-TOGETHER LUNCH Lunch is

an ideal time to entertain friends. Spend the morning in the kitchen (you can even set the table the night before) and enjoy a leisurely afternoon with your friends, knowing that you'll still have your evening to yourselves.
>Portions at lunch tend to be smaller, and we tend to indulge in wine less, so lunchtime entertaining can also be cost-effective. This menu can double as a lovely Sunday brunch.

Asparagus Fonterelle

Puff Pastry Baked Peameal Pork with Mustard Sour Cream

Warm Crunchy Snow Peas

Strawberry Pavlovas

ASPARAGUS FONTERELLE

We wish we could lay claim to the original version of this dish, but it's a French classic. This adaptation, though, is pure Olson.

3 lb	1.5 kg	fresh asparagus
6	6	large eggs
5 Tbsp	65 mL	unsalted butter
		coarse salt and ground black pepper
2 Tbsp	25 mL	chopped fresh chives

Peel asparagus by holding it against palm of your hand and peeling downward. Trim fibrous end and wash. Bring a pot of water to a boil and salt generously. Prepare a bowl filled with ice water. Add asparagus and cook, uncovered, until tender, 4 to 5 minutes. Drain asparagus and toss immediately into ice water. Once completely cooled, drain and chill until ready to serve.

Place eggs in cool water and bring slowly up to a boil. Boil for 1 minute, shut off heat and let eggs sit for 6 minutes. Drain and immerse eggs in cold water to chill. This should produce eggs that are just a little past soft boiled. Peel eggs, and chop finely.

To serve asparagus, melt butter in a small pan, stir in chopped egg and season to taste. Keep warm. Warm asparagus for 2 minutes in a pot of simmering water, drain and place on a platter. Spoon warm egg mixture over and garnish with chopped chives. Serve immediately.

SERVES 8

ANNA Peeling your asparagus is recommended for the wider spears — that way you don't have to trim the stems as short and they'll taste sweeter. Don't bother peeling asparagus that is pencil-thin — you'll have nothing left!

MICHAEL This is a great recipe if you want to recreate the buttery richness of a hollandaise sauce without the effort.

PUFF PASTRY BAKED PEAMEAL PORK WITH MUSTARD SOUR CREAM

This recipe is very versatile. Serve it for Sunday brunch, a lunch gathering or a holiday breakfast.

FOR PUFF PASTRY PEAMEAL PORK

½ cup	125 mL	ricotta cheese
1 cup	250 mL	grated medium cheddar cheese
½ tsp	2 mL	Hungarian or Spanish paprika
1	1	14-oz (397-g) package frozen puff pastry, thawed to room temperature
1	1	2-lb (1-kg) whole peameal pork loin
1	1	egg whisked with 1 Tbsp (15 mL) water for egg wash
1 Tbsp	15 mL	poppy seeds

FOR MUSTARD SOUR CREAM

1¼ cups	300 mL	sour cream
¼ cup	50 mL	coarse grain mustard
3 Tbsp	45 mL	thinly sliced green onion
½ tsp	2 mL	ground black pepper

For pork, preheat oven to 400°F (200°C). Combine ricotta, cheddar and paprika. On a lightly floured surface, roll out puff pastry to ¼-inch (5-mm) thick rectangle, about 10 inches (25 cm) by 8 inches (20 cm). Spread ricotta filling over pastry, leaving a 1-inch (2.5-cm) border free of filling. Dry off any excess moisture from peameal loin and place centered on filling. Fold pastry around peameal loin, sealing edges by pinching them together. Place pastry on a parchment-lined baking sheet seam side down. Brush pastry with egg wash and sprinkle with poppy seeds. Bake for 10 minutes at 400°F (200°C), then reduce heat to 350°F (180°C) and bake for 55 minutes, until pastry is a rich golden brown. Remove from oven and let rest 15 minutes before slicing.

For mustard sour cream, stir all ingredients together and chill until ready to serve.

To serve, slice ½-inch (1-cm) portions of peameal and dollop Mustard Sour Cream on the side.

SERVES 8

ANNA Now sold coated in cornmeal, brined pork loin was originally covered in ground dried peas to absorb excess juices.

MICHAEL This is "Canadian Night at the Oscars" — peameal bacon dressed up with cheddar cheese and wrapped in a "red carpet" of rich puff pastry. What would Joan Rivers say?

WARM CRUNCHY SNOW PEAS

This is one occasion when we still favor the al dente, crunchier style of cooking vegetables.

1 lb	500 g	snow peas
2 Tbsp	25 mL	extra virgin olive oil
¼ cup	50 mL	sliced green onion, cut on the bias
2 Tbsp	25 mL	chopped fresh mint
		coarse salt and ground black pepper

Trim stems from snow peas and pull out any fibrous strings. Heat a sauté pan over medium-high heat and add olive oil. Add snow peas and toss until bright green, about 3 minutes. Add green onion, mint and seasonings. Serve immediately.

SERVES 8

ANNA If you miss a few strings when you clean your snow peas, just argue that you included dental floss!

MICHAEL Snow peas have to be just about the fastest vegetable to cook. The price might appear daunting at the grocery store, but remember that snow peas are very light.

STRAWBERRY PAVLOVAS

The delight of this meringue dessert is the lovely pink color of the berry cream and the caramelized crunch topping, which slowly dissolves as it comes into contact with those sweet strawberry juices. Call it a "Pavlova Brûlée" for lack of a better term!

FOR MERINGUE

4	4	egg whites at room temperature
¾ cup	175 mL	sugar
1 tsp	5 mL	cornstarch
1 tsp	5 mL	fresh lemon juice

FOR CREAM

1 cup	250 mL	whipping cream
3 Tbsp	45 mL	crème fraîche or sour cream
2 Tbsp	25 mL	sugar
⅓ cup	75 mL	puréed fresh strawberries

FOR FRUIT

2 cups	500 mL	fresh strawberries
½ cup	125 mL	sugar
1 Tbsp	15 mL	corn syrup
2 Tbsp	25 mL	water

ANNA I've applied to other sweets the trick of using cornstarch in pavlovas — to hold in moisture and make a soft-centered, marshmallow-like dessert. A teaspoon (5 mL) of cornstarch in my chocolate chip cookie recipe keeps them chewy — guaranteed!

MICHAEL Pavlova was created in honor of Anna Pavlova, the famous Russian ballerina. Australia and New Zealand have each adopted it as their national dessert, and you often see it topped with passion fruit, native to those tropical climates.

For meringue, preheat oven to 275°F (140°C). Trace eight 2½-inch (6-cm) circles onto 2 sheets of parchment paper, turn paper over (so ink doesn't transfer to meringue) and line baking sheets. In a mixer fitted with the whisk attachment or with electric beaters, whip egg whites until frothy. While whipping, gradually add sugar and beat until stiff peaks form. By hand, fold in cornstarch and lemon juice until incorporated. Dollop and spread onto traced circles. Bake for 25 to 40 minutes, until meringue lifts easily from parchment paper. If meringue starts to show signs of coloring, reduce oven temperature slightly. Allow to cool.

For cream, whip cream to medium peaks and fold in crème fraîche or sour cream, sugar and puréed strawberries. Chill until ready to serve.

Wash, hull and quarter strawberries and chill. In a small saucepot, bring sugar, corn syrup and water to a boil. Cook without stirring for 3 to 4 minutes, until mixture turns light brown. Pour syrup onto a sheet of greased parchment paper and allow to cool. Pulse the cooked caramelized sugar in a food processor to grind finely.

To serve, place a meringue disk onto each plate and dollop with strawberry cream. Arrange strawberries over cream and sprinkle generously with sugar. Serve immediately.

MAKES 8 PAVLOVAS

CASUAL BISTRO

We really get into French bistro food when entertaining. The work is done ahead of time, so you can feel like a guest in your own little French bistro, indulging in rich, big flavors and simple, relaxed presentations. >This menu is for a larger group. Don't be afraid to imitate the French in their cozy little bistros — pack everyone close together around the table, use mismatched plates, put on a Paolo Conte CD and get in the spirit. Bon appétit!

Sherry Onion Tarts

Classic Cassoulet

Endive Walnut Salad

Chocolate Pots de Crème

SHERRY ONION TARTS

These tarts are perfect to start a bottle of wine, white or red.
Make miniature versions for your next cocktail party.

FOR CARAMELIZED ONIONS

1 Tbsp	15 mL	unsalted butter
1 Tbsp	15 mL	extra virgin olive oil
2 lb	1 kg	onions, sliced
2 tsp	10 mL	chopped fresh tarragon
1/4 cup	50 mL	dry sherry
		coarse salt and ground black pepper

FOR TARTS

1/3 cup	75 mL	unsalted butter, melted
1 clove	1 clove	garlic, minced
1	1	1 lb (454 g) package frozen phyllo pastry, thawed

FOR GARLIC CUSTARD

1 cup	250 mL	2% milk
1 clove	1 clove	garlic, minced
2 tsp	10 mL	grated lemon zest
4	4	large egg yolks
1 tsp	5 mL	sugar
3 Tbsp	45 mL	cornstarch
1/2 tsp	2 mL	fine salt
2 Tbsp	25 mL	unsalted butter

ANNA To change these a bit, use puff pastry instead of phyllo dough. To save time you can even use store-bought tart shells or vol-au-vent pastry cases, found in the grocery store's freezer section.

MICHAEL The key ingredient of our fragrant caramelized onions, sherry, is also an excellent drink to have with them. A fino (dry) or amontillado (semi-dry) is best.

For caramelized onions, melt butter and oil in a sauté pan over medium heat and add onions. Cook, stirring occasionally, until they are a rich brown color, about 30 minutes. Add tarragon and sherry, and stir until sherry is absorbed. Season to taste and set aside to cool.

For tart shells, preheat oven to 350°F (180°C). Melt butter with minced garlic. Layer 4 sheets of phyllo pastry on top of each other, brushing each layer with garlic butter (remember to keep unused phyllo covered with a damp towel). Cut into squares and line twelve 3-inch (8-cm) tart shells, trimming off excess. Bake shells for 15 to 18 minutes, until they're a light golden brown. Allow to cool. Fill each tart with about 2 Tbsp (25 mL) of caramelized onions.

For garlic custard, heat milk with garlic and lemon zest to just below a simmer. In a bowl, whisk together egg yolks, sugar, cornstarch and salt. Gradually whisk hot milk into egg mixture, whisking constantly until all milk has been added. Return custard to pot, and continue whisking over medium heat until thickened and glossy, about 4 minutes. Remove from heat and stir in butter. Transfer to a bowl and cover with plastic wrap directly touching surface of custard. Chill completely.

To assemble tarts, preheat oven to 400°F (200°C). Whisk custard to soften slightly and spoon it into baked tart shells and bake for 3 to 5 minutes, until tops brown just slightly.

Serve warm.

MAKES TWELVE 3-INCH (8-CM) TARTS

CLASSIC CASSOULET

Cassoulet hails from the French town of Castelnaudary in the Languedoc region, and the recipe title refers to the terracotta pot, or *cassole,* in which the dish is slowly cooked. This version has taken only a few turns from an authentic recipe (many claim authenticity), for the sake of time and the availability of ingredients. We'd rather you make a respectable variation of cassoulet than none at all.

4 strips	4 strips	double-smoked or regular bacon, diced
3	3	shallots, sliced
4 cloves	4 cloves	garlic, minced
2 tsp	10 mL	chopped fresh thyme
dash	dash	nutmeg
2	2	14-oz (398-mL) cans navy beans, rinsed and drained
4	4	smoked or cooked duck (or chicken) legs, meat pulled from the bone (or chicken)
¾ lb	375 g	smoked pork sausage, diced
1 cup	250 mL	white wine
		coarse salt and ground black pepper
1 cup	250 mL	fine dry breadcrumbs

Preheat oven to 350°F (180°C). In a pan over medium heat, cook bacon until crispy and remove, leaving fat in the pan and reserving bacon. Add shallots, garlic, thyme and nutmeg and sauté for 3 minutes. Add beans, meat and white wine and bring up to a simmer. Season to taste and add cooked bacon. Pour into a baking dish (terracotta is traditional) and sprinkle with breadcrumbs.

Bake for 40 minutes until bubbling.

SERVES 10

ANNA A true cassoulet uses duck confit — duck legs slowly cooked in their own fat until the meat melts off the bone — which can be found in some fine food stores. As we've said in the recipe, though, chicken is just as delicious.

MICHAEL A traditional cassoulet bakes for over 3 hours, and there are as many recipes for this dish as there are French chefs and homemakers who make it. It's possible, though, to achieve a lovely, rich flavor in less time.

ENDIVE WALNUT SALAD

The French tradition of a salad following the entrée is worthy of note.
A salad of bitter greens cleanses the palate after a rich course and aids digestion.

FOR SALAD

1 cup	250 mL	walnut pieces
4 heads	4 heads	Belgian endive
1 cup	250 mL	radicchio
2	2	green onions, chopped

FOR FRENCH VINAIGRETTE

1/4 cup	50 mL	red wine vinegar
1 tsp	5 mL	Dijon mustard
1 tsp	5 mL	honey or sugar
1 clove	1 clove	garlic, minced
		fine salt and ground black pepper to taste
3/4 cup	175 mL	extra virgin olive oil

Preheat oven to 350°F (180°C). Spread walnut pieces on a baking sheet and toast for 10 to 12 minutes, until lightly browned. Allow to cool and store in an airtight container until ready to use.

For salad, cut bottom off endive and peel away leaves, arranging pretty ones around a platter. Chop remaining leaves into 1/2-inch (1-cm) pieces. Chop radicchio into shreds, toss with cut Belgian endive and place in center of platter. Sprinkle with chopped green onion and walnut pieces.

For vinaigrette, whisk red wine vinegar with Dijon mustard, honey or sugar, garlic and salt and pepper until fully blended. Slowly pour in oil, whisking constantly. Vinaigrette can be prepared in advance and whisked to emulsify. Drizzle over salad and serve immediately.

SERVES 10

ANNA I remember the first time I tried Belgian endive. I was 12 years old, and my mom and I went out for dinner before going to the *Nutcracker* ballet. I felt so fancy to be presented with this unusual salad green, and I even thought it tasted pretty good.

MICHAEL Belgian endive is such a cool lettuce because of its shape — it dresses up any salad plate by building height and texture. Don't buy endive with green tips — it will have a strong, bitter taste. The tips should be pale yellow, showing that they haven't been exposed to light.

CHOCOLATE POTS DE CRÈME

Pots de crème are simply crème brûlées without the burnt sugar layer.
With a rich, chocolate custard such as this, who needs burnt sugar?

2½ cups	625 mL	whipping cream
1½ cups	375 mL	2% milk
2 tsp	10 mL	lemon zest
12 oz	375 g	bittersweet chocolate, chopped
12	12	large egg yolks
⅓ cup	75 mL	sugar
2 tsp	10 mL	vanilla

Preheat oven to 300°F (150°C) and arrange ten 5-ounce (150-g) ramekins in a baking dish with at least a 2-inch (5-cm) lip. Bring cream, milk and lemon zest to just below a simmer and pour over chopped chocolate. Let sit one minute, then gently stir until chocolate has melted completely.

In a separate bowl, whisk egg yolks, sugar and vanilla together. Place bowl on a damp tea towel to prevent slipping, and gradually ladle chocolate cream into eggs, whisking constantly until all cream has been added. Strain custard mixture and ladle into prepared ramekins. Bring pan to the open oven door and rest it there while pouring in boiling water halfway up the ramekins. Cover with a piece of aluminum foil that has been poked with a skewer (this will prevent a skin from forming on top of the custards). Bake for 30 to 35 minutes, until the custards are set around the outside but still have a little jiggle in the middle. Remove from baking pan, cool on the counter to room temperature and then chill for at least four hours before serving.

To serve, garnish pots de crème with a little grated chocolate, a dollop of whipped cream, a little sprinkle of cocoa powder or "au naturel."

MAKES 10 POTS DE CRÈME

ANNA Add a little instant coffee powder (1 tsp/5 mL) to make mocha pots de crème, or a little orange zest for another twist.

MICHAEL I love the simplicity of classic French bistro desserts. No fancy sauces or garnishes, just a quality sweet to finish your meal.

NEW GUESTS

>Entertaining isn't always a choice, as much as you might wish it to be. There's always the obligation of welcoming into your home people you've never met before or perhaps know only casually.

>The challenge in entertaining new guests is not to get nervous. Remember, your guests are probably more nervous than you are, and they don't have the luxury of being in their own home.

>Here are a few simple rules to keep in mind:

1 Always ask your guests beforehand if they have any food allergies or aversions. This avoids the embarrassment of serving something they can't eat.

2 Consider inviting your new guests into the kitchen, even for just a few minutes. The comfort zone of the kitchen can relax both you and your guests.

3 Clean your washroom! Like many restaurants, you may not be ultimately judged on your meal but on the condition of your washroom!

IMPRESS YOUR BOSS

Tension may build as the clock ticks closer to the arrival of your boss for dinner. You're probably not as relaxed as you were last weekend when you had your friends over for a barbecue and a bottle of wine — but don't fear! A successful meal awaits you.

>The menu below is showy enough to please the greater powers — it's certainly big on flavor — but its impressiveness won't overwhelm your effort or finances.

Smoked Salmon Pizza

Veal Tenderloin with Horseradish Cream

Shallot Roasted Potatoes

Garlic Rapini

Lemon Olive Oil Cake with Steeped Citrus

SMOKED SALMON PIZZA

Roll the pizza dough as thinly as possible for a dainty, crispy-crusted appetizer.

1 recipe	1 recipe	pizza dough (page 21)
8 oz	250 g	cream cheese at room temperature
4 tsp	10 mL	chopped fresh dill
4 tsp	10 mL	chopped fresh chives
4 oz	100 g	smoked salmon
½	½	red onion, sliced
1 lb	450 g	asparagus, trimmed and blanched
3 Tbsp	45 mL	capers

Prepare pizza dough as specified on page 21 and let rise for 1 hour.

To assemble pizzas, preheat oven to 500°F (260°C) and sprinkle a baking sheet with cornmeal (or rub with olive oil). Beat cream cheese to soften and add chopped dill and chives.

On a lightly floured surface, turn out dough and cut into 2 pieces. Cover 1 piece of dough with a tea towel. Press the other piece of dough flat with your hands and start pulling and shaping it into a thin disk, less than ¼ inch (5 mm) thick. If dough starts to spring back, just let it rest 5 minutes, then resume stretching. Place flattened dough onto prepared pan and spread with cream cheese. Repeat with other piece of dough. Bake for 12 minutes, until edges of pizza turn light brown. Remove pizzas and top with smoked salmon, red onion, asparagus and capers, and pop back in the oven for 2 more minutes, just to warm through.

Cool for 2 minutes, then slice and serve.

SERVES 4

ANNA This is a great idea for a brunch dish, topped with a poached egg. If asparagus is out of season, use slices of avocado instead.

MICHAEL I love this pizza with a dry white wine like Pinot Gris or Sauvignon Blanc.

VEAL TENDERLOIN WITH HORSERADISH CREAM

A roast is a perfect entrée for entertaining because the oven does all the work! Veal tenderloin makes such a delectable, mild roast — perfect for pairing with other interesting flavors. If you'd rather use beef tenderloin, the results are just as spectacular. >The secret to a perfectly cooked roast is a small investment in a reliable oven thermometer. We use a probe thermometer that is inserted into the core of the roast, and whose digital gauge sits outside the oven. Our cue to start warming the sauce and vegetables is when the meat is 10 degrees below its target internal temperature.

2½ lb	1.25 kg	veal tenderloin roast
1 Tbsp	15 mL	extra virgin olive oil
2 tsp	10 mL	coarse salt
1 tsp	5 mL	ground black pepper
2 tsp	10 mL	chopped fresh thyme or rosemary
2 cloves	2 cloves	garlic, minced

FOR HORSERADISH CREAM

½ cup	125 mL	white wine
1 cup	250 mL	whipping cream
2 Tbsp	25 mL	extra hot prepared horseradish
		OR 3 Tbsp (45 mL) freshly grated horseradish
		fine salt and ground black pepper to taste

Preheat oven to 300°F (150°C). Clean veal tenderloin of any outside fat (or ask the butcher to do this for you) and let roast come up to room temperature for 20 minutes before placing in oven. Combine olive oil, salt, pepper, thyme and garlic, and rub over surface of veal tenderloin. Place on a roasting rack in a roasting pan and insert a temperature gauge. Cook for 1 to 1½ hours, depending on the temperature desired, about 1 hour for medium-rare — 130°F (55°C) — and 1½ hours for medium-well — 145°F (65°C). Let rest for 15 minutes before carving. Remember that the roast will cook an additional 5°F (20°C) as it sits and rests.

While roast is in the oven, prepare horseradish cream. Heat white wine over medium heat in a small saucepot and reduce by half its volume. Add whipping cream and bring to just below a simmer. Add horseradish, season to taste and serve. The sauce can also be prepared fully in advance, chilled and reheated before serving.

To serve, carve tenderloin into 4 sections and spoon sauce over the plate just touching the meat a bit.

SERVES 4

ANNA I like this sauce with beef or pork roast as much as with veal. If you want to use freshly grated horseradish, add an extra 1 Tbsp (15 mL) and let it steep in the reducing wine to draw out more flavor.

MICHAEL This roast is a great meal for a sophisticated occasion, but the minimal effort doesn't show in the final result. Plus, any leftovers can be turned into spectacular gourmet sandwiches.

SHALLOT ROASTED POTATOES

Shallots are like mild onions with a hint of garlic — a real chef's trick to building fine flavors.

1¼ lb	625 g	red mini potatoes, washed and halved
½ lb	250 g	shallots, peeled
3 cloves	3 cloves	garlic, peeled
3 Tbsp	45 mL	extra virgin olive oil
		coarse salt and ground black pepper

Preheat oven to 300°F (150°C). Toss potatoes, shallots and garlic with olive oil, salt and pepper. Place in a baking dish and cover with foil. Bake for 30 minutes, covered, then remove foil and bake for another 30 to 45 minutes, until fork tender.

SERVES 4

ANNA Fine dining fit to impress doesn't mean you have to make each item on the plate overly elaborate. A simply prepared and properly seasoned potato dish such as this can speak far more eloquently than a fancier concoction.

MICHAEL My advice is to use your onions interchangeably. If you can't find a shallot, you can always take a leek! (Anna always groans at that one.)

GARLIC RAPINI

Healthy, healthy, healthy! The sharp bitterness of rapini makes you feel you're doing your body good, and its distinctive taste offsets the richness of other tastes. For a palate-cleansing vegetable course, delicious all on its own, replace the garlic in this recipe with 2 tsp (10 mL) of finely grated lemon zest.

1 bunch	1 bunch	rapini
2 Tbsp	25 mL	extra virgin olive oil or butter
2 cloves	2 cloves	garlic, minced
		coarse salt and ground black pepper

Trim bottoms of rapini, peel off large leaves, wash and reserve separately from stems. Prepare a bowl of ice water for immersing rapini. Bring a pot of water up to a boil and salt generously. Add rapini stems and blanch, uncovered, for 3 minutes, until tender but still firm. Drain and shock rapini stems in ice water. Drain ice water and chill rapini until ready to heat.

Heat a sauté pan over medium heat and add olive oil. Add rapini stems and leaves and stir to wilt leaves. Add garlic and sauté 1 minute more until leaves are fully wilted and stems are heated through. Season to taste and serve immediately.

SERVES 4

ANNA Bitter greens served with a richly sauced entrée add body and cleanse the palate (and will perhaps ease any guilt from eating so richly).

MICHAEL Rapini is bitter — like me after being forced to watch a Hugh Grant movie!

LEMON OLIVE OIL CAKE WITH STEEPED CITRUS

Dessert can be a challenge when you're entertaining new guests. Not everyone is a chocoholic. Some people have small appetites. And the pressure's on because it's your last chance to impress! I find a citrus dessert the best option. I do like this cake as a dessert, but I'll wrap up a portion for the guests to take home — it's delicious served warm for breakfast the next day!

FOR CAKE

1	1	large egg
1	1	large egg white
1¼ cups	300 mL	sugar
⅔ cup	150 mL	extra virgin olive oil
¾ cup	175 mL	2% milk
2 Tbsp	25 mL	lemon zest
1 cup	250 mL	all-purpose flour
¼ tsp	1 mL	baking powder
¼ tsp	1 mL	baking soda
dash	dash	salt

FOR STEEPED CITRUS

2	2	navel oranges
2	2	tangerines
2	2	blood oranges, or grapefruit
2 Tbsp	25 mL	extra virgin olive oil

For cake, preheat oven to 350°F (180°C) and grease and flour an 8-inch (20-cm) cake pan. Whisk egg, egg white, sugar, olive oil, milk and lemon zest. In another bowl, stir together flour, baking powder, baking soda and salt. Add flour mixture to olive oil mixture and stir slowly just until blended. Scrape batter into prepared pan and bake for 45 to 55 minutes, until a skewer inserted in the center of the cake comes out clean. Let cool in the pan and serve at room temperature, dusted with icing sugar and with steeped citrus on the side.

For steeped citrus, remove peel, pith and membranes from oranges by lopping off the top and bottom of the orange with a serrated knife and slicing down the sides of the orange on a cutting board. Using a paring knife, slice in between the membranes to loosen and pull out skin-free orange segments. Toss in a bowl with olive oil and serve next to olive oil cake.

MAKES ONE 8-INCH (20-CM) CAKE

ANNA This is a smash hit if you're not a baker by nature but want to impress someone with a delicious dessert. Easy method, simple ingredients, and it can all be made well in advance!

MICHAEL The olive oil quality is very important in this recipe. Use only extra virgin. A finer, greener olive oil imparts a more effective flavor.

YOU'RE BRINGING WHO? WHEN? Great … just great. The love of your life calls to say there are four out-of-towners visiting the office. Before you can argue, your sweetie adds that the dinner invitation has already been extended, so there's no backing out. What to do?

>First, pour yourself a glass of wine (you deserve it) and then shove everything into the closets. Next, strategically place tea lights to shadow obvious dust bunnies (do they qualify as house pets?). Then, dinner.

>Below is a straight-shooting, delicious menu that can be prepared in a snap – perfect for late spring, summer or early fall, so that you can, smiling the whole while, shove your spontaneous guests out on the deck with a drink and let your spouse entertain them while watching the grill. Do all this, and as a reward next week there will be a quiet dinner for two!

Mussels in Garlic Fennel Cream

Spice-Rubbed Grilled Chicken

Tuscan Grape Tomato Bread Salad

Simple Summer Squash

Goat Cheese Torte with Limoncello Cream and Berries

MUSSELS IN GARLIC FENNEL CREAM

Serving a big bowl of steamed mussels can be a great icebreaker because it's a communal activity. You pass around the bowl and everyone can help themselves. Even if there are guests who don't like mussels, there's always the deliciously garlicky cream to be sopped up with fresh baguette.

4 lb	2 kg	fresh cultivated mussels
2 Tbsp	25 mL	extra virgin olive oil
1/2 cup	125 mL	sliced onion
1 1/2 cups	375 mL	thinly sliced fennel bulb
3 cloves	3 cloves	garlic, thinly sliced
2 sprigs	2 sprigs	fresh tarragon
1/2 cup	125 mL	white wine
1 cup	250 mL	whipping cream
		coarse salt and ground black pepper
		fresh baguette, for dipping

To clean mussels, rinse 2 or 3 times in cold water, tossing with your hands. To store before serving, place them in a colander on a plate and cover with a damp tea towel.

Heat a large soup pot over medium-high heat and add oil. Add onion and sauté for 1 minute, then add sliced fennel. Sauté for another 3 minutes then add garlic and tarragon. Add mussels and stir to coat. Pour in white wine and bring up to a simmer before adding cream. Cover pot and cook until all mussels have opened, about 5 minutes. Spoon mussels into a serving bowl with a slotted spoon. Return cream to a simmer and season. Remove tarragon sprigs, pour cream and vegetables over mussels and serve with a fresh baguette.

SERVES 6

ANNA Big bowls of mussels served family-style with a large loaf of bread to be torn and dunked make a great icebreaker and can bring a group of strangers together, literally breaking bread.

MICHAEL Be sure that your mussels are tightly closed before cooking. If one is slightly open, tap it on the counter — if the shell closes, then it's fine. If it stays open, toss it out.

SPICE-RUBBED GRILLED CHICKEN

Part of impressing people with a meal is getting their mouths watering even before they sit down. This will definitely do the trick.

FOR SPICE RUB

2 Tbsp	25 mL	ground cumin
1 Tbsp	15 mL	ground coriander
2 tsp	10 mL	Spanish paprika
2 tsp	10 mL	celery salt
2 tsp	10 mL	coarse salt
1 tsp	5 mL	ground black pepper
1 tsp	5 mL	onion powder
1 tsp	5 mL	garlic powder

FOR CHICKEN

6	6	6-oz (175-g) boneless chicken breasts
1/3 cup	75 mL	cider vinegar

Heat grill on high heat for 10 minutes. Combine all ingredients for spice rub in a bowl, and coat chicken breasts thoroughly (this can be done up to 2 hours in advance). Grill chicken on high heat for 5 minutes, then turn chicken over, reduce heat to medium, cover grill, and cook until chicken is almost done, 12 to 15 minutes. During the last few minutes of cooking, drizzle liberal spoonfuls of cider vinegar over chicken breasts, turning once and repeating with vinegar on other side. Remove from grill and serve immediately.

SERVES 6

ANNA Found in many fine food stores, Spanish paprika differs from Hungarian paprika because of its distinctive smokiness, achieved by drying the peppers over an open fire. In a pinch, any paprika will do.

MICHAEL Intense flavor-building doesn't have to be time-consuming. Barbecuing is a fantastic ploy since it can draw your guests outside (and away from potential chaos in the kitchen) and it creates a relaxed atmosphere.

TUSCAN GRAPE TOMATO BREAD SALAD

We love side dishes that make a dinner plate look different from the standard "meat and potatoes," and this fits the bill. The crunch of garlic croutons is just barely softened by the sweet juices of ripe tomatoes. Grape tomatoes make a great option if summer field tomatoes aren't yet in season.

4 cups	1 L	French or Italian bread, cut into 1-inch (2.5-cm) cubes, crusts left on
7 Tbsp	105 mL	extra virgin olive oil
1 Tbsp	15 mL	minced garlic
		coarse salt and ground black pepper
2 cups	500 mL	grape tomatoes
1	1	green onion, chopped
1 Tbsp	15 mL	balsamic vinegar
½ cup	125 mL	fresh basil leaves

Preheat oven to 350°F (180°C). Toss cubed bread with 4 Tbsp (50 mL) olive oil, 2 tsp (10 mL) minced garlic, 1 tsp (5 mL) salt and ½ tsp (2 mL) black pepper and spread on a baking sheet. Toast bread for 15 to 18 minutes, stirring occasionally, until bread is evenly but lightly toasted. Let cool completely before combining with other ingredients. The toasted bread can be prepared a day in advance and stored in a sealed bag.

Cut the grape tomatoes into quarters and toss with remaining 3 Tbsp (45 mL) olive oil, 1 tsp (5 mL) minced garlic, 1 tsp salt (5 mL), ½ tsp (2 mL) black pepper, green onion and balsamic vinegar. One hour before serving, toss tomatoes with bread cubes and basil leaves and let sit at room temperature. Juices that naturally seep from tomatoes will gently soften the bread cubes.

SERVES 6

ANNA Emergency! Last-minute guests arrive, and all you have for a starch is a loaf of day-old bread. No worries — this salad is best when made with stale bread.

MICHAEL Never EVER store your tomatoes in the fridge — always store them on the kitchen counter. We try to leave them for about a week before using — then they're usually just ripe enough. Tomatoes from the farmers' market are another story — use those plump gems as soon as you can!

SIMPLE SUMMER SQUASH

Sometimes the best way to create impressive flavor is to keep things simple. Summer squash, coaxed with a little seasoning, can have more than enough taste and color.

1½ lb	750 g	summer squash
2 Tbsp	25 mL	extra virgin olive oil
1 clove	1 clove	garlic, minced
2 Tbsp	25 mL	finely grated Parmesan cheese
		coarse salt and ground black pepper

Slice squash into thin medallions. Heat a sauté pan over high heat with olive oil. Add squash and sauté until centers just begin to show signs of going translucent, about 4 minutes. Add garlic and sauté 1 minute more. Stir in Parmesan cheese, season to taste and serve immediately.

SERVES 6

ANNA Summer squash is different from yellow zucchini. It's pale yellow, often with a crook neck and a wide bottom. My mom used to cook summer squash all the time. I've come to love it.

MICHAEL Few vegetables don't punch out with their own flavor, but this is one of them (eggplant is another). With just a little seasoning, though, it can develop true character.

GOAT CHEESE TORTE WITH LIMONCELLO CREAM AND BERRIES

People rarely guess that fresh goat cheese is the base for this torte. Like a fallen soufflé, it leaves a great sunken center to fill with cream and fruit.

FOR GOAT CHEESE TORTE

6 oz	175 g	fresh goat cheese
3 Tbsp	45 mL	sugar
4	4	large eggs, separated

FOR LIMONCELLO CREAM

3/4 cup	175 mL	whipping cream
2 Tbsp	25 mL	sugar
1 tsp	5 mL	finely grated lemon zest
2 Tbsp	25 mL	limoncello

FOR BERRIES

1 cup	250 mL	fresh raspberries
1 cup	250 mL	fresh blueberries
1 cup	250 mL	fresh blackberries
		icing sugar for dusting

For goat cheese torte, preheat oven to 350°F (180°C) and grease and sugar an 8-inch (20-cm) cake pan. Cream goat cheese to soften and beat in sugar. Add egg yolks, one at a time, stirring well after each addition. In a separate bowl, whip egg whites with electric beaters until they hold a stiff peak. Fold one-third of the egg whites into the goat cheese until blended, then gently fold in the remaining two-thirds. Scrape batter into prepared pan and bake for 25 to 30 minutes, until the cake has risen and turned an even golden brown. Let cool to room temperature, but don't worry when the center of the cake falls — it's supposed to. It leaves you with a lovely space to fill with cream and berries. Remove cake from pan and peel away parchment.

For limoncello cream, whip cream to soft peaks and whisk in sugar, lemon zest and limoncello. Dollop cream over top of torte.

For berries, wash and gently toss together. Spoon berries over limoncello cream and dust with icing sugar immediately before serving.

Goat cheese torte and cream can be made up to 4 hours in advance. Simply assemble immediately before serving.

MAKES ONE 8-INCH (20-CM) TORTE

ANNA This is a great, showy dessert that takes very little time, and you can change it to suit the season. A cranberry compote makes it perfect for autumn, while rhubarb preserves would be pretty for spring.

MICHAEL A new twist on cheesecake, this can be made with any fruit in season.

COCOONING

>Cocooning implies winter, and these menus are great against the blast of winter's worst. The trip to the gym can happen tomorrow — for now, make the house smell great.

BREAD IN THE OVEN
Is there any kitchen smell better than that of baking bread? After years of cooking and baking, this is still the task we both enjoy the most.

Sweet Potato Scones

Hand-Kneaded Sourdough

Whole Wheat Slicing Loaf

Lemon Blueberry Loaf

SWEET POTATO SCONES

These are a cake-style scone, like a Southern flaky biscuit. We love adding raisins — great for breakfast.

2 cups	500 mL	all-purpose flour
2 Tbsp	25 mL	baking powder
1 tsp	5 mL	ground cinnamon
1 tsp	5 mL	fine salt
1/2 cup	125 mL	cold unsalted butter, cut into pieces
2 cups	500 mL	mashed cooked sweet potato
3/4 cup	175 mL	sugar
1/2 cup	125 mL	raisins
2 Tbsp	25 mL	2% milk

Preheat oven to 350°F (180°C). Combine flour, baking powder, cinnamon and salt in a bowl and cut in butter with your fingers, or a mixer, until it's a rough crumbly texture. In a separate bowl, combine sweet potato and sugar and add to flour, stirring until dough comes together and is an even consistency. Stir in raisins.

On a lightly floured surface, roll or pat out dough to 3/4-inch (2-cm) thickness and cut into desired shapes. Place scones on a parchment-lined baking sheet and brush with milk. Bake for 18 to 20 minutes until lightly browned around the edges. Cool for 10 minutes before eating.

MAKES 12 LARGE SCONES

ANNA Use squash or pumpkin instead of sweet potatoes, without adjusting the recipe at all.

MICHAEL I love apricot jam on these for breakfast.

HAND-KNEADED SOURDOUGH

The hint of rye flour in the starter adds that familiar sour taste of a sourdough bread. Begin this recipe a day ahead — the starter needs time to ferment and develop flavor.

FOR STARTER

1		1	package instant dry yeast
1 cup		250 mL	warm water (105°F/40°C)
1 Tbsp		15 mL	instant skim milk powder
3/4 cup		175 mL	whole wheat flour
1/4 cup		50 mL	rye flour

FOR DOUGH

2 cups		500 mL	warm water (105°F/40°C)
6 cups		1.5 L	unbleached bread flour
1 Tbsp		15 mL	coarse salt
			cornmeal, for sprinkling

ANNA Hand-kneading dough is a relaxing but muscle-toning activity. The kneading action should come from the shoulders and upper arms, where you have more strength, not just the wrists. Do enough hand-kneading and you can treat yourself to a professional massage and have your back kneaded!

Starter should be prepared at least one day in advance. Combine yeast and water and allow to sit for 5 minutes to dissolve. Stir in milk powder and flours, just until blended. Cover starter and set aside at room temperature for a day.

For dough, blend starter with water using a wooden spoon. Add 5 cups (1.25 L) of bread flour and salt and mix until dough becomes too stiff to work. Turn dough out onto a work surface and knead, adding the remaining 1 cup (250 mL) of flour as you go. To knead, use the ball of your hands and push the dough away from you, stretching it. Fold the stretched dough over, turn 90 degrees, and stretch again. Dough is sufficiently kneaded when it has a smooth appearance and springs back when poked. Place dough in an oiled bowl, cover bowl with plastic wrap and set in a warm, draft-free place to rise for 2 hours.

Punch the dough down and turn out onto a work surface. Divide dough in half and shape into 2 boules, or rounds, by rolling in a circular motion on a work surface — the goal is to create a taut outer surface to hold in the air that the yeast produces. Place boules on a baking tray sprinkled with cornmeal and cover with a tea towel. Let rise for 45 minutes.

Preheat oven to 425°F (220°C) and place a baking pan filled with 2 cups (500 mL) water on the lower rack. Brush the tops of the boules with water and score 3 slashes into top of bread with a sharp knife. Bake for 15 minutes, then reduce oven temperature to 375°F (190°C) and bake until bread is a rich golden brown color, and sounds hollow when the bottom is tapped, about 40 minutes total. Allow bread to cool at least 20 minutes before slicing.

MAKES TWO 1-LB (500-G) LOAVES

MICHAEL Bread is the cornerstone of our culinary culture, and even though Anna is the baker in our house, I've been making bread for as long as I've been a chef. There's nothing more gratifying than using the simplest of ingredients and working them by hand to create food that we normally take for granted.

WHOLE WHEAT SLICING LOAF

The smell of this bread baking will remind you of your childhood (or perhaps adult) visits to historical sites or pioneer villages, where they recreate a hearth kitchen. This is the perfect bread for toasted tomato sandwiches or a slathering of jam.

2½ cups	625 mL	warm water (105°F/40°C)
½ cup	125 mL	instant skim milk powder
1	1	package instant dry yeast
¼ cup	50 mL	honey
5 cups	1.25 L	whole wheat flour
1 cup	250 mL	all-purpose flour
1 Tbsp	15 mL	coarse salt
1	1	egg beaten with 1 Tbsp (15 mL) milk, for glazing

Stir water, skim milk powder, yeast and honey together and let sit 5 minutes. Stir in flours and salt. If using a stand-up mixer, knead with a dough hook for 8 minutes on medium-low speed, and if kneading by hand, knead for 12 minutes. Place dough in a lightly oiled bowl, cover bowl with plastic wrap and place in a warm, draft-free place to rise for an hour.

Punch down dough and turn out onto a lightly floured work surface. Divide dough into 3 pieces, and roll out each piece into a rectangle (or oval) 9 inches (23 cm) wide by 12 inches (30 cm) long and about the thickness of pizza dough. Roll up dough from the short end and place into a greased 9 x 5-inch (2-L) loaf pan. Repeat with remaining pieces, cover dough with tea towels and let rise 30 minutes.

Preheat oven to 375°F (190°C). Brush tops of loaves with egg wash and slice a lengthwise slit across the tops. Bake for 45 minutes. Let bread cool for 15 minutes, then turn out loaves from pans to finish cooling.

MAKES THREE 9 x 5-INCH (2-L) LOAVES

ANNA Rolling out risen bread dough as flat as a pizza crust helps you to shape the bread evenly. Once the bread is rolled, feel free to add a filling that could be spiralled in, such as 1 cup (250 mL) of grated cheddar cheese per loaf, or a layer of pesto.

MICHAEL It's important to tap bread loaves out of their pans to finish cooling. If left in the pans, the bread will steam and get a soggy crust.

LEMON BLUEBERRY LOAF

A great one for the freezer, for surprise quests or for the kids' bake sales.

FOR LOAF

6 Tbsp	90 mL	unsalted butter at room temperature
2/3 cup	150 mL	sugar
1 Tbsp	15 mL	finely grated lemon zest
1½ Tbsp	22 mL	vanilla
1	1	large egg at room temperature
2	2	large egg yolks at room temperature
1 cup +1 Tbsp	250 mL +15 mL	all-purpose flour
½ cup	125 mL	pastry flour
2 tsp	10 mL	baking powder
½ tsp	2 mL	fine salt
6 Tbsp	90 mL	buttermilk
1 cup	250 mL	fresh or frozen blueberries

FOR GLAZE

1/3 cup	75 mL	fresh lemon juice
½ cup	125 mL	sugar

For loaf, preheat oven to 350°F (180°C) and grease and sugar a 9 x 5-inch (2-L) loaf pan. In a large bowl, cream butter and sugar until smooth. Stir in lemon zest and vanilla. Beat in egg and egg yolks, until fully incorporated. In separate bowl, sift 1 cup (250 mL) all-purpose flour, pastry flour, baking powder and salt. Add flour to butter mixture alternately with buttermilk, starting and finishing with the flour. Be sure to scrape the sides of the bowl often for an even texture. Toss blueberries with remaining all-purpose flour and fold gently into cake batter. Scrape batter into prepared pan and spread to level. Bake on center rack of the oven for 50 to 60 minutes, until a tester inserted in the center of the cake comes out clean.

For glaze, stir lemon juice and sugar in a small saucepot over medium heat until sugar is dissolved. As soon as cake comes out of the oven, pierce holes in it with a skewer and pour syrup over slowly. Allow cake to cool for 20 minutes, then turn it out onto a plate to cool completely before slicing.

MAKES ONE 9 x 5-INCH (2-L) LOAF
SEE PHOTO ON PAGE 60

ANNA Pound cake gets its name because the original recipe called for a pound of butter, a pound of eggs, a pound of sugar and a pound of flour. And you'll only weigh 4 pounds more after eating all of that! Good thing this version is a little lighter.

MICHAEL If you don't have loaf tins or you want to transport this loaf, use the disposable aluminum ones.

A WINTER'S TALE
A fragrant, slow-cooked meal using winter flavors cheers us up in harsh weather. It's tempting to try to recreate the taste of summer and satisfy your craving for fresh flavors, but you'll end up disappointed by dry produce that costs far more than it should.

White Bean Soup

Black Beer Braised Short Ribs

Brown Rice

Cumin-Scented Cauliflower

Coconut Cream Pie

<LEMON BLUEBERRY LOAF, PAGE 59

WHITE BEAN SOUP

A hearty bean soup can warm even the coldest person after an afternoon of shoveling snow or sledding.

2 strips	2 strips	bacon, diced
1 cup	250 mL	diced onion
1/2 cup	125 mL	diced celery
2 cloves	2 cloves	garlic, minced
2 tsp	10 mL	chopped fresh thyme
2	2	14-oz (398-mL) cans white navy or kidney beans
4 cups	1 L	chicken stock or water
		coarse salt and ground black pepper
		extra virgin olive oil for garnish

In a medium saucepot over medium heat, sauté bacon until crisp and remove to drain on paper towel. In the same pot, cook the onions and celery until translucent, about 5 minutes. Add garlic and thyme and cook 1 minute more. Rinse and drain the beans, reserving 1/2 cup (125 mL). Add beans and chicken stock or water to saucepot, bring to a simmer, cook 20 minutes and purée. Add reserved beans and reheat. Season to taste and garnish with a drizzle of olive oil and the reserved bacon bits.

SERVES 6

ANNA This has to be one of the fastest soups ever to make — on the table in no time. That said, like all good soups, this one tastes better the second day.

MICHAEL A puréed soup doesn't have to be as thick as a dip. Even a soup such as this should be eaten with a spoon, not a fork.

BLACK BEER BRAISED SHORT RIBS

How about filling the house with the warm stewy scent of braising beef ribs?
These take hours, but it's cold outside — you're not going anywhere.

7 lb	3 kg	beef short (braising) ribs, square cut
		coarse salt and ground black pepper
2 Tbsp	25 mL	extra virgin olive oil
2 cups	500 mL	diced onions
¾ cup	175 mL	diced carrots
½ cup	125 mL	diced celery
2 cloves	2 cloves	garlic, minced
1	1	14-oz (455-mL) can diced tomatoes
1	1	12-oz (355-mL) can dark beer
½ cup	125 mL	dark brown sugar, packed
1 Tbsp	15 mL	crushed coriander seeds
1	1	orange, zest and juice
2	2	bay leaves
1	1	fresh jalapeño pepper (optional)

Season ribs with salt and pepper. In a large heavy-bottomed casserole over medium-high heat, brown short ribs in oil in batches and remove. Reduce heat to medium and sauté the onions, carrots and celery until onions are translucent, about 5 minutes. Add garlic and cook 1 minute more, then add remaining ingredients. Return ribs to the casserole, bring to a boil, reduce to a simmer, cover and cook 2½ hours, or until rib meat comes away from the bone easily. Remove ribs carefully, skim off excess fat and season sauce to taste. Serve sauce spooned over short ribs in a pasta bowl.

SERVES 6

ANNA The beer's sweetness and the orange zest create a pleasant surprise, especially when countered with a little chili pepper heat.

MICHAEL Beef short ribs are squares of wide rib bones with as much gristle as meat. The slow cooking breaks down the tough tissue to make this a succulent cut. The easiest way to remove excess fat? Put the pot in the fridge after it has cooled and skim off the fat pieces the next day.

BROWN RICE

Brown rice is a tasty way to add fiber to your diet. Give it extra time on the stove, though — it takes longer to cook than white rice.

2 cups	500 mL	water
1 cup	250 mL	brown rice
1	1	bay leaf
1/2 tsp	2 mL	fine salt
1 tsp	5 mL	unsalted butter
4	4	whole cloves

Run water over rice and wash until water runs clear. Drain. Bring water to a boil and add remaining ingredients. Allow to return to boil, then cover and simmer slowly for 40 minutes or until water is absorbed into rice. Remove from heat, let stand a few minutes, remove cloves and gently fluff with a fork before serving.

SERVES 6

CUMIN-SCENTED CAULIFLOWER

Adding fragrance to this supper makes it an appealing mid-winter meal.
Who needs Mexico's hot sun? We don't!

1 Tbsp	15 mL	unsalted butter
1	1	small onion, diced
1	1	red bell pepper, seeded and diced
1 tsp	5 mL	whole cumin seeds
1 tsp	5 mL	freshly grated ginger
		coarse salt
6 cups	1.5 L	cauliflower florets
2/3 cup	150 mL	water
1 Tbsp	15 mL	fresh coriander, chopped
1	1	lime, cut in 6 wedges

Melt butter in a saucepot over medium heat and add onion and pepper, cooking until tender, about
5 minutes. Add cumin and ginger and sauté 1 minute further with a pinch of salt. Stir in cauliflower
and add water. Cover and simmer over medium heat 8 minutes, or until the cauliflower breaks
easily with a fork. Top with coriander and serve with lime wedge.

SERVES 6

ANNA This sounds like such a down-home meal,
but we'd proudly serve it to guests. A properly
cooked meal is a work of art, no matter how
humble the ingredients.

MICHAEL We once accidentally overcooked our
cauliflower until all the florets exploded. We
drained the water, stirred in yogurt, cumin and a little cheese, and we had a tasty cauliflower purée!

COCONUT CREAM PIE

A macaroon crust makes this a tropical dream. Let the sun shine in, if only in your mind.

FOR CRUST

2	2	egg whites
½ cup	125 mL	sugar
3 Tbsp	45 mL	all-purpose flour
½ tsp	2.5 mL	vanilla
2 cups	500 mL	unsweetened coconut

FOR COCONUT FILLING

⅔ cup	150 mL	sugar
2½ Tbsp	37 mL	cornstarch
¼ cup	50 mL	fine salt
2¼ cups	550 mL	coconut milk
2	2	whole large eggs
2	2	large egg yolks
1 tsp	5 mL	vanilla
2 Tbsp	25 mL	unsalted butter
1 cup	250 mL	unsweetened coconut, lightly toasted

FOR CREAM TOPPING

1½ cups	375 mL	whipping cream
¼ cup	50 mL	sugar
1 Tbsp	15 mL	skim milk powder
½ cup	125 mL	diced dried pineapple

ANNA The filling for this pie, and many cream pies, is a pastry cream. Didn't know you were using a "chef-y" technique, did you?

MICHAEL Our storage buffet used to be the pie fridge of Keith's Restaurant in Fonthill, Ontario. It was, and still is, known for its excellent pies. The kitchen had a ruler for measuring the lemon meringue pies, so they could fit into the fridge.

To prepare crust, preheat oven to 275°F (140°C). Stir together egg whites, sugar, flour and vanilla until sugar has half-dissolved. Stir in coconut until evenly coated with egg mixture. Grease a 9-inch (23-cm) pie plate and press in crust, dipping your fingers in a cup of cool water while doing this to prevent the mixture from sticking. Bake for 35 to 45 minutes, rotating pan halfway through baking. Crust will be a rich, golden brown around the edges. Allow to cool in pie plate.

For filling, stir sugar, cornstarch and salt together in a heavy-bottomed saucepot. Whisk in coconut milk, whole eggs and egg yolks. Heat custard on low heat, whisking constantly for 5 minutes. Increase heat to medium and continue whisking until custard thickens and becomes glossy, about 5 more minutes. Remove from heat and strain. Stir in vanilla, butter and coconut and stir until butter has melted. Pour immediately into cooled pie shell, let sit on the counter for 15 minutes, then chill completely before topping with cream, at least 4 hours.

For cream topping, whip cream to medium peaks, and whisk in sugar and skim milk powder (the skim milk powder stabilizes the cream) and stir in dried pineapple. Top coconut custard with whipped cream.

MAKES ONE 9-INCH (23-CM) PIE

COUCH POTATOES We're told to fear carbohydrates, but we'd hate to see potatoes fall completely out of favor. They're cheap, tasty and, best of all, comforting. Potatoes make great sponges for other flavors — take advantage of their full potential.

Brandade de Morue

Potato Salmon Torta

Golden Delicious Cake with Fudgy Frosting

BRANDADE de MORUE

Buy salt cod at your grocery store's fish department. It can be stored in your pantry, but because of its fishy smell we prefer to buy it as we need it.

¼ lb	125 g	dried salted cod
2	2	medium baking potatoes
4 Tbsp	50 mL	extra virgin olive oil
2 cloves	2 cloves	garlic, minced
¼ cup	50 mL	whipping cream
dash	dash	ground black pepper
2 Tbsp	25 mL	chopped Italian parsley

Break salt cod into pieces and soak in water for 2 hours, rinsing and changing water 4 times, to remove excess salt (or cover with water and soak in fridge overnight).

Peel and dice potatoes and cook in boiling, salted water until tender. Drain and roughly mash with a fork or potato masher and set aside. To the pot in which potatoes were cooked, add olive oil and garlic and sauté over medium heat for 2 minutes. Add drained and rinsed cod pieces and toss with garlic oil. Add potatoes and cream to pot and stir until warmed through. Stir in black pepper and parsley and serve in small bowls.

SERVES 4

ANNA Traditionally, salt cod is soaked for 12 to 24 hours, but rinsing the cod every half hour for a few hours clears the fish of its salt. For added sweetness, soak the fish in milk.

MICHAEL This is a poor man's dish found in every Mediterranean culture, with Italian, Spanish and Portuguese versions as well as this French variation. The method may vary a little, but the humble ingredients of preserved fish and potatoes stay the same. True comfort food.

POTATO SALMON TORTA

This is one of those beautiful foods — relatively simple to make — that works with comforting, familiar flavors, but it's absolutely gorgeous when you slice into it to reveal a layer of spinach potato topped with a salmon layer. The torta presents well because we use a springform pan to make a tall, straight-sided pie, but a regular 9-inch (23-cm) pie pan will also work.

FOR POTATO LAYER

2	2	large Yukon Gold potatoes
2 cloves	2 cloves	garlic, peeled
1/2 cup	125 mL	sour cream
2 Tbsp	25 mL	unsalted butter
dash	dash	ground nutmeg
4 cups	1 L	spinach leaves, washed and trimmed
		coarse salt and ground black pepper

FOR SALMON LAYER

2 Tbsp	25 mL	extra virgin olive oil
2	2	shallots, sliced
1 1/2 lb	750 g	salmon fillet, diced
		coarse salt and ground black pepper
8 oz	250 g	cream cheese at room temperature
2	2	hard boiled eggs

FOR ASSEMBLY

1	1	recipe pie pastry (page 248)
1	1	egg mixed with 2 Tbsp (25 mL) water for egg wash

ANNA I love crossing savory cooking with pastry techniques, and a pie such as this is really fun to make. Try changing your flavors a bit. Add 1 cup (250 mL) of grated cheddar cheese to the potatoes and use 1 1/2 pounds (750 g) of cooked ground pork or beef instead of the salmon for a shepherd's pie variation.

MICHAEL I like these recipes, too, because I can get involved in the pastry kitchen, so to speak. Usually when we make this together, we switch roles: I make the pie dough, while Anna makes the filling. This is another of those perfect make-ahead recipes ideal for freezing.

For potato layer, peel and dice potatoes and boil with garlic in salted water until tender. Drain and roughly mash potatoes and garlic with sour cream, butter and nutmeg and season. While still warm, stir in spinach leaves to wilt. Cool completely.

For salmon layer, heat a sauté pan over medium-high heat and add olive oil and shallots. Stir for 1 minute, then add diced salmon. Sauté salmon until just evenly pink but cooked, and remove from heat. Season salmon and break in pieces of softened cream cheese. Grate egg over mixture and stir together until evenly combined. Adjust seasoning if necessary and chill completely.

To assemble, preheat oven to 400°F (200°C). On a lightly floured surface, roll out two-thirds of pie dough to just less than 1/4 inch (5 mm) thick. Line an 8-inch (20-cm) springform pan with pastry so that it hangs over the sides. Spoon the potato filling into the bottom of the pan and top with salmon filling, pressing down to fill and level. Roll out remaining dough and place over salmon filling. Trim edges and pinch together to seal. Brush top of torta with eggwash, snip a few airholes on top of torta and place pan on a baking tray. Bake for 15 minutes at 400°F (200°C), then reduce oven temperature to 350°C (180°C) and bake until torta is a rich, golden brown color, about 35 minutes.

Allow torta to cool 15 minutes before slicing, or chill completely and serve cold with mixed greens.

SERVES 6 TO 8

GOLDEN DELICIOUS CAKE WITH FUDGY FROSTING

Can't decide whether to make a vanilla or chocolate cake? Well, here you can get the best of both worlds (and you'll use this frosting for all other cakes you make).

FOR CAKE

1 cup	250 mL	unsalted butter at room temperature
2 cups	500 mL	sugar
2 tsp	10 mL	vanilla
4	4	large eggs at room temperature
2 3/4 cups	675 mL	pastry flour
1/2 tsp	2 mL	baking powder
1/4 tsp	1 mL	baking soda
1/2 tsp	2 mL	fine salt
1 cup	250 mL	buttermilk at room temperature

FOR FROSTING

1 1/2 cups	375 mL	unsalted butter at room temperature
1/2 cup	125 mL	cream cheese at room temperature
12 oz	360 g	bittersweet or semisweet chocolate, chopped, melted and cooled to room temperature
2 tsp	10 mL	vanilla
1/4 tsp	1 mL	fine salt
2 1/2 cups	625 mL	icing sugar, sifted

For cake, preheat oven to 325°F (160°C) and grease and flour three 9-inch (23-cm) round cake pans.

Beat butter in a mixer fitted with the paddle attachment, or with electric beaters, until light and fluffy. Add sugar and beat until fluffy. Beat in vanilla and add eggs, one at a time, blending well after each addition. In a separate bowl, sift flour, baking powder, baking soda and salt. Add flour, 1/2 cup (125 mL) at a time, mixing on a lower speed and alternating with buttermilk until all has been added and batter is smooth. Scrape batter evenly into the 3 prepared pans (I use a measuring cup to dole out the batter equally) and level with a spatula. Give the cake pans a gentle tap on the counter to loosen up any trapped air bubbles. Bake on center oven rack for 30 to 40 minutes, rotating pans halfway through cooking, until a tester inserted in the center of the cake comes out clean. Cool cakes for 20 minutes, then turn out on a rack to cool completely.

For frosting, beat butter and cream cheese on high speed, scraping sides frequently, until light and fluffy. Reduce speed and add melted chocolate. Add vanilla, salt and icing sugar and beat until smooth.

To frost the cake, top one layer with icing and spread. Place second cake layer on top. Ice the top of the cake and finish with the sides. Chill cake to set, but it's best stored at room temperature.

SERVES 12

ANNA Whenever my mom asked me what kind of cake I wanted for my birthday, this was the style I'd request. Now I can make my cake and eat it, too!

MICHAEL I like this cake because the frosting sets, and when cutting into a slice you can peel off a little of the icing first and eat it like candy.

KIDS

>Kids can be our toughest critics. Even if they're being polite and eating something they don't like, you can read their faces like a book! At the same time, nothing beats that look of satisfaction as children dig hungrily into a plate full of their favorite foods.

>For special occasions like birthday parties, you feed children or young adults as a group. You're going to have enough to worry about (such as putting breakables out of reach) without spending all your time in the kitchen. The menus in this section can be prepared ahead of time and cooked just before serving — so you can keep an eye on more important things.

BIRTHDAY PARTY

Since nap time isn't a recognized birthday party activity, meal time is the only chance you have to get 12 kids to sit down together (and even that can be a challenge). With appealing goodies on the table, you might have 10 minutes to pick up the confetti and tipped-over chairs in the other room.

Individual Cheese "Fondues"
Baked Sweet Potato Fries
Mini Hamburgers
Chocolate Birthday Cheesecake

INDIVIDUAL CHEESE "FONDUES"

What a great way to sneak vegetables into the meal without the kids noticing!
And don't worry — this is a great, cheesy dipping sauce that you don't serve in a
fondue pot. No open flames on the table, please!

FOR VEGETABLES

1½ cups	375 mL	cauliflower florets
1½ cups	375 mL	broccoli florets
1½ cups	375 mL	snow peas
1½ cups	375 mL	carrot sticks
1½ cups	375 mL	celery sticks

FOR CHEESE FONDUE

4 cups	1 L	grated mild cheddar cheese
4 cups	1 L	grated Swiss cheese
2 Tbsp	25 mL	cornstarch
1 tsp	5 mL	dried mustard powder
½ tsp	2 mL	garlic powder
2 cups	500 mL	2% milk

Vegetables can be prepared a day in advance and stored in sealable bags until ready to serve.
Arrange vegetables on individual plates. Place a ramekin or cup on each plate for the fondue.

To prepare fondue, toss grated cheeses with cornstarch, mustard powder and garlic powder.
Heat milk in a saucepot over medium heat until just below a simmer. Add cheese mixture and
stir with a wooden spoon until melted completely and fondue just begins to bubble. Remove
from heat and allow to cool for 10 minutes. Spoon into dipping cups and serve.

Fondue can be prepared a day in advance and reheated in the microwave for convenience.

SERVES 12 KIDS (OR 6 ADULTS)

ANNA If you've got a crowd of older kids (8+),
put the fondue in a coffee cup and arrange the
vegetables on the saucer around the cup.

MICHAEL Forget the kids! This is my kind of snack:
I'll grab any opportunity to play with my food!

BAKED SWEET POTATO FRIES

There's something incredibly satisfying about the salt/sweet combination of these fries. Deep frying sweet potatoes can result in a soggy fry, or else an over-cooked one, due to the sugars in the potato. Baking is a simpler and healthier alternative to frying, without sacrificing one little bit of taste.

3 lb	1.5 kg	sweet potatoes
3 Tbsp	45 mL	extra virgin olive oil
1 Tbsp	15 mL	coarse salt
1 tsp	5 mL	Spanish (mild) paprika

Preheat oven to 450°F (230°C) and place a baking sheet in the oven to preheat. Peel and cut sweet potatoes into 1/2-inch (1-cm) thick sticks about 3 inches (8 cm) long. Toss with olive oil, salt and paprika. Remove baking sheet from oven. Spread sweet potato fries in a single layer on the baking sheet and cook for 20 to 30 minutes, stirring gently occasionally until fries are cooked through and browned.

SERVES 12 KIDS (6 ADULTS)

ANNA Sweet potato fries are delicious served to grownups with a spicy ketchup or with mayonnaise with a little added lemon juice.

MICHAEL Don't limit your "fries" to regular potatoes or sweet potatoes. Try parsnips for a baker's cupboard taste or pumpkin for a mellow flavor.

MINI HAMBURGERS

Mini hamburgers bring out the kid in each of us. Don't limit this dish just to kids' parties. These make great hors d'oeuvres or a coffee table snack during the big game!

2½ lb	1.25 kg	lean ground beef
2	2	large eggs
½ cup	125 mL	breadcrumbs
1 Tbsp	15 mL	soy sauce
1 tsp	5 mL	dried mustard powder
1 tsp	5 mL	ground cumin (optional)
1 tsp	5 mL	fine salt
½ tsp	2 mL	ground black pepper
24	24	small dinner rolls
		cheese, bacon and other toppings of your choice

Preheat grill to medium high heat or preheat oven to 400°F (200°C). Combine ground beef with eggs, breadcumbs, soy sauce, mustard powder, cumin (if adding), salt and pepper until it's an even texture. Use a ¼ cup (50 mL) ice cream scoop or your hands and make meatball-sized portions of beef. Flatten mini burgers and place on a baking tray. Grill or bake burgers until well done, 12 to 15 minutes. To serve, finish with desired toppings, or let everyone dress their own and serve on split small dinner rolls.

The mini burger patties can be made a day or more in advance and frozen. Simply thaw in the fridge before cooking.

MAKES 18 MINI BURGERS
SERVES 12 KIDS (6 ADULTS)

ANNA I like these burgers for a crowd of kids because even children of the same age have different appetites. Some kids will eat one burger and some may have three, but you're rarely left with half-eaten burgers.

MICHAEL Use this recipe to make great meatballs for a spaghetti dinner or for a large meatball sandwich on a panini bun.

CHOCOLATE BIRTHDAY CHEESECAKE

Chocolate, oh yeah! This is an irresistible combination — a brownie bottom and a fluffy, mousse-like chocolate, cream-cheese filling that doesn't need to be baked. This is another great make-ahead recipe to keep that party simple and smooth-sailing.

FOR BROWNIE LAYER

1 cup	250 mL	unsalted butter
1 cup	250 mL	cocoa powder
1¾ cups	425 mL	sugar
4	4	large eggs at room temperature
2 tsp	10 mL	vanilla
1¼ cups	300 mL	all-purpose flour
1 tsp	5 mL	baking powder
½ tsp	2 mL	fine salt

FOR CHEESECAKE LAYER

6 oz	175 g	semi-sweet chocolate, chopped
2	2	8-oz (250-g) packages of cream cheese at room temperature
½ cup	125 mL	sugar
1 tsp	5 mL	vanilla
1½ cups	375 mL	whipping cream
10	10	Oreo cookies, cut in half

For brownie layer, preheat oven to 350°F (180°C). Grease a 10-inch (25-cm) springform cake pan and line bottom and sides with parchment paper. Melt butter and pour into a larger bowl. Sift cocoa into butter and stir in sugar. Add eggs to mixture, blending well after each addition. Stir in vanilla. In a separate bowl, combine flour, baking powder and salt (don't sift). Add to cocoa mixture and blend. Pour into pan and bake for 35 minutes, until firm. Cool completely before filling.

For cheesecake layer, place chopped chocolate in a bowl over a pot of gently simmering water (be sure bowl does not touch the water) and stir to melt. Remove from heat. Beat cream cheese until fluffy with electric beaters or in a stand mixer with the whisk attachment on high speed. Slowly add sugar while mixing and beat in vanilla. Pour in whipping cream and whip into cream cheese on high speed, until mixture becomes firm and holds a peak. Scrape chocolate into mixture and blend quickly. Scrape filling onto brownie base and spread evenly.

To garnish, remove springform pan and arrange Oreo cookie halves around top of cake.

SERVES 12 KIDS

ANNA Make sure to save a piece for yourself to enjoy after the kids are gone and you've cleaned up after the hurricane, and you're ready to put your feet up.

MICHAEL My beverage pairing suggestion: ice-cold milk.

FOR TWEENS AND TEENS

The bottomless pit of a teenager's stomach can be a challenge to fill. There seem to be only two main areas of appetite fulfillment: pizza and Mexican. Since we provide a great Design-Your-Own Pizza dinner on page 21, here we supply a tasty menu of Mexican delights. >In Canada, good Mexican restaurants aren't as plentiful as in the US, but we still have access to the ingredients to cook Mexican at home. With flavors such as garlic, cumin, coriander and lime, our culinary boundaries are open to let the free trade begin!

Chicken Tortilla Soup

Beef Enchiladas

Red Rice

Black Bean Coriander Salad

Cinnamon "Fried" Ice Cream Sundaes

CHICKEN TORTILLA SOUP

Despite the long list of ingredients, this soup is a snap to make. We love to serve this for lunch on a cold, wintry day — a great replacement for chili.

2 Tbsp	25 mL	extra virgin olive oil
4	4	boneless, skinless chicken breasts, diced
1 cup	250 mL	diced onion
½ cup	125 mL	diced celery
¼ cup	50 mL	peeled and diced carrot
2 Tbsp	25 mL	ground cumin
4 tsp	20 mL	ground coriander
4 tsp	20 mL	chili powder
3 cloves	3 cloves	garlic, minced
3 Tbsp	45 mL	finely minced jalapeño pepper (optional)
2	2	28-oz (796-mL) cans diced tomatoes
4 cups	1 L	water or beer
		coarse salt and ground black pepper
⅓ cup	75 mL	chopped fresh coriander
2 Tbsp	25 mL	fresh lime juice
4 cups	1 L	corn tortilla chips

Heat olive oil in a soup pot over medium-high heat. Add diced chicken and sauté until browned, about 4 minutes. Remove from pan and set aside. Reduce heat to medium and add onions, celery and carrot. Sweat vegetables for 5 minutes, until onions are translucent. Stir in cumin, coriander, chili powder, garlic and jalapeño, if using, and stir for one minute. Add tomatoes and water (or beer) and bring up to a simmer. Return chicken to pot and simmer, partially covered, until chicken is cooked and carrots are tender, 15 to 20 minutes. Season to taste.

Immediately before serving, stir in chopped coriander and lime juice. Lightly crush tortilla chips and place ½ cup (125 mL) of chips into each soup bowl. Ladle soup over chips and serve.

SERVES 6 TEENS (8 ADULTS)

ANNA Like any good soup, this one tastes better the next day. If you're making it a day ahead, add the coriander and lime juice right before you serve it. If you're reheating the soup as leftovers, you may have to add a little more coriander and lime to bring their sharpness back.

MICHAEL The first time Anna made this soup I wondered why she put the crumbled tortilla chips in the bottom of the bowl, since the temptation as a chef is to use them as a garnish on top. Remember your tomato soup as a kid, with the squashed-up saltine crackers? Well, this is better!

BEEF ENCHILADAS

Make this entrée a day ahead to save time, or assemble and freeze the enchiladas for your next potluck contribution.

2 Tbsp	25 mL	extra virgin olive oil
3 lb	1.5 kg	lean ground beef
1 cup	250 mL	diced onion
4 cloves	4 cloves	garlic, minced
2 Tbsp	25 mL	minced jalapeño pepper
1 Tbsp	15 mL	ground cumin
2 tsp	10 mL	ground coriander
2 tsp	10 mL	coarse salt and ground black pepper
2 cups	500 mL	tomato salsa
16	16	large flour tortillas
1	1	14-oz (398-mL) can refried beans
1 cup	250 mL	green tomatillo sauce
		OR 1 cup (250 mL) tomato salsa
3 cups	750 mL	grated Monterey Jack cheese
3 cups	750 mL	grated medium Cheddar cheese
3/4 cup	175 mL	sour cream
1/2 cup	125 mL	chopped green onion

Heat oil in a large sauté pan over medium-high heat. Add ground beef and cook until well done. Remove beef, draining off excess fat and return pan to medium heat. Add onions and sauté until translucent, about 5 minutes. Add garlic, jalapeño pepper and spices and cook 1 minute more. Return beef to pan and add 1 cup (250 mL) of tomato salsa with 1/2 cup (125 mL) of water and simmer until liquid is absorbed. Remove from heat and season to taste.

Preheat oven to 375°F (190°C) and grease two 11 x 7-inch (2-L) baking dishes. To assemble enchiladas, spread out 4 tortillas (or as many as you'd like to fit on your counter) and spoon about 1/2 cup (125 mL) of beef mixture in the center of each. Top with a generous dollop of refried beans and sprinkle with a mix of cheddar and Monterey Jack cheeses (about 2 Tbsp [25 mL] of each). Spoon a little of the green tomatillo sauce (if available) or tomato salsa over cheese, but leave about 1 1/2 cups (375 mL) of sauce for the tops of the enchiladas. Roll up tortillas into a large cigar shape, tucking in the ends so the filling does not leak out. Place enchiladas in prepared baking dishes, close together and repeat process until all tortillas are filled. Sprinkle enchiladas with remaining cheese and salsa and bake for 25 to 30 minutes, or until cheese is melted and bubbling. Let cool for 5 minutes, then top with dollops of sour cream and green onion and serve.

MAKES 16 ENCHILADAS

ANNA I learned a lot about Mexican cooking when I worked in Texas. These dishes satisfy the cravings I still have for those fantastic, brash flavors.

MICHAEL What I love about Mexican food is the wonderful fragrance of chilis, spices, coriander, corn and lime intermingled. With that combination, feel free to use ground pork, chicken or turkey instead of ground beef.

RED RICE

Flavor and simplicity go hand in hand. Perfect as part of a Mexican fiesta, this rice is also great under a piece of grilled fish.

2½ cups	625 mL	long grain white rice
dash	dash	fine salt
2 tsp	10 mL	chili powder
2	2	bay leaves
2 Tbsp	25 mL	unsalted butter
3 Tbsp	45 mL	tomato paste
2/3 cup	150 mL	chopped green onion
1/3 cup	75 mL	chopped fresh coriander
2 tsp	10 mL	coarse salt

ANNA I have a mental block when it comes to cooking rice. I either overcook it until it's squishy and sticks to the bottom of the pot, or it's still crunchy. See, even a professional chef has a food nemesis.

Bring 5 cups (1.25 L) water up to a boil and add rice, a dash of salt, chili powder and bay leaves. Cover pot, reduce heat to a simmer and cook rice without lifting lid until water has been absorbed, about 20 minutes (you can peek after 15 minutes). Remove bay leaves and add remaining ingredients, stirring until warm and evenly blended.

SERVES 6 TEENS (8 ADULTS)

MICHAEL I love cooking rice (Anna will always let me cook it for her). Take this rice recipe in a different direction by adding 2 Tbsp (25 mL) chopped jalapeño, 1/4 cup (50 mL) green chili sauce, 1 cup (250 mL) drained canned kidney beans and 1 cup (250 mL) fresh or frozen corn kernels.

BLACK BEAN CORIANDER SALAD

Feeding a group of teens is easy with make-ahead dishes like this. It's even easier if your teenaged "host" gives you a hand in the kitchen or really plays the part of host by making the whole meal. What a sense of pride!

1	1	14-oz (398-mL) can black beans
1/2 cup	125 mL	chopped green onion
1/2 cup	125 mL	diced red bell pepper
1 cup	250 mL	diced fresh tomato
1/4 cup	50 mL	chopped coriander
2 cloves	2 cloves	garlic, minced
2 Tbsp	25 mL	fresh lime juice
		fine salt and ground black pepper
1 tsp	5 mL	freshly grated lime zest
1	1	avocado, diced

ANNA Sometimes I purée all these ingredients together for a black bean dip, with a dollop of sour cream on top.

MICHAEL I use this recipe (in smaller amounts) as a salsa for grilled chicken or pork.

Drain and rinse black beans until the water runs clear. Toss together all ingredients except avocado, season to taste and chill. Immediately before serving, toss in avocado.

SERVES 6 TEENS (8 ADULTS)

CINNAMON "FRIED" ICE CREAM SUNDAES

Mika, Michael's daughter, is a young teen, and this dessert is just her sort of thing.

FOR CINNAMON "FRIED" ICE CREAM

8 cups	2 L	vanilla ice cream
1½ tsp	7 mL	cinnamon
2 cups	500 mL	cornflake crumbs
¼ cup	50 mL	light brown sugar, packed
3 Tbsp	45 mL	unsalted butter, melted

FOR CHOCOLATE SAUCE

1 cup	250 mL	water
⅔ cup	150 mL	sugar
½ cup	125 mL	Dutch process cocoa powder
1 tsp	5 mL	instant coffee
1 tsp	5 mL	cinnamon
½ cup	125 mL	whipping cream

FOR GARNISH

whipped cream
toasted pecans or peanuts

For cinnamon "fried" ice cream, soften ice cream on kitchen counter for 10 minutes. Beat cinnamon into ice cream with electric beaters and refreeze until firm. Combine cornflake crumbs, brown sugar and melted butter. Scoop ice cream balls, roll them in crumbs and refreeze for up to 2 hours (any longer and they will become soggy).

For chocolate sauce, bring water and sugar to a boil for 3 to 5 minutes. Sift cocoa powder and whisk in with instant coffee and cinnamon, and return to a boil. Reduce heat to medium-low, add cream and whisk until sauce thickens, about 3 minutes. Sauce can be served warm or chilled.

To make sundaes, place 2 ice cream balls in a bowl and pour chocolate sauce around. Top with whipped cream and toasted nuts and serve.

SERVES 6 TEENS (8 ADULTS)

ANNA Another easy ice cream dessert for a group of teens — the make-your-own-sundae station. Lots of fruit and crunchy toppings make everybody happy.

MICHAEL To save time, skip the step of adding cinnamon to the ice cream. Simply work it into the crunchy coating.

NECESSITY

>Yes, it's obvious that food is a necessity, but what we mean in this section goes beyond mere function. Good technique is a necessary part of cooking, so we've included menus using the BASICS, with each recipe focusing on an important cooking technique — a translation of our culinary school instruction. BUDGET is definitely a function of necessity. When wearing our chef whites, we enjoy cooking with foie gras, truffles and lobster but, like you, our waistlines and wallets can't afford to eat like that all the time. But less money doesn't mean less flavor. We're also pleased to introduce CRAVINGS as a necessity — sometimes you "need" chocolate. It goes beyond a mere whim. And where would we be without BREAKFAST, the most important, and most often ignored, meal of the day?

BASICS

>This is our chance to provide a crash-course cooking school curriculum. Our aim is to make you comfortable with a few new techniques or to expand your understanding of what you've already been doing for years!

START WITH THE SAUCES

The first course often required at professional cooking schools (after Safety in the Kitchen 101) is Sauces. There's a finite number of common proteins we cook at home (chicken, pork, beef and fish, mainly) but once you've mastered a few sauce techniques, your flavor combinations become infinite.

>Auguste Escoffier, master chef and executive chef of the Hotel Ritz in Paris at the turn of the last century, broke classical sauce preparation into six basic categories: tomato, Espagnole, demi-glace, béchamel, hollandaise and velouté. Though a true Espagnole sauce on a menu is rare, there are many variations of the other classics. Restaurants rely on demi-glace, or reductions of veal stock as a key sauce, but this labor-intensive and costly preparation is hardly practical to produce at home.

>We've provided a menu that uses some basic sauce techniques, along with some recommended flavor variations. Try your hand at it and don't be afraid to get creative!

Old School Warm Spinach Salad with Bacon and Mushroom
Tagliatelle with Hearty Beef Tomato Ragout
Challah Bread Pudding with Crème Anglaise

OLD SCHOOL WARM SPINACH SALAD WITH BACON AND MUSHROOM

A warm vinaigrette is a wonderful thing. Heat heightens the flavor of everything it touches and requires substantially less oil than many chilled vinaigrettes.

6 cups	1.5 L	washed spinach leaves, trimmed of stems
6 slices	6 slices	bacon, diced
6 Tbsp	90 mL	extra virgin olive oil
1 cup	250 mL	sliced white mushrooms
1 clove	1 clove	garlic, minced
½ tsp	2 mL	dried mustard powder
3 Tbsp	45 mL	red wine vinegar
		coarse salt and ground black pepper
3	3	hard boiled eggs, peeled and chopped
⅔ cup	150 mL	sliced red onion (about ½ an onion)

ANNA I worked as a server at an old-fashioned hotel (perhaps I'm dating myself!) that would serve caesar salad and this salad prepared table-side. To prepare a salad in front of an audience requires confidence, or in its absence, an ability to distract guests so that they notice you more than the salad you're making. Note that only 6 Tbsp (90 mL) of olive oil is required in this recipe to make the vinaigrette — a very small amount as salad dressings go.

Arrange spinach leaves on plates or a serving platter.

Cook bacon until crispy in a large sauté pan. Remove bacon, drain excess fat and return pan to medium heat. Add 2 Tbsp (25 mL) of oil and mushrooms and sauté for 2 to 3 minutes, until soft but not fully cooked. Stir in garlic and mustard powder. Add vinegar, season lightly and stir for one minute. Stir in remaining olive oil, remove from heat and adjust seasoning. Spoon dressing over spinach leaves and top with reserved bacon, chopped egg and red onion. Serve immediately.

SERVES 6

MICHAEL These days you can buy spinach in baby leaves — full, tied bunches or cello packs. Whichever style you choose, be sure to wash the spinach well and trim off the tough stems.

TAGLIATELLE WITH HEARTY BEEF TOMATO RAGOUT
ANNA A few birthdays ago, I gave Michael a pasta machine with all the bells and whistles. We've had lots of fun playing with it in the kitchen and fine-tuning our technique. It makes a great gift for the foodie in your family.

MICHAEL When we make pasta at home, we always start with a small bowl of the noodles with just a little olive oil, salt and pepper to savor our efforts.

TAGLIATELLE WITH HEARTY BEEF TOMATO RAGOUT

As this is the "cooking class" section of the book, we thought we'd present you with our recipe for perfect pasta dough. Of course, if you focus all your attention on the sauce, then a good-quality, fresh, store-bought pasta will do just fine > The pasta sauce is derived from a classic tomato sauce. Stewing beef, slowly braised, creates an aromatic and rich sauce that's perfect for a chilly November night.

FOR PASTA DOUGH

2¹/₃ cups	575 mL	all-purpose flour
1/2 tsp	2 mL	fine salt
3	3	large eggs
1 Tbsp	15 mL	water

FOR HEARTY BEEF RAGOUT

2 Tbsp	250 mL	extra virgin olive oil	2 sprigs	2 sprigs	fresh thyme
1¹/₂ lb	750 g	stewing beef, cubed	1 sprig	1 sprig	fresh rosemary
2 Tbsp	25 mL	all-purpose flour	1 cup	250 mL	red wine
3/4 cup	175 mL	diced onion	1	1	28-oz (796-mL) can
1/2 cup	125 mL	diced carrot			diced tomato
1/2 cup	125 mL	diced celery	coarse salt and ground black pepper
2 cloves	2 cloves	garlic, minced	olive oil, salt and pepper for pasta
2	2	bay leaves	Parmesan cheese for garnish

For pasta, pulse flour and salt in a food processor. With the processor running, add eggs and water and pulse until dough is a rough, crumbly texture. Turn dough onto a work surface, shape into 2 disks and wrap in plastic. Allow to chill at least an hour before rolling. Roll pasta into thin sheets through a pasta machine, according to manufacturer's instructions. If you don't have a tagliatelle-size cutter, roll the pasta into lasagne sheets and cut into 1/2-inch (1-cm) strips. Toss tagliatelle with a little flour or semolina, shape into nests and let dry until ready to cook. If not using within 4 hours, wrap and refrigerate pasta.

For the beef ragout, heat a large stockpot over medium-high heat and add 1 Tbsp (15 mL) olive oil. Toss beef cubes in flour. Shake off excess flour and sear beef in pot until browned on all sides, doing this in batches so as not to overcrowd the pot. Remove beef and reduce heat to medium. Add remaining 1 Tbsp (15 mL) olive oil. Add onion, carrots and celery and sauté for 5 minutes, until onion becomes translucent. Add garlic, bay leaves, thyme and rosemary and cook 1 minute more. Pour in red wine and bring up to a simmer. Simmer for 5 minutes, then add tomatoes. Return beef to the pot and return to a gentle simmer. Cover pot and simmer for 2¹/₂ to 3 hours, until the beef easily shreds with a fork.

Remove pot from heat, pull out beef and allow to cool slightly. Pull meat into shreds. Remove herb stems and bay leaves from sauce and stir in beef. Season with salt and pepper and return to a simmer.

To cook pasta, bring a large pot of water to a boil. Once boiling, salt water generously — about 1 tsp (5 mL) for every 4 cups (1 L) — and add pasta. Cook until just tender (tasting is the best way to check) and drain. Toss warm pasta with a little olive oil, salt and pepper and place in serving bowl. Ladle pasta sauce over and top with Parmesan cheese shavings.

SERVES 6

CHALLAH BREAD PUDDING WITH CRÈME ANGLAISE

Bread pudding may seem like a homey comfort food, but when you make it, you use a classic French custard ratio in the pudding, and the sauce demonstrates another classic French custard technique (even though the sauce translates as English cream).

5 Tbsp	70 mL	unsalted butter, melted
5 cups	1.25 L	cubed challah egg bread (with crusts)
4 Tbsp	50 mL	dried cherries or cranberries
3	3	large eggs
½ cup	125 mL	sugar
2¼ cups	550 mL	half-and-half cream
2 tsp	10 mL	vanilla
		sugar for sprinkling

Preheat oven to 350°F (180°C). Brush the sides of a 9-inch (23-cm) square baking dish with some of the melted butter. In baking dish, toss bread cubes with remaining melted butter and add dried cherries or cranberries.

Whisk together eggs and sugar. Whisk in cream and vanilla. Pour over bread cubes and press down gently on bread to help liquid soak in. Let stand for about 15 minutes.

Place baking dish into a larger pan and pour boiling water around baking dish, halfway up sides. Sprinkle top of pudding with sugar. Bake for 50 to 60 minutes, until the center of the pudding springs back when pressed. Remove baking dish from water bath. Serve warm with Crème Anglaise.

MAKES ONE 9-INCH (23-CM) SQUARE BAKING DISH
SERVES 6 TO 9

CRÈME ANGLAISE

1 cup	250 mL	half-and-half cream
1 tsp	5 mL	vanilla
2	2	large egg yolks
¼ cup	50 mL	sugar

Bring cream with vanilla to just below a simmer. Whisk together egg yolks and sugar. Gently whisk cream into egg mixture and return to pot. With a wooden spoon over medium-low heat, stir sauce until it coats the back of the spoon, about 4 minutes. Strain and chill.

MAKES ABOUT 1⅓ CUPS (325 ML)

ANNA Crème anglaise is a versatile sauce, which can be infused with many flavors. Try an Earl Grey tea bag, 1 tsp (5 mL) green tea powder, 2 cinnamon sticks or 1 tsp (5 mL) instant coffee powder for variety.

MICHAEL Feel free to use any type of bread in the pudding: cinnamon, raisin, brioche, baguette or even croissants for real decadence.

GREAT GRILLING
Sure, most guys with a six-pack of beer and a pair of tongs will tell you they know how to grill, but there's a knack to great grilling that goes beyond lighting a bonfire that can be seen from the moon.
>Different grilling temperatures produce different results — that's obvious, but creating airflow changes by covering and uncovering, and even the type of grill you use, can alter the final product. Also to be considered are the flavors that pair with grilled food. Can delicate herbs like mint stand up to charred vegetables? You bet! In fact, a really talented grill guy or girl will tell you that you can heighten or soften the taste of foods depending on the technique you use.

Charred Hot Pepper Dip

MO's Saucy Beef Ribs

Grilled Zucchini with Mint and Basil

Grilled Eggplant with Miso

Grilled Garlic Pita Crisps

Flame-Kissed Pineapple and Peaches with Lemon Ice

CHARRED HOT PEPPER DIP

A grilled dinner implies dining on the deck or patio. This dip makes a great starter to a supper outdoors, perhaps while a game of horseshoes, badminton or bocce is in progress; or perhaps while you're relaxing on the hammock — every swing to the left gets you within reach of the dip.

FOR DIP

4	4	fresh jalapeño peppers
1	1	sweet onion, such as Vidalia, Bermuda or Spanish
1	1	14-oz (398-mL) can chickpeas, drained and rinsed
3 Tbsp	45 mL	extra virgin olive oil
3 Tbsp	45 mL	fresh lime juice
1 clove	1 clove	garlic, roughly chopped
2 Tbsp	25 mL	chopped fresh coriander
2 tsp	10 mL	finely grated lime zest
1½ tsp	7 mL	coarse salt

FOR DIPPING

Tortilla chips
Snow peas
Cherry tomatoes
Cucumber wedges

ANNA My folks often come to visit and are always complimentary about our cooking, but Mom has a sensitive stomach and can't take spicy foods. A great substitute for the jalapeño peppers in this dip is to grill one red bell pepper. Purée the charred skin along with the flesh of the pepper for that real grilled taste, without the heat.

Heat grill on high (or until charcoal briquettes turn half white) and grill whole jalapeño peppers, turning often, until skin is charred, about 5 minutes. Place peppers in a resealable bag and let cool for 15 minutes. While peppers are cooling, peel and slice sweet onion into circles ½ inch (1 cm) thick and grill until marked on both sides, about 8 minutes. Remove from grill and roughly chop. Slice cooled jalapeño peppers open lengthwise, scrape out seeds and roughly chop.

In a food processor, purée peppers and onion with remaining dip ingredients and season to taste. Dip can be served chilled or at room temperature, or stored chilled until ready to serve.

To serve, arrange dippable items of your choosing (see above for suggestions) around a bowl of dip.

SERVES 8

MICHAEL Unfortunately, you can't tell by looking at a jalapeño how hot it's going to be. Some can be as mild as a green bell pepper and some can blow your head off! If you're not sure how much heat you want, add half the peppers to the recipe, taste and then add more if you wish. And be careful: either wear rubber gloves when seeding your peppers, or else take care not to touch your eyes, nose or other delicate parts, even after washing your hands. The capsaicin that gives peppers their heat can stay on your hands for a few hours, even a day.

MO'S SAUCY BEEF RIBS

Ready to get messy? Messy, but definitely happy!

FOR BARBECUE RUB

2 Tbsp	25 mL	ground cumin
2 Tbsp	25 mL	ground coriander seed
2 Tbsp	25 mL	Spanish paprika (mild)
1 Tbsp	15 mL	fine salt
2 tsp	10 mL	garlic powder
2 tsp	10 mL	ground black pepper
½ tsp	2 mL	cayenne pepper (optional)

FOR SAUCY RIBS

3–4 racks	3–4 racks	beef ribs, taken from the prime rib roast (about 8 bones per rack)
1 cup	250 mL	barbecue sauce (your favorite variety)
½ cup	125 mL	cider vinegar
½ cup	125 mL	fancy molasses

For barbecue rub, combine all ingredients and set aside until ready to use.

For a gas grill, preheat to medium and for charcoal, burn long-lasting briquettes until they turn three-quarters white. Score backside of ribs with a sharp knife to open up the tissue, without piercing the meat (this allows the spice flavors in). Rub barbecue rub vigorously over all sides of the ribs, pressing well with your hands to make it stick. Start grilling ribs on one side, covered for 20 minutes. Reduce grill heat (if gas) to medium-low and turn ribs after another 20 minutes. The convection heat of a covered grill will keep air and heat circulating, while concentrating the smoke and spice flavors. Continue cooking and turning ribs every twenty minutes, for at least 2 hours (you may have to re-fuel your charcoal barbecue).

While ribs are cooking, prepare barbecue sauce. Stir prepared sauce with cider vinegar and molasses. When ribs are 20 minutes from finishing, brush glaze on both sides. Repeat glazing two more times.

To serve, remove ribs from grill to a cutting board and slice into single rib portions. Stack on a large platter and dig in!

SERVES 8
SEE PHOTO ON PAGE 94

ANNA Beef ribs are my absolute favorite barbecue food, and they're far more affordable than pork ribs. Make sure that you have a roll of paper towels handy and that you're not wearing your favorite white T-shirt — it won't be white for long!

MICHAEL Beef ribs might not be front and center at the meat counter, but ask your butcher for them because there may be stock hidden in the freezer. If you use charcoal to cook these ribs and you need to temper the heat a little, cut off some airflow by closing the vents for a bit.

GRILLED ZUCCHINI WITH MINT AND BASIL

Served at room temperature, this is more of a salad than a hot vegetable side dish.

1½ lb	750 g	green zucchini (about 3 large)
4 Tbsp	50 mL	extra virgin olive oil
¾ cup	175 mL	loosely packed fresh basil leaves
⅓ cup	75 mL	loosely packed fresh mint leaves
		coarse salt and ground black pepper

Preheat grill to medium-high. Trim ends off zucchini and slice lengthwise into strips just less than ½-inch (1 cm) thick. Grill zucchini (without oil) about 5 minutes on each side, until strips are pliable and lightly marked. Remove from heat and let cool. Chop zucchini strips into 1-inch (2.5-cm) lengths and toss with olive oil. Chop basil and mint by hand and toss with zucchini. Season and chill until ready to serve.

Grilled zucchini is best if served just below room temperature but not ice cold.

SERVES 8

ANNA I was amazed the first time Michael made this dish. The combination of mint and basil is absolutely brilliant!

MICHAEL Zucchini is affordable year-round and very easy to cut and cook — no peeling required! Be sure to season it generously to bring out its full potential.

<MO'S SAUCY BEEF RIBS, PAGE 93

GRILLED EGGPLANT WITH MISO

Miso is fermented soybean paste available in Asian food stores and health food stores.

1 lb	500 g	purple eggplant (1 large)
2 Tbsp	25 mL	light miso paste
2 Tbsp	25 mL	minced onion
1 Tbsp	15 mL	minced fresh ginger
1 Tbsp	15 mL	soy sauce
1 Tbsp	15 mL	fresh lime juice
3 Tbsp	45 mL	extra virgin olive oil
3 Tbsp	45 mL	chopped fresh Italian parsley

ANNA Michael's inspiration for this dish is Nasu Dengako, a miso-topped eggplant appetizer we order every time we go out for Japanese food.

MICHAEL Although salty (which is why salt isn't an ingredient in this recipe), miso paste is a low-fat, vegetable-based protein that can be stirred into vinaigrettes, soups and grilling glazes.

Preheat grill to medium-high heat. Trim ends of eggplant and slice into lengths less than 1/2 inch (1 cm) thick. Grill without oil about 5 minutes on each side, until eggplant is pliable and has light grill marks. Remove slices from grill and stack in a bowl. The residual heat will continue to cook the eggplant all the way through. Slice eggplant into thin strips and return to bowl.

In a separate bowl, stir miso paste, minced onion, ginger, soy sauce and lime juice until smooth. Stir in olive oil and toss with eggplant. Spoon into a serving bowl and sprinkle with chopped parsley. Chill until ready to serve.

SERVES 8

GRILLED GARLIC PITA CRISPS

These are crispy and warm — great for scooping up sauce and the last bits of veggies and herbs off your plate.

4	4	pocket pita breads
4 Tbsp	50 mL	extra virgin olive oil
1 clove	1 clove	garlic
		coarse salt and ground black pepper
2 Tbsp	25 mL	chopped Italian parsley

Gently open up pita breads and brush with olive oil. Cut garlic clove in half and rub over pitas. Grill over medium heat (or remaining heat from the grill after making MO's Saucy Beef Ribs, page 93) until just crispy, about 2 minutes on each side. Season, sprinkle with parsley and cut into quarters to serve.

SERVES 8

ANNA Before the days of tortilla chips, my mom made this as a summer dipper — a great invention that's still trendy.

MICHAEL My college roommate Chris and I would challenge each other with puns. "Havarti?" was our usual greeting, followed by "I falafel" and "Well, that's a pita!"

FLAME-KISSED PINEAPPLE AND PEACHES WITH LEMON ICE

The natural sugars in these fruits caramelize as they grill, making a sort of fruit brûlée.

1	1	small pineapple
4	4	peaches
2 Tbsp	25 mL	unsalted butter, melted

Preheat grill to medium-high heat. Peel pineapple, remove eyes and slice into 16 spears. Quarter and pit peaches, leaving skins on. Brush fruit lightly with melted butter and grill for 2 to 3 minutes on each side, just to warm. Serve fruit warm with lemon ice.

SERVES 8

ANNA Switch to a lime ice for a twist, or even grapefruit for an extra mouth-puckering edge.

MICHAEL Grocery stores regularly carry great quality pineapples, and many will peel and core it for you.

LEMON ICE
So refreshing — and fat-free, too!

2 cups	500 mL	sugar
2 cups	500 mL	water
2 cups	500 mL	fresh lemon juice
2	2	egg whites

Bring sugar and water up to a simmer in a saucepot over medium-high heat. Simmer for 5 minutes then cool completely.

Stir lemon juice with chilled syrup. Whisk in egg whites, pour into ice cream maker and churn. Spoon ice into a container and freeze until firm.

MAKES ABOUT 8 CUPS (2 L)

GET BAKED

Turn on the oven and get ready to roll … literally! We've got a great menu that includes some straight-forward and fundamental baking techniques. It's amazing — once you've spent some time baking, you realize how much flexibility and creativity you have in a craft you've been taught requires precision and formula. Unleash the baker within!

Pissalidière Tart on Tender Greens

Herbed Salmon in Brioche with Saffron Yogurt

Lemon Chiffon Cake with Coconut Raspberry Cream

ANNA The method for this puff pastry is called Dutch, Rough or Blitz puff, since you work the butter immediately into the dough, as opposed to the French method in which a slab of butter is folded into a pasta-like dough — lots of elbow grease required!

MICHAEL This is the pizza of Southern France, a savory tart with great warm-weather flavors not smothered by cheese.

PISSALIDIÈRE TART ON TENDER GREENS

This is a classic Provençal tart, and for today's baking lesson, you're going to make puff pastry from scratch. Difficult? Not at all. Just give yourself a little time for the dough to chill between foldings.

PUFF PASTRY DOUGH FOR TARTS

1¾ cups	425 mL	all-purpose flour
¾ cup	175 mL	pastry flour
1¼ tsp	6 mL	salt
1½ cups	375 mL	unsalted butter, cut into pieces and chilled
1½ tsp	7 mL	fresh lemon juice
⅔ cup	150 mL	ice water

Place flours and salt in a mixing bowl or an electric mixer fitted with the paddle attachment. Cut cold butter into dry ingredients until it is the texture of coarse meal, with some small pieces of butter still visible (they will get smoothed out when folded). Combine lemon juice and water and add to dough all at once. Mix until dough just comes together. Shape into a flat rectangle, wrap and chill for at least 2 hours before rolling.

Turn dough onto a lightly floured surface and roll lengthwise to create a large rectangle, about ¾ inch (2 cm) thick. Fold both short ends into the center of the rectangle, then fold dough in half where the first 2 folds meet. Chill for 1 hour. Roll pastry again lengthwise to same thickness. Fold dough in thirds and chill for 1 hour. Repeat process once more, folding in thirds, chilling for at least 1 hour before using.

SERVES 8

PISSALIDIÈRE TARTS ON TENDER GREENS

1	1	recipe Puff Pastry Dough (above)
		OR one 14-oz (394-g) package frozen puff pastry, thawed
½ cup	125 mL	thinly sliced onion
2 cups	500 mL	cherry or grape tomatoes
1	1	small tin anchovy fillets
¾ cup	175 mL	kalamata olives, pitted
¼ cup	50 mL	extra virgin olive oil
½ cup	125 mL	fresh basil leaves
4 cups	1 L	mixed tender greens or mesclun mix
¼ cup	50 mL	French Vinaigrette, page 35

Preheat oven to 400°F (200°C). On a lightly floured surface, roll out puff pastry to just less than ¼ inch (5 mm) thick. Cut 8 disks 4 inches (10 cm) in diameter, re-rolling pastry if necessary. Arrange disks on a parchment-lined baking sheet and pierce with a fork. Top each pastry disk with some onion slices. Slice tomatoes in half and arrange over disks (be random — this is a rustic tart). Place anchovy fillets and olives over tarts. Drizzle with olive oil and bake for 15 to 18 minutes, until pastry is a rich, golden brown. Tear basil leaves roughly and sprinkle over tarts.

Toss washed salad greens with French Vinaigrette and arrange ½ cup (125 mL) of greens onto each plate. Top with warm tart and serve immediately.

SERVES 8

HERBED SALMON IN BRIOCHE WITH SAFFRON YOGURT

Imagine little muffins of buttery dough surrounding an herb-slathered morsel of salmon hidden inside. Hungry yet?

FOR DOUGH

½ cup	125 mL	milk, room temperature
1 Tbsp	15 mL	dry active yeast
2 Tbsp	25 mL	rum (any kind)
3 cups	750 mL	all-purpose flour
2 Tbsp	25 mL	sugar
1 tsp	5 mL	fine salt
6	6	large eggs at room temperature
1½ cups	375 mL	unsalted butter at room temperature

FOR FILLING

1 cup	250 mL	basil
¼ cup	50 mL	minced shallot
2 tsp	10 mL	chopped fresh thyme
½ cup	125 mL	fresh parsley
2 Tbsp	25 mL	fresh mint
		coarse salt and ground black pepper
4 Tbsp	50 mL	breadcrumbs
2 Tbsp	25 mL	extra virgin olive oil
8	8	3-oz (75-g) salmon fillets, skin and pinbones removed
1	1	egg mixed with 2 Tbsp (25 mL) cold water for brushing

ANNA If you've never made bread before, then brioche is the first one to try. It's a forgiving dough, even if you're not sure if you've under- or over-kneaded it or if you let it sit in the fridge an extra day.

MICHAEL A modern version of the classic Russian coulibiac, fish cooked in pastry provides an elegant touch to a sophisticated dinner.

To prepare dough, sprinkle yeast over milk in the bowl of a mixer fitted with the paddle attachment. Allow to dissolve for 5 minutes.

Mix remaining ingredients, except butter, on low speed for 5 minutes. Switch to a dough hook attachment and knead on medium speed for 5 minutes.

Add butter a bit at a time until it has all been incorporated. You may have to pull the dough off the hook once or twice to work the butter into it. Knead for 5 minutes more. The dough may look very soft, but it will come together. Place in a bowl, cover, and allow to rise at room temperature for 1 hour, then chill overnight in the fridge.

For filling, purée all ingredients except salmon and egg wash in food processor and set aside. Divide dough into 6 pieces. On a lightly floured surface, roll out 1 portion of dough to just shy of ½ inch (1 cm) thick. Spread herb filling in center of disk and place salmon, flat side up, on herbs. Fold over brioche and pinch edges of pastry together. Repeat with remaining dough and salmon and place on a parchment-lined baking sheet. Cover with plastic wrap and let rise for 20 minutes.

Preheat oven to 375°F (190°C). Brush parcels with egg wash and bake for 18 to 25 minutes, until pastry is a rich, golden brown.

To serve, slice each parcel in half with a serrated knife, arrange on plate and spoon a pool of yogurt sauce (recipe opposite) in front.

SERVES 8

SAFFRON YOGURT SAUCE
(FOR THE HERBED SALMON IN BRIOCHE RECIPE OPPOSITE)

2 Tbsp	25 mL	fresh lemon juice
pinch	pinch	saffron threads
1½ cups	375 mL	plain yogurt
		fine salt

Stir lemon juice and saffron threads together and let sit for 10 minutes, to extract saffron color and flavor. Stir lemon juice into yogurt and season to taste. Chill until ready to serve, stirring once before spooning onto plates.

MAKES 1½ CUPS (375 ML)

LEMON CHIFFON CAKE WITH COCONUT RASPBERRY CREAM

This chiffon cake follows a classic sponge method in which egg whites are whipped and folded into an egg yolk base. It's lemon pound cake's fluffy, tangy cousin.

FOR CAKE LAYERS

2¼ cups	550 mL	pastry flour
1½ cups	375 mL	sugar
2 tsp	10 mL	baking powder
1 tsp	5 mL	fine salt
½ cup	125 mL	canola or vegetable oil
7	7	large eggs, separated
3	3	egg whites
½ cup	125 mL	water
¼ cup	50 mL	fresh lemon juice
2 tsp	10 mL	finely grated lemon zest
1 Tbsp	15 mL	cream of tartar
		icing sugar for dusting

ANNA Turning the cake upside down to cool is the most critical step in making this cake. Even if you accidentally under- or overwhip your egg whites, your cake will completely recover if cooled upside down.

MICHAEL I like a dessert like this on a buffet table: it has height, takes up space and feeds a lot of people.

Preheat oven to 325°F (160°C). In a large bowl, combine flour, all but 2 Tbsp (25 mL) of sugar, baking powder and salt. Make a well in the center and add oil, egg yolks, water, lemon juice and zest. Beat until smooth with hand mixer. In a stand mixer or with a hand mixer, beat egg whites until frothy. Add cream of tartar and beat until soft peaks form. Beat in 2 Tbsp (25 mL) remaining sugar until stiff peaks form. Gently fold one-third of egg whites into batter, then fold in remaining two-thirds. Pour batter into ungreased tube pan. Run a knife through batter to burst any large air bubbles and bake for 1 hour or until cake springs back when touched (don't open oven door until at least 50 minutes have passed). Invert pan and cool for 1½ hours. Loosen sides with a long metal spatula and remove core of pan.

Serve in slices with a dollop of Coconut Raspberry Cream on the side.

MAKES ONE 10-INCH (25-CM) TUBE CAKE

COCONUT RASPBERRY CREAM

1 cup	250 mL	fresh raspberries
2 cups	500 mL	whipping cream
2 Tbsp	25 mL	icing sugar
1 cup	250 mL	sweetened coconut, lightly toasted
½ tsp	2 mL	vanilla

Crush ½ cup (125 mL) of raspberries with a fork to extract juices and set aside. Whip cream to medium peaks and whisk in icing sugar, coconut and vanilla. Stir in crushed raspberries and chill until ready to serve.

To serve, dollop beside a slice of chiffon cake and sprinkle remaining raspberries over.

MAKES 4 CUPS (1 L)

BUDGET

>Cooking on the cheap doesn't mean opening a tin can. We each learned in our university years that buying a whole chicken and roasting it provides multiple tasty meals for lots less than prepared or frozen products.

>"Budget" can also apply to a shortage of time — our most valuable commodity. When time is limited, we need to eat well to keep up our stamina to make it through to the weekend.

MONDAY NIGHT SUPPER

Cook un-boring! On our frequent trips to Ikea, we sometimes treat ourselves to lunch in the restaurant. We're amazed at the value of a complete dinner served promptly, which doesn't qualify in the least as fast food. We've replicated this meal at home, much to our amusement.

Scandinavian Meatballs in Mushroom Sauce

Boiled New Potatoes

Almond Broccoli

Easy Cranberry Sauce

Date Shortbread Squares

SCANDINAVIAN MEATBALLS IN MUSHROOM SAUCE

If you're like us, you make a double batch of meatballs and freeze half for a quick meal later. This meatball recipe also cooks nicely into an Italian tomato sauce.

FOR MEATBALLS

1½ lb	750 g	ground beef
⅓ cup	75 mL	minced onion
¼ cup	50 mL	dry breadcrumbs
1	1	large egg
1 clove	1 clove	garlic, minced
4 shakes	4 shakes	Worcestershire sauce
1½ tsp	7 mL	fine salt
1 tsp	5 mL	ground black pepper

FOR MUSHROOM SAUCE

2 Tbsp	25 mL	extra virgin olive oil
½ cup	125 mL	diced onion
1 lb	500 g	button mushrooms, sliced
1 clove	1 clove	garlic, minced
2 Tbsp	25 mL	all-purpose flour
1½ cups	375 mL	low-sodium beef or chicken stock
3 Tbsp	45 mL	bottled steak sauce
3 shakes	3 shakes	Worcestershire sauce
2 Tbsp	25 mL	dry vermouth
		coarse salt and ground black pepper

For meatballs, combine ground beef with remaining ingredients. Scoop or shape small meatballs, about ½ inch (1 cm) across and chill until ready to cook.

For mushroom sauce, heat 1 Tbsp (15 mL) of oil in a large sauté pan on medium-high heat. Sear meatballs to brown on all sides, but not cook completely. Remove from pan and reserve. Reduce heat to medium and add remaining oil. Add onion and sauté until translucent, about 5 minutes. Add mushrooms and sauté until tender and any excess liquid has evaporated. Add garlic and flour and stir to coat mushrooms, cooking for 2 minutes. Pour in about ½ cup (125 mL) of stock, stirring constantly, until it has been absorbed by the flour. Switch to a whisk and whisk in remaining broth. Stir in steak sauce, Worcestershire sauce and vermouth and bring up to a simmer. Add meatballs and cover, letting simmer until meatballs are cooked through, about 10 minutes. Season with salt and pepper and serve.

SERVES 4

ANNA Add an extra 2 cups (500 mL) of chicken stock to this recipe, make the meatballs smaller, and you've got yourself a lovely meatball mushroom soup.

MICHAEL Sometimes I need a comfort-food evening, and Anna knows this is just what I'm looking for.

BOILED NEW POTATOES

There's something to be said for simplicity! It's sometimes tempting to overwork food, especially for a chef. Often the best results happen when you do the least!

1 lb	500 g	mini white or red potatoes
1 Tbsp	15 mL	unsalted butter
		coarse salt and ground black pepper

Cover mini potatoes with cold salted water and bring up to a simmer, uncovered, over medium-high heat. Simmer until potatoes are tender and pierce easily with a knife. Drain and return potatoes to pot. Over low heat stir in butter, season and serve.

SERVES 4

ALMOND BROCCOLI

Almond green beans may be a cafeteria standard, but that's because they're tasty, and almond broccoli is just as nice.

¼ cup	50 mL	slivered almonds
1 head	1 head	broccoli
1 Tbsp	15 mL	unsalted butter
½ tsp	2 mL	finely grated orange zest
		coarse salt and ground black pepper

To toast almonds, either spread nuts on an ungreased baking sheet and toast in a 350°F (180°C) oven for 10 minutes, stirring once, or lightly toast in a sauté pan, stirring constantly over medium heat until golden. Set aside.

Trim florets from broccoli and cut stem into bite-size pieces. Peel some of the stem to make the pieces more tender. Bring a pot of salted water to a boil. Add broccoli all at once and boil, uncovered, until tender, about 4 minutes. Drain water and return broccoli to pot. On low heat, stir in toasted almonds, butter, and orange zest. Season to taste and serve immediately.

SERVES 4

ANNA Orange zest keeps heavy vegetables light-tasting. The zest's citrus is more fragrant than the juice and won't turn green veggies brown (the juice would).

MICHAEL Don't throw away the broccoli stems. Peel away the tough outer layer and cook the stems along with the florets.

EASY CRANBERRY SAUCE

The Swedish accompaniment to this meal is lingonberry sauce, but as lingonberries are hard to come by in Canada, we substituted cranberries.

1½ cups	375 mL	fresh or frozen cranberries
⅔ cup	150 mL	water
⅔ cup	150 mL	sugar
1 tsp	5 mL	finely grated orange zest
½ tsp	2 mL	vanilla

Simmer all ingredients in a saucepot over medium heat until cranberries have "popped" and are tender. Remove from heat and chill until ready to serve.

MAKES ABOUT 1½ CUPS (375 ML)

ANNA For a fresh cranberry sauce, omit the water and pulse all the ingredients in a food processor.

MICHAEL See, cranberry sauce isn't just for Thanksgiving turkey. Try serving this sauce with your next cheese or pâté platter.

DATE SHORTBREAD SQUARES

More delicate than the earthy, oaty date squares you typically find, these freeze
well for holiday cookie plates.

FOR DATE FILLING

2 cups	500 mL	pitted dates
1 Tbsp	15 mL	unsalted butter
2 tsp	10 mL	finely grated lemon zest
1 tsp	5 mL	cinnamon
3/4 cup	175 mL	water

FOR SHORTBREAD

1 1/2 cups	375 mL	all-purpose flour
1/2 cup	125 mL	sugar
4 Tbsp	50 mL	cornstarch
1/2 tsp	2 mL	baking powder
1/4 tsp	1 mL	salt
3/4 cup	175 mL	unsalted butter, cut into pieces and chilled
1 tsp	5 mL	vanilla

For filling, place all ingredients in a pot and bring to a boil. Remove from heat and let dates
sit and soak until they are at room temperature. Purée until smooth and set aside.

Preheat oven to 350°F (180°C). In a bowl or in a mixer fitted with the paddle attachment, combine
flour, sugar, cornstarch, baking powder and salt. Cut in butter and vanilla until the mixture has an
even crumbly texture. Press two-thirds of the crumble into the bottom of a parchment-lined 8-inch
(20-cm) square pan. Spread date mixture over pressed shortbread and sprinkle remaining crumble
evenly over date mixture. Bake for 35 to 40 minutes, until the top of the crumble turns very light
brown. Allow to cool before cutting into squares.

MAKES ONE 8-INCH SQUARE (20-CM) PAN

ANNA I grew up with cookies more than squares,
so as an adult I developed this recipe for a cookie/
square blend.

MICHAEL I love the scent of dried fruits and simmering spices. It reminds me of Mom's Vinetarta,
an Icelandic prune cardamom torte.

PLOTTING LEFTOVERS

When we know we're going to be pressed for time but want to eat properly (no fast food, please), planning a day ahead helps. It's funny — we often teach evening cooking classes together, and when we get home after feeding 24 people a 3-course meal, we're famished and don't feel at all like cooking.

>These recipes serve 8 people in one seating but are geared to two 4-person meals, with a few adaptations so it doesn't feel like you're eating the same meal twice.

Sweet Pepper Braised Chicken Thighs

Laurel Basmati Rice (Day 1)

Buttered Pappardelle (Day 2)

Boston Greens with Maple Vinaigrette

Cardamom Carrot Cake

SWEET PEPPER BRAISED CHICKEN THIGHS

Yum! This is one of our weekday staples. Cooking the chicken in a sweet pepper stew adds flavor to the chicken and creates a rich sauce. On the first day, serve the chicken with the pepper pieces and juices over rice. On day two, purée the sauce and pull the chicken off the bone for a pasta dish that looks nothing like the dinner you had the night before.

2 Tbsp	25 mL	extra virgin olive oil
5 lb	2.2 kg	skinless chicken thighs
1½ cups	375 mL	roughly diced onion
¾ cup	175 mL	diced celery
2½ cups	625 mL	seeded and roughly chopped red bell pepper
2 cloves	2 cloves	garlic
3 cups	750 mL	chicken stock or water
1 Tbsp	15 mL	chopped fresh thyme
2	2	bay leaves
		coarse salt and ground black pepper
2 Tbsp	25 mL	cold unsalted butter (optional)

Heat olive oil in a large heavy-bottomed pot over medium-high heat. Add chicken thighs (in 2 batches) and sear on both sides until brown, about 3 minutes per side. Remove and set aside. Reduce heat to medium-low and add onion and celery, sautéeing until translucent, about 5 minutes. Add peppers and garlic and sauté 2 minutes more. Flood pepper mixture with stock or water, add thyme and bay leaves and bring up to a simmer. Return chicken thighs to liquid, cover and simmer gently for 45 minutes to 1 hour, until chicken is cooked through and peppers are tender.

Remove chicken thighs and bay leaves and purée sauce until smooth (an immersion blender works best) and strain. Return sauce and chicken together to the pot and bring to just below a simmer. Season and stir in butter to enrich the sauce, if desired.

SERVES 4 (PLUS 4 THE NEXT DAY)

ANNA I learned to make this dish at a fine dining restaurant in Vail, Colorado. It pleased discerning diners, and it pleased me with its minimal effort, so it should please you and your family.

MICHAEL The great thing about this meal is that while the chicken simmers you've got about 45 minutes to get some other things done before supper's ready.

LAUREL BASMATI RICE (Day 1)

3 cups	750 mL	water
1 tsp	5 mL	coarse salt
1½ cups	375 mL	basmati rice
2	2	bay leaves
½ tsp	2 mL	ground black pepper

Bring water to a boil in a medium saucepot and add salt. Stir in rice and bay leaves and cover, reducing heat to medium. Cook for 20 minutes, without lifting lid until 15 minutes have passed. Remove bay leaves and add pepper. Fluff up rice with a fork before serving.

SERVES 4

ANNA The fragrant combination of basmati rice and bay laurel is irresistible. If you're out of bay leaves, try a little rosemary.

MICHAEL Bay leaves have been used since Roman times (can you picture the crowns of laurel?), but don't use those from the same era. Buy dried spices in small quantities and replace them every 6 months.

BUTTERED PAPPARDELLE (Day 2)

1 package	1 package fresh lasagne noodles
2 Tbsp	25 mL	unsalted butter
		coarse salt

Bring a large pot of water up to a boil and salt generously. Slice lasagne sheets into strips 2 inches (5 cm) wide and immerse in boiling water. Cook until tender (tasting is the best way to check doneness) and drain. Return pasta to the pot and toss with butter and salt.

SERVES 4

ANNA I like how the wide strips of pappardelle hold the chicken pieces and slatherings of sauce.

MICHAEL Get creative: with sheets of fresh lasagne, you can invent your own cuts of pasta.

BOSTON GREENS WITH MAPLE VINAIGRETTE

A little sweetness in a vinaigrette adds depth of flavor, giving your palate an opportunity to savor all the tastes.

FOR MAPLE VINAIGRETTE

2 Tbsp	25 mL	white wine vinegar
1/4 tsp	1 mL	dried mustard powder
2 Tbsp	25 mL	pure maple syrup
6 Tbsp	90 mL	extra virgin olive oil
1/2 tsp	2 mL	coarse salt
1/4 tsp	1 mL	ground black pepper
2 Tbsp	25 mL	chopped fresh chives

FOR SALAD

1	1	small head Boston lettuce, washed and torn
1/2 cup	125 mL	thinly sliced celery
1	1	orange, cut into segments
		coarse salt and ground pepper

For vinaigrette, whisk vinegar, mustard powder and maple syrup until evenly blended. Slowly drizzle in olive oil while whisking. Stir in salt, pepper and chives and chill until ready to serve.

For salad, place Boston lettuce in a bowl and top with celery and orange. Toss with vinaigrette, sprinkle lightly with salt and pepper and serve.

SERVES 4

ANNA You can use honey instead of maple syrup, or try a little marmalade to bring out the taste of the orange.

MICHAEL I like to buy hydroponic Boston lettuce. With the roots still attached, it lasts longer in the fridge, and there's very little waste.

CARDAMOM CARROT CAKE

This is a moist spice cake. The applesauce adds moisture while the cardamom is an unexpected flavor that's great with carrots.

FOR CAKE

³/₄ cup	175 mL	vegetable oil
³/₄ cup	175 mL	light brown sugar, packed
3	3	large eggs
¼ cup	50 mL	honey
1 tsp	5 mL	finely grated orange zest
1²/₃ cups	400 mL	all-purpose flour
1 tsp	5 mL	baking powder
½ tsp	2 mL	baking soda
½ tsp	2 mL	fine salt
1 tsp	5 mL	ground cardamom
2 cups	500 mL	grated carrot
½ cup	125 mL	unsweetened applesauce

FOR FROSTING

½ cup	125 mL	cream cheese at room temperature
¼ cup	50 mL	unsalted butter at room temperature
1½ cups	375 mL	icing sugar, sifted
1½ tsp	7 mL	vanilla

Preheat oven to 325°F (160°C) and grease a 9-inch (23-cm) round cake pan. Whisk together oil, brown sugar, eggs, honey and orange zest. In a separate bowl, sift flour, baking powder, baking soda, salt and cardamom and stir into wet mixture to blend. Stir in carrot and applesauce and pour into prepared pan. Bake for 75 to 90 minutes, until a tester inserted in the center of the cake comes out clean. Allow to cool completely before frosting.

To prepare frosting, beat cream cheese and butter together. Beat in icing sugar until smooth and stir in vanilla. Spread over cooled cake and chill until ready to serve.

MAKES ONE 9-INCH (23-CM) ROUND CAKE

ANNA Cut the fat in this recipe in half by replacing some of the vegetable oil with more applesauce.

MICHAEL For kicks, try the Orange Honey Carrots (page 238) with a dash of cardamom.

CRAVINGS

>Cravings go beyond mere necessity. Have you ever felt, at a family occasion, like elbowing your frail Aunt Mathilda out of the way so that you can get that last slice of cheesecake? That's a craving.

>Yes, we sometimes crave bitter green vegetables or red meat or milk when we might be a little vitamin or mineral deficient, but in this section we're speaking of those primal cravings with no foundation in nutrition or reason. Think moderation later — indulge now!

GIMME CHOCOLATE

Chocolate — the most primal of food cravings! How can a flavor that has touched our palates only since Christopher Columbus (unless of course you have Aztec blood in you) feel like a requirement for our very existence as human beings?

>We don't have an answer to that question, but we do have the recipes.

Cheater Chocolate Mousse

Spanish Hot Chocolate

Chocolate Orange Cake

Chocolate Pistachio Truffles

CHOCOLATE PISTACHIO TRUFFLES

Truffles aren't difficult to make. Before you know it, you'll be sitting in front of the TV with your frou-frou slippers on, eating bonbons.

FOR GANACHE

1 cup	250 mL	whipping cream
12 oz	350 g	bittersweet chocolate, chopped
1 Tbsp	15 mL	brandy (optional)

FOR COATING

6 oz	175 g	dark or white chocolate, chopped and melted
½ cup	125 mL	coarsely chopped unsalted pistachios

Heat the cream to just below a simmer and pour over chocolate. Stir gently to blend, stir in brandy, if using, and cool to room temperature. Beat with a whisk to make a little fluffy, then let cool in the fridge for about half an hour before making truffles.

Cold hands are good for this task. Roll teaspoonfuls of chocolate filling into balls. Place on a baking tray and chill completely. Dip truffles in melted chocolate (using a toothpick), dip immediately in chopped pistachios and place on a cooling rack to set.

MAKES ABOUT 30

ANNA Make the ganache ahead of time and freeze it, then scoop it right from the freezer. You can coat the truffles in different things: other chopped nuts, coconut, cocoa powder or icing sugar. What's most important is that you use the best quality chocolate available. It really makes a difference.

MICHAEL Not a candy guy myself, I like to serve these morsels with coffee to guests.

PERFECT WITH COFFEE

We're a coffee generation. Embrace it! We have some perfect accompaniments to serve with that fresh-brewed pot of coffee. A little bite with your mug of joe can soften the hard edge of caffeine a touch. And don't worry: we're not the least bit offended if you serve these nibbles with tea.

Sour Cream Doughnuts

Cranberry Pecan Biscotti

Special Occasion Strawberry Coffee Cake

SOUR CREAM DOUGHNUTS, PAGE 122>

SOUR CREAM DOUGHNUTS

This recipe also qualifies for our "Frying Time" menu but, really, what goes better with a cup of coffee than a fresh, warm doughnut?

½ cup	125 mL	sour cream
½ cup	125 mL	buttermilk
½ cup	125 mL	sugar
1	1	large egg
½ tsp	2 mL	fine salt
2 cups	500 mL	all-purpose flour
¾ tsp	4 mL	baking soda
dash	dash	ground nutmeg
		vegetable oil for frying
		icing sugar for dusting

Whisk sour cream, buttermilk, sugar, egg and salt together. Sift together flour, baking soda and nutmeg and add to sour cream mixture, stirring just to blend. Let dough sit while heating oil.

Heat 2 inches (5 cm) of oil in a high-sided pot to 350°F (180°C), measured on a fryer or sugar thermometer. With a small ice cream scoop, or with a tablespoon, drop spoonfuls of dough carefully into oil. Let cook until doughnuts are a deep brown on one side, about 4 minutes, before turning and cooking to the same color on the other side. Remove doughnuts with a slotted spoon and drain on paper towel.

Let doughnuts cool 10 minutes, then sift icing sugar on top and serve.

MAKES 24 DOUGHNUT BITES
SEE PHOTO ON PAGE 121

ANNA These doughnuts are absolutely irresistible when served warm. If you want to serve these at breakfast, make the batter the night before and chill it. Then you can scoop and make these fresh in the morning.

MICHAEL Try these drizzled with a little maple syrup for a Canadian treat.

CRANBERRY PECAN BISCOTTI

It would be silly not to include a biscotti recipe in this chapter. It's a coffee shop staple, after all.

2 cups	500 mL	all-purpose flour
1 tsp	5 mL	baking powder
1 tsp	5 mL	ground cinnamon
1/4 tsp	1 mL	baking soda
1/4 tsp	1 mL	fine salt
1/2 cup	125 mL	unsalted butter at room temperature
3/4 cup	175 mL	sugar
2	2	large eggs
1 tsp	5 mL	vanilla
1 cup	250 mL	pecan halves
1 cup	250 mL	dried cranberries

Preheat oven to 350°F (180°C). Sift flour, baking powder, cinnamon, baking soda and salt into a bowl and set aside. Cream butter and sugar until smooth. Add eggs, one at a time, and mix in well. Stir in vanilla. Add flour mixture and stir just until blended. Stir in pecan halves and cranberries. Turn dough out onto a lightly floured surface and divide into 2. With floured hands shape each piece into a log 12 inches (30 cm) long by 3 inches (8 cm) wide and place on a parchment-lined baking tray. Bake for 25 minutes and let cool for 15 minutes.

Reduce oven temperature to 325°F (160°C). Slice biscotti logs on an angle into cookies about 1/2 inch (1 cm) thick and return to baking tray. Bake for 20 minutes, flipping cookies over halfway through baking. Allow biscotti to cool completely, then pack in an airtight container to store for up to 6 weeks.

MAKES ABOUT 3 1/2 DOZEN BISCOTTI

ANNA I find that nuts are often interchangeable in biscotti recipes, depending on the style. A recipe such as this one, which starts with butter, is good for tender nuts like pecans, walnuts, pistachios or cashews, while a recipe that starts with eggs or oil (and will make a harder biscotti) is good for almonds or hazelnuts.

MICHAEL I like the indestructible nature of biscotti — perfect for holiday cookie tins or the large cookie jar, stacked high.

SPECIAL OCCASION STRAWBERRY COFFEE CAKE

This isn't a weekday, leave-the-knife-in-the-pan coffee cake but a "company's coming" coffee cake, when you have to plug in the extra coffee maker that usually lives in the basement.

½ cup	125 mL	vegetable oil
1 cup	250 mL	sugar
3	3	large eggs, separated
1 tsp	5 mL	finely grated lemon zest
½ tsp	2 mL	vanilla
⅓ cup	75 mL	2% milk
1¼ cups	300 mL	pastry flour
1½ tsp	7 mL	baking powder
¼ tsp	1 mL	fine salt
½ cup	125 mL	finely chopped walnuts
2 cups	500 mL	sliced fresh strawberries
½ cup	125 mL	whipping cream, whipped to soft peaks

Preheat oven to 350°F (180°C) and grease and flour two 8-inch (20-cm) cake pans. Beat vegetable oil, ½ cup (125 mL) sugar and egg yolks until fluffy. Stir in lemon zest and vanilla. Stir in milk. Sift together pastry flour, baking powder and salt and gently stir into butter mixture until blended. Spread evenly into the prepared pans. Whip egg whites with electric beaters until frothy. Gradually add the remaining ½ cup (125 mL) sugar and whip until whites hold a stiff peak. Fold in chopped walnuts and spread over cake batter. Bake for 30 to 35 minutes, until a tester inserted in the center of the cake comes out clean. Cool cakes completely in the pan.

To assemble, turn one cake out onto a plate, meringue side down. Top cake with half the strawberries and cream. Place second cake layer on top, meringue side up, and top with remaining cream and fruit. Chill until ready to serve.

MAKES ONE 8-INCH (20-CM) COFFEE CAKE

ANNA This is such a pretty, ladies' cake, especially with the strawberries — perfect for a shower or bridge party. Of course, raspberries or blackberries would be just as wonderful. During the brief season when fresh red currants are available, use them as a feminine garnish on top.

MICHAEL I'll go check out antique stores or putter around the yard while you ladies have your get-together. Just leave me a piece, please.

FRYING TIME

It must be the texture contrast created by deep-fat frying that is so satiating. A crispy exterior yielding to a warm soft center — whether a french fry, mushroom cap or falafel — it's all great.

Coconut Shrimp with Citrus Dipping Sauce

Falafel Sandwiches

Strawberry Fritters with Honey Cream

COCONUT SHRIMP WITH CITRUS DIPPING SAUCE

These make great pass-around hors d'oeuvres at cocktail parties. I don't think caterers could survive without a variation of this recipe in their repertoire.

FOR SHRIMP

3/4 lb	375 g	raw 21/25 or 31/40 shrimp, peeled and de-veined
1/2 cup	125 mL	cornstarch
3/4 tsp	4 mL	fine salt
1/4 tsp	1 mL	ground black pepper
3 cups	750 mL	sweetened shredded coconut
3	3	large egg whites
		vegetable oil, for frying

FOR CITRUS DIPPING SAUCE

2 Tbsp	25 mL	fresh lime juice
2 Tbsp	25 mL	fresh orange juice
1/4 cup	50 mL	honey
1 tsp	5 mL	freshly grated ginger
1 tsp	5 mL	Dijon mustard
		salt and hot sauce

For shrimp, run a paring knife down the back of each shrimp, to split it open without cutting all the way through (this is "butterflying"). Toss cornstarch, salt and pepper together in one bowl and pour coconut into another bowl. In a third bowl, whip egg whites until frothy.

Pour enough vegetable oil into a high-sided pot to a depth of 2 inches (5 cm), and heat to 350°F (180°C), using a fryer or sugar thermometer to measure the temperature. Dredge each shrimp in cornstarch, shake off excess, then dip into egg whites, again shaking off excess, then press shrimp into coconut. Fry a few shrimp at a time until cooked through, 1 to 2 minutes. Drain cooked shrimp on a paper towel and arrange on a serving bowl with Citrus Dipping Sauce.

For Citrus Dipping Sauce, whisk all ingredients together and season to taste. Chill until ready to serve.

SERVES 6

ANNA For a seafood mix, follow the same technique using sea scallops and crab fingers. The Citrus Dipping Sauce is a good one to serve with spring rolls or Vietnamese salad rolls. If you're entertaining and want to get ahead, you can fry these shrimp ahead of time and keep them warm in a 200°F (85°C) oven.

MICHAEL There's a steakhouse that Anna and I regularly visit that features these on their menu. When we're there for dinner, I immediately start fantasizing about the crispy coconut hiding a succulent shrimp inside … mmmm.

FALAFEL SANDWICHES

These Middle Eastern sandwiches are made with chickpea "meatballs," for lack of a better term. Load them up with your favorite toppings.

FOR FALAFELS

1¼ cups	300 mL	dried chickpeas
2 cloves	2 cloves	garlic, minced
½ cup	125 mL	minced onion
½ cup	125 mL	chopped fresh coriander
¼ cup	50 mL	chopped Italian parsley
1 tsp	5 mL	coarse salt
¾ tsp	4 mL	ground cumin
½ tsp	2 mL	ground coriander
½ tsp	2 mL	ground black pepper
½ tsp	2 mL	baking soda
3 Tbsp	45 mL	sesame seeds
		vegetable oil for frying

FOR SANDWICHES

6	6	soft pita, with pockets
¼ cup	50 mL	tahini sauce (sesame paste thinned with a little water)
		hot sauce (optional)
1 cup	250 mL	diced tomato
3 cups	750 mL	shredded iceberg lettuce
½ cup	125 mL	shredded cucumber or red cabbage

ANNA One of my first jobs as a teenager was working at "A Taste of Cheese," a little cheese shop and deli owned by a Middle Eastern couple who taught me how to make these sandwiches. This was quite some time ago (not to date myself!), before this style of food became trendy, and for years it was hard to find tahini paste. Now this sesame paste, a healthy addition to salad dressings or potato and pasta salads, is a grocery store staple.

MICHAEL This is the ultimate vegetarian/vegan lunch. Full-flavored and filling, the pita bread combines with the chickpea falafels to create a complete protein.

For falafels, soak chickpeas in water to cover in the fridge overnight. Drain and rinse well. Purée chickpeas in a food processor with remaining ingredients except vegetable oil and sesame seeds. Make meatball-sized balls of mixture and roll between your hands. Flatten falafels and press in some sesame seeds.

Heat 2 inches (5 cm) of oil in a high-sided pot to 350°F (180°C). Gently drop in a few falafels and cook for 3 minutes, turning halfway through cooking. Use a slotted spoon to remove falafels and drain on paper towel. Falafels can be served warm or at room temperature or refrigerated and warmed in the microwave to serve later.

To assemble sandwiches, open pita carefully halfway. Crumble in 2 or 3 falafels and drizzle with tahini sauce and hot sauce (optional). Top with tomato, lettuce and cucumber or red cabbage. Fold one flap of pita over filling and roll up tightly. Wrap in waxed paper and serve.

SERVES 6

STRAWBERRY FRITTERS WITH HONEY CREAM

What a pleasant surprise this makes from other deep-fried desserts.

4 cups	1 L	strawberries
1 cup	250 mL	vegetable oil
1 cup +2 Tbsp	250 mL +25 mL	all-purpose flour
½ tsp	2 mL	baking powder
dash	dash	fine salt
1	1	large egg
1 cup	250 mL	cold water
		icing sugar for dusting

Wash and hull strawberries and place on a baking sheet lined with paper towel to dry.

Heat oil in a pot over medium-high heat to 350°F (180°C). This will take about 8 minutes. Combine 1 cup (250 mL) flour with baking powder and salt. Whisk in egg and cold water until smooth. Dust each strawberry with a little flour, shake off and dip into batter. Using a pair of tongs, place fritter in hot oil and cook for 2 minutes on each side. Remove to drain on a paper towel. Cook fritters together, leaving ½ inch (1 cm) between them as they fry in the pot.

SERVES 6

ANNA This is one recipe in which firm strawberries, even out-of-season berries, work best, because they won't leak their juices.

MICHAEL Serve these with vanilla ice cream or a chocolate sauce for dunking.

HONEY CREAM

½ cup	125 mL	whipping cream
2 Tbsp	25 mL	sour cream
2 Tbsp	25 mL	honey

Whip cream to soft peaks and stir in sour cream and honey.

Chill until ready to serve with strawberry fritters.

SERVES 6

BREAKFAST

>Breakfast can be a great time to meet before the day starts full-on. Weekend morning meals have a sense of occasion about them, and the coffee always tastes better when you have time to savor it.

SATURDAY FUEL
Whether Mom or Dad makes the meal, a tasty sit-down breakfast can be enjoyed without too much preparation time or much of a mess.

Honeydew with Lime

Warm Tomato Salsa

Montecristo French Toast

HONEYDEW WITH LIME

You'll be amazed at how a little lime juice can snap up honeydew. We also like to use this technique when serving melon with prosciutto.

½	½	honeydew melon, seeds removed
1	1	lime

Slice melon into 8 wedges and sprinkle generously with lime juice.

SERVES 4

ANNA I took it as a compliment when someone called this their favorite dessert, one they could make themselves (not a baker, I guess!).

MICHAEL Be sure to wash your melons with soap and water before cutting. They grow on the ground, after all!

WARM TOMATO SALSA

This salsa is great with scrambled eggs or inside an omelette.

2 Tbsp	25 mL	extra virgin olive oil
2 cups	500 mL	cherry or grape tomatoes, halved
1 clove	1 clove	garlic, minced
1 tsp	5 mL	red wine vinegar
2 Tbsp	25 mL	chopped green onion
2 Tbsp	25 mL	chopped fresh coriander
		coarse salt and ground black pepper

In a sauté pan over medium-high heat add oil. Once oil is hot add tomatoes and garlic and toss to warm through. Stir in vinegar, green onion and coriander and season to taste. Serve warm.

SERVES 4

MONTECRISTO FRENCH TOAST

When was the last time you made a Montecristo sandwich? That long, huh? The combination of ham and cheese dipped in egg and cooked like French toast is a perfect way to fuel the gang for a day of errands and housework — and maybe even a little fun.

1/2 loaf	1/2 loaf	French bread
8 slices	8 slices	Black Forest ham
8 slices	8 slices	Monterey Jack cheese
3	3	large eggs
1 cup	250 mL	2% milk
dash	dash	ground nutmeg
2 Tbsp	25 mL	vegetable oil

Cut bread into 1½-inch (4-cm) slices and, with a paring knife, cut a slit in the center of each slice, creating a pocket. Wrap a slice of ham around each slice of cheese and insert it into the center of the bread. Whisk eggs with milk and nutmeg.

Preheat a skillet or large fry pan over medium heat and heat oil. Dip stuffed bread slice in egg mixture, coating both sides. Fry for about 4 minutes on each side, reducing heat if necessary, until cheese is melted. Serve with Warm Tomato Salsa (opposite page).

SERVES 4
SEE PHOTO ON PAGE 134

ANNA Montecristos predate quesadillas, but using flour tortillas and skipping the egg dip saves a little time.

MICHAEL Cook your Montecristos on low heat so that your toast browns nicely while the cheese has time to melt.

SUNDAY BRUNCH
We love one menu that can be two meals. On a few occasions, we've enjoyed brunch for over four hours! Now that's leisure.

Spiced Poached Fruits

Muesli and Honey Yogurt

Maple-Glazed Peameal

Asiago and Pepper Strata

Pecan Streusel Coffee Ring

<MONTECRISTO FRENCH TOAST, PAGE 133

MAPLE-GLAZED PEAMEAL

Two Canadian favorites, peameal and maple, united as they were meant to be.

1½ lb	750 g	sliced peameal bacon
1 Tbsp	15 mL	unsalted butter
3 Tbsp	45 mL	pure maple syrup
½ tsp	2 mL	Dijon mustard

Heat a skillet or large sauté pan over medium-high heat and cook peameal bacon about 4 minutes on each side, browning lightly. Remove peameal and reduce heat to medium-low. Add butter to pan and stir in maple syrup and mustard. Return peameal to pan and toss to coat. Serve immediately.

SERVES 8

ASIAGO AND PEPPER STRATA

Mix up this savory bread pudding the evening before and then bake it fresh in the morning.

5 Tbsp	70 mL	unsalted butter
1 cup	250 mL	diced onion
1½ cups	375 mL	diced red bell pepper
2 Tbsp	25 mL	chopped fresh basil
1 Tbsp	15 mL	chopped fresh marjoram
6 cups	1.5 L	cubed day-old baguette
2	2	large eggs
2 cups	500 mL	2% milk
½ cup	125 mL	half-and-half cream
2 tsp	10 mL	Dijon mustard
1½ tsp	7 mL	fine salt
½ tsp	2 mL	black pepper
2 cups	500 mL	grated Asiago cheese

ANNA This is a favorite weeknight supper for us. We call it the "clean the fridge" supper because so many different foods can taste great in it.

MICHAEL To save time, you can always use green onions instead of the regular onion, and use jarred red peppers to bypass the sautéing step.

Preheat oven to 350°F (180°C). Butter the sides of a 6-cup (1.5-L) baking dish and melt the remaining butter in a sauté pan over medium heat. Add onion to pan and cook until translucent, about 4 minutes. Add diced pepper and sauté 4 minutes more until soft. Remove from heat and let cool.

Toss pepper mixture with bread cubes, basil and marjoram in a large bowl. In a separate bowl, whisk eggs, milk, cream, mustard, salt and pepper. Pour over bread and add Asiago. Toss well and let stand for about 15 minutes. Pour mixture into prepared baking dish.

Place baking dish in a water bath and cover. Bake for 55 to 65 minutes, uncovered for the last 20 minutes of cooking, until the center of the strata springs back when pressed. Let cool for 10 minutes before slicing and serving.

SERVES 8

PECAN STREUSEL COFFEE RING

This pecan twist coffee cake is really fun to make and freezes well if you don't finish eating it all.

FOR DOUGH

2 tsp	10 mL	instant dry yeast
1/4 cup	50 mL	warm water
1/2 cup	125 mL	2% milk at room temperature
1	1	large egg
2 Tbsp	25 mL	sugar
2 1/2 cups	625 mL	all-purpose flour
1/2 tsp	2 mL	fine salt
1/2 cup	125 mL	unsalted butter at room temperature
4 oz	125 g	cream cheese at room temperature

FOR STREUSEL FILLING

1 cup	250 mL	dark brown sugar, packed
1 cup	250 mL	breadcrumbs
1 Tbsp	15 mL	ground cinnamon
1/2 tsp	2 mL	ground cardamom
2/3 cup	150 mL	unsalted butter
1 cup	250 mL	chopped pecans
1	1	large egg white

For dough, dissolve yeast in water in the bowl of a stand mixer and let sit for 5 minutes. Add milk, egg and sugar and blend. Add flour and salt and mix for 1 minute to combine. Add butter and cream cheese and knead for 5 minutes on medium speed. Place dough in a lightly oiled bowl, cover and let rest 1 hour.

For streusel, combine brown sugar, breadcrumbs, cinnamon and cardamom. Cut butter until it's a rough crumbly texture. Sprinkle in chopped pecans.

Preheat oven to 350°F (180°C). On a lightly floured surface, roll out dough into a rectangle 1/2 inch (1 cm) thick. Sprinkle two-thirds of the streusel filling over the dough and roll up lengthwise. Slice the roll lengthwise to expose the pecan filling and twist to create a knotted, rough look. Place roll in a greased bundt or angel cake pan, pinching the two ends gently together. Let rise 20 minutes. Bake 30 minutes, cool for 15 minutes, then turn out ring onto a parchment-lined baking sheet. Brush top of ring with egg white and sprinkle with remaining streusel. Return ring to oven for 12 minutes, then allow to cool before slicing and serving.

SERVES 8 TO 12

ANNA I love the brown sugar caramel bits that ooze out and get crunchy on the outside of the streusel ring as it bakes. I guess it's a symptom of being a pastry chef: I'm used to snacking on the overcooked bites from the oven's "hot spot."

MICHAEL Sometimes Anna makes this coffee cake for just the two of us. After we get our fill, I bring the rest into work where it disappears faster than you can say "hungry chef."

ADVENTURES

>Culinary adventures are memory builders. We love asking people about their most memorable meal. For some, it's a momentous event like a marriage proposal or a special birthday, but for others TRAVEL plays a big part. We tend to plan our vacations together with food in mind, so we've replicated a few menus that reflect our travels and discoveries. Staying at home can also count as an adventure, especially when the plan is a trip to the local FARMERS' MARKET. Sometimes it takes traveling abroad to make us truly appreciate how much we have at home.

>We also count BEER and WINE as topics worthy of adventure status because the journey our palates take as we try new food and drink combinations draws us beyond the familiar borders of our kitchens and dining rooms.

TRAVEL

>Travel is an important inspiration for the way we cook at home. For months before our vacation, we plot our journey online, searching out restaurants and ingredients that best reflect our destination, and for months after we've returned, we spend hours in the kitchen trying to replicate our favorite meal. We're thrilled to share with you the results, which we hope are just the beginning of many more adventures.

SPAIN Our trip to Madrid and the Basque region of Spain was about six years in the dreaming and planning. We can't begin to get into the details of every meal (we could — and torture you with the photo albums, too) but this menu does try to capture the simplicity and elegance of Spanish cuisine. You must also check out the Ribeye Steak a la Plancha (page 190) for another fantastic Spanish cooking technique.

Shrimp and Mushroom Tarts
Potato Tortilla
Seafood and Sausage Paella
Almond Flan

SHRIMP AND MUSHROOM TARTS

We enjoyed these as we packed like sardines into a tapas bar in San Sebastián. The tarts were easy to pop into our mouths as we were jostled by the crowds fueling up before an important soccer match.

1 Tbsp	15 mL	extra virgin olive oil
1/3 cup	75 mL	finely minced onion
2 Tbsp	25 mL	finely minced green pepper
2 cloves	2 cloves	garlic, minced
1 cup	250 mL	minced button mushrooms
1/2 cup	125 mL	plain tomato sauce
2 Tbsp	25 mL	brandy
1/4 cup	50 mL	whipping cream
1 cup	250 mL	minced salad shrimp
		coarse salt and ground black pepper
12	12	frozen tart shells, baked
		parsley and grated Parmesan cheese for garnish

In a sauté pan over medium-high heat, add oil, onion and pepper. Sauté for 5 minutes until onion is tender. Add garlic and mushrooms and sauté until mushrooms are soft and pan is dry. Add tomato sauce, brandy and cream and cook 5 minutes to reduce. Add shrimp to warm through, and season to taste. Spoon into baked tart shells and garnish with chopped parsley and Parmesan cheese. Serve warm.

MAKES 12 TARTS

ANNA The styles of tapas bars depend on the location in Spain. In San Sebastián, the bar was packed to overflowing with tarts and little skewers (called *pinxos*) of tasty snacks.

MICHAEL This tart is the Spanish equivalent of our Mushroom Asiago Tarts (page 266). Make both for your next cocktail party: they complement each other nicely.

POTATO TORTILLA

A real Spanish tortilla has nothing to do with corn or flour flatbreads. It's all about potatoes, sliced and cooked and bound with eggs to make a great potato pie, for lack of a better term.

½ cup	125 mL	extra virgin olive oil
4	4	russet potatoes, peeled and cut into thin slices
		coarse salt
1	1	onion, thinly sliced
4	4	large eggs

Heat an 8-inch (20-cm) pan with oil over medium heat and layer potato slices around pan, seasoning lightly with salt and alternating with onions. Cook slowly until potatoes are tender (lift occasionally to prevent browning). They shouldn't stick together. Remove the potatoes from pan, draining oil, except for 2 Tbsp (25 mL).

In a bowl whisk eggs together and add potatoes to coat. Heat the reserved oil in same pan over medium-high heat and add potato mixture to pan, spreading it evenly. Lower heat to medium and when egg begins to brown remove pan from heat, top with a plate, invert and flip tortilla back into pan with browned side up. Cook for 2 minutes, then flip tortilla 2 or 3 more times until evenly cooked.

Remove from pan and serve warm or at room temperature (traditionally at room temperature).

Get creative with your tortilla — add a little roasted red pepper, salt cod, chorizo, shrimp or crab to dress it up.

MAKES 8 WEDGES

ANNA Baking potatoes, also known as russet or Idaho potatoes, are important to this dish. Their mealy texture stays tender, and they make good french fries, too.

MICHAEL Slow-cooking the eggs with the potato is the key to success. Keep peeking under the potatoes to make sure the tortilla isn't browning too quickly. You want to avoid an eggy crust.

SEAFOOD AND SAUSAGE PAELLA

Paella is all about the saffron, which hails from La Mancha in central Spain, and the short-grain rice that comes from the coastal region near Valencia, though we use arborio rice in this recipe since it's more easily available. The seasonings — well, that's up to you.

3 Tbsp	45 mL	extra virgin olive oil
1 cup	250 mL	diced onion
1½ cups	375 mL	arborio rice
6 cups	1.5 L	chicken stock or water
½ cup	125 mL	diced celery
1	1	diced red bell pepper
1 Tbsp	15 mL	fresh thyme, chopped
2 cloves	2 cloves	garlic, chopped
pinch	pinch	saffron threads
1 tsp	5 mL	smoked paprika or 2 tsp (10 mL) regular Spanish paprika
2	2	chorizo sausages, diced
2	2	tomatoes, diced
1 lb	500 g	clams, washed
1 lb	500 g	mussels, cleaned
1 lb	500 g	white, firm fleshed fish, diced
1 lb	500 g	bay or sea scallops
1 lb	500 g	shrimp, peeled and deveined
1 cup	250 mL	frozen peas
		coarse salt and ground black pepper

In a large pan, heat oil over medium heat and sauté onion until translucent, about 5 minutes. Add rice and sauté for 4 minutes, to coat with oil but not brown. Add one-third of the chicken stock and simmer for 5 minutes, stirring often. Add celery, pepper, thyme, garlic, saffron, paprika and another third of the stock, stirring often. Stir in sausage and tomatoes and let simmer another few minutes. Add clams and cook, covered, for 3 minutes. Stir in mussels and fish. Cover (adding remaining stock if needed) and cook 3 minutes. Add scallops, shrimp and peas and cook just until shrimp are pink. Season to taste and serve immediately.

SERVES 8 TO 10

ANNA I've heard that there are two basic styles of paella: a fishermen's or seafood paella and a hunter's or meat paella. I was once told never to mix the two, but I saw the seafood and meat blend on a few menus in Spain, so perhaps that's just an old señora's tale.

MICHAEL I've made paella more than once at the lake for our summer barbecues. I place my giant paella pan on a stock rocket, a propane-fueled portable burner that's about 2 feet (60 cm) across. An easy way to make a one-pot meal for a large group!

ALMOND FLAN

This smooth, silky custard refreshes you more than it fills you.

1¾ cups	400 mL	sugar
2 Tbsp	25 mL	water
6	6	large eggs
2½ cups	625 mL	2% milk
½ cup	125 mL	whipping cream
3 Tbsp	45 mL	all-purpose flour
1 tsp	5 mL	vanilla
1 tsp	5 mL	almond extract

Preheat oven to 375°F (190°C). In a sauté pan melt 1 cup (250 mL) sugar over high heat with 2 Tbsp (25 mL) water. Cook the sugar without stirring until golden brown (3 to 4 minutes) and pour into an ungreased 9-inch (23-cm) round cake pan. Swirl sugar around bottom to coat. Place pan in a baking dish with a 2-inch (5-cm) lip.

In a large bowl, whisk eggs. Add remaining ¾ cup (175 mL) sugar, milk, whipping cream, flour, vanilla and almond extract, and whisk until well blended. Pour over caramelized sugar and carry to oven door. Pour boiling water around pan, coming up at least halfway, and place carefully in oven. Bake for 55 to 60 minutes until a tester inserted in the center comes out clean. Remove pan from water bath and let cool 30 minutes.

This dessert is delicious served warm, but it can also be served after being chilled for at least 4 hours. To plate, run a palette knife around the outside edge of the custard, invert the pan over a plate and lift.

MAKES ONE 9-INCH (23-CM) FLAN

ANNA Last year, Michael invited me to judge his culinary classes on their final practical exam. On top of zucchini fritters, cobb salad and spanikopita, I had to taste 75 crème caramels over 3 days. Needless to say, I wasn't craving custard for dessert those evenings. (P.S. the students did a great job!)

MICHAEL We recently went to a Portuguese christening luncheon, and the center of attention, second only to my grand-nephew, Magnus, was the flan on the dessert table. Baked in an angel cake pan, it shone with its melted caramelized sugar top and jiggly custard.

SOUTH CAROLINA

Our memories sometimes play tricks on us, and a memory can seem happier than the actual event on which it's based — but that's okay. We fell in love with Charleston, South Carolina, our honeymoon destination. Yes, after fabulous dinners we enjoyed romantic evening walks through the Battery district. Here up north, we've recreated some signature Carolinian dishes. Oh, and by the way, the honeymoon has never ended.

Shrimp and Grits

Buttermilk Fried Chicken

Angel Biscuits

Stewed Okra

Peach Pie with Peach Ice Cream

SHRIMP AND GRITS

This is definitely what we call "high-low" food. All the best restaurants in Charleston had this on their menu, yet you could always order it at the neighborhood diner. It makes a great appetizer and a great surprise in place of risotto.

2 Tbsp	25 mL	extra virgin olive oil
1 cup	250 mL	finely minced onion
1/2 cup	125 mL	finely diced celery
1/2 cup	125 mL	finely diced red bell pepper
2 cloves	2 cloves	garlic, minced
2 1/2 cups	625 mL	water or chicken stock
2/3 cup	150 mL	cornmeal grits
2 lb	1 kg	white shrimp, peeled and cleaned
1 Tbsp	15 mL	chopped fresh tarragon
2 Tbsp	25 mL	chopped fresh chives
2 Tbsp	25 mL	fresh lemon juice
4 oz	125 g	cream cheese at room temperature
2 Tbsp	25 mL	unsalted butter
		coarse salt and ground black pepper

Heat olive oil in a large saucepot over medium heat. Add onions, celery and bell pepper and sauté for 5 minutes, until onions become translucent. Add garlic and sauté 1 minute more. Flood vegetables with water or chicken stock and bring up to a simmer. Pour in grits slowly, whisking constantly. Reduce heat to medium-low, switch to a wooden spoon and continue stirring until almost all the liquid has been absorbed by the grits. Add shrimp and stir until they turn pink. Stir in tarragon, chives, lemon juice, cream cheese and butter, and stir until cheese melts in. Season to taste and spoon into serving bowls.

SERVES 12

ANNA I've always loved grits, especially for breakfast with a pat of butter and a little raspberry jam swirled in.

MICHAEL We get our grits after crossing the border, but if you don't have access to grits, use regular cornmeal as a tasty alternative.

BUTTERMILK FRIED CHICKEN

It's all in the buttermilk! Marinating adds such sweetness and juiciness to chicken, whether it's grilled, baked or fried. Ask your butcher to "joint" or cut up the chicken into even-sized pieces.

FOR MARINADE

4 cups	1 L	buttermilk
1/4 cup	50 mL	Dijon mustard
3 Tbsp	45 mL	fine salt
4 tsp	20 mL	ground black pepper
1 tsp	5 mL	cayenne pepper
2	2	3 1/2-lb (1.75-kg) fryer chickens, cut into equal pieces

FOR FRYING

6 cups	1.5 L	all-purpose flour
1 Tbsp	15 mL	baking powder
1 Tbsp	15 mL	coarse salt
1 tsp	5 mL	ground black pepper
6 cups	1.5 L	peanut or canola oil, for frying

For marinade, whisk together buttermilk, mustard, salt and peppers. Pour over cut-up chicken, cover and refrigerate for at least 6 hours and up to a day, stirring occasionally.

For frying, whisk flour with baking powder, salt and pepper in a large flat dish. Lift chicken pieces out of marinade and, without shaking off excess, coat with flour. Let chicken sit in flour, turning occasionally, while heating oil.

Pour oil into a large, heavy-bottomed pot or pan, so that oil only comes halfway up the sides. Heat oil over medium-high until it reaches 350°F (180°C) (a fryer thermometer is a great tool here). Add 4 pieces of chicken to the pot and reduce heat to medium-low. Fry chicken for 5 minutes, adjusting the heat so it hovers between 280°F (145°C) and 300°F (150°C) (oil should be constantly bubbling) then turn over. Fry 7 minutes more then turn chicken again, frying about another 3 minutes. Transfer chicken to a paper towel-lined baking sheet to drain (and check for doneness by opening chicken or using a probe thermometer).

Return oil heat to 350°F (180°C) and repeat process with remaining chicken. Cooked chicken can be transferred to an unlined baking sheet and kept warm in a 250°F (120°C) oven. Serve warm or chill overnight and serve on a picnic!

SERVES 12

ANNA I got this recipe and cooking method from "Big Troy" when I worked in New Orleans. To show your appreciation when eating a great piece of fried chicken, it's Southern tradition to say, "Mmm, good scald on that chicken, honey!"

MICHAEL Many thanks to "Big Troy" for showing my wife how to make this chicken. We now have a cast iron fryer skillet just for this job.

ANGEL BISCUITS

Angel biscuits get their name because they're lighter than air. Letting the dough rise overnight is well worth the wait. Using yeast helps create the fluffy texture, while the buttermilk gives these biscuits their Southern charm.

2½ tsp	12 mL	one package instant dry yeast
¼ cup	50 mL	sugar
3 Tbsp	45 mL	warm water (body temperature)
6 cups	1.5 L	all-purpose flour
1 tsp	5 mL	baking soda
1 tsp	5 mL	baking powder
1 tsp	5 mL	fine salt
1 cup	250 mL	cold unsalted butter, cut into pieces
2 cups	500 mL	buttermilk

Stir yeast, a pinch of the sugar and water together and set aside. Sift flour, remaining sugar, baking soda, baking powder and salt into a large bowl. Cut the butter into the flour until it's a rough crumbly texture. Stir the yeast mixture into the buttermilk and add all to the flour. Mix until a sticky dough comes together, wrap and chill overnight.

The next day, preheat oven to 425°F (220°C). On a generously floured surface (dough will be sticky), roll out dough to ½ inch (1 cm) thick and fold over, pressing down gently. Using a 2-inch (5-cm) round cutter, cut out biscuits and place on a parchment-lined baking sheet. Bake 10 to 12 minutes, until just lightly browned.

Serve biscuits warm or freeze and reheat to serve later.

MAKES 24 BISCUITS

ANNA Folding over the dough in the method adds flakiness and creates a natural break point for splitting the biscuit to butter it.

MICHAEL The English may have scones, but Southerners love their biscuits. As in all baking, unsalted butter counts in this recipe.

STEWED OKRA

If you've never tried okra, you're in for a treat, and a bit of a surprise, too!
This mild-tasting vegetable has a sweet green taste and a slippery consistency

2 lb	1 kg	fresh okra
3 strips	3 strips	bacon, diced
1 cup	250 mL	diced onion
1/2 cup	125 mL	diced celery
2 cloves	2 cloves	garlic, minced
1 cup	250 mL	diced tomato
1 Tbsp	15 mL	chopped fresh oregano
2 tsp	10 mL	chopped fresh thyme
		coarse salt and ground black pepper
dash	dash	hot sauce
2/3 cup	150 mL	dry breadcrumbs
1/3 cup	75 mL	grated Parmesan cheese

To prepare okra, wash it and drain. Trim off stem ends, cut into 1/2-inch (1-cm) pieces and reserve.

In a large sauté pan over medium heat, cook diced bacon until crispy. Remove bacon from pan and add onion and celery to remaining drippings. Cook onions for 5 minutes, stirring often, until translucent, then add garlic and cook one minute more. Add okra and stir to coat. Add tomato, oregano and thyme and bring mixture up to a simmer, stirring occasionally until okra is fork-tender, about 10 minutes.

Preheat oven to 375°F (190°C). Season okra to taste, stir in reserved cooked bacon and pour into a casserole dish. Combine breadcrumbs and Parmesan and sprinkle over okra. Bake for about 15 minutes, until breadcrumbs have browned and okra is bubbling. Let sit for 5 minutes before serving.

SERVES 12

ANNA As a kid I lived in Georgia, where Mom used to puzzle over what to do with this Southern staple (she's a Yankee, herself). I always enjoyed her sautéed okra with toasted breadcrumbs.

MICHAEL Gumbo is a New Orleans seafood soup that uses okra as a thickener. Anna has a good recipe for that, too.

PEACH PIE WITH PEACH ICE CREAM

We couldn't possibly serve anything but this epitome of Southern dining to finish this meal.

FOR CRUST

5 cups	1.25 L	all-purpose flour
1 tsp	5 mL	fine salt
1 cup	250 mL	cold unsalted butter
1 cup	250 mL	vegetable shortening
¼ cup	50 mL	fresh lemon juice
		about 1 cup (250 mL) ice cold water

ANNA When it comes to making pie for a crowd, more is always better. That way there's always enough for seconds, or a great big slice for you after you've done the dishes and can put your feet up.

MICHAEL If you're making individual pies from a large pie recipe you can usually use the same filling proportions — but double the crust recipe.

FOR PEACH FILLING

12 cups	3 L	peeled and sliced fresh peaches
2 cups	500 mL	sugar
6 Tbsp	90 mL	cornstarch
1 tsp	5 mL	cinnamon
dash	dash	fine salt
		1 egg mixed with 2 Tbsp (25 mL) cold water, for brushing
		mixture of sugar and cinnamon for sprinkling

For crust, combine flour with salt. Cut in butter and shortening until dough is a roughly even crumbly texture. Add lemon juice and water and blend just until dough comes together. Shape into a disk, wrap and chill for 30 minutes.

Cut dough into 4 equal pieces. On a lightly floured surface, roll out dough into a circle large enough to fit a 9-inch (23-cm) pie pan. Line pan with pastry and trim edges. Repeat with second pie shell and chill until ready to fill.

Preheat oven to 400°F (200°C). Toss peaches with sugar, cornstarch, cinnamon and salt to coat. Fill pie shells with fruit. Roll out remaining 2 pieces of pastry and top each pie. Tuck excess dough under bottom dough and pinch edges together to create a seal. Brush tops of pie shells with egg-wash and sprinkle with cinnamon sugar. Snip holes in crust with scissors to allow steam to escape and place pies on a baking sheet. Bake pies at 400°F (200°C) for 20 minutes, then reduce heat to 350°F (180°C) and bake for about 40 minutes more, until filling is bubbling. If crust edge is browning too quickly, cover edges with a thin strip of aluminum foil. Let pie cool for at least an hour before slicing and serve with Peach Ice Cream (below).

MAKES TWO 9-INCH (23-CM) PIES

PEACH ICE CREAM

8 cups	2 L	peeled and diced peaches
1 cup	250 mL	icing sugar, sifted
		juice of 1 lemon
2½ cups	625 mL	whipping cream

Purée peaches with icing sugar until smooth then add icing sugar and lemon juice. Purée again to blend and chill thoroughly. Whip the cream to soft peaks and fold into peach purée. Pour mixture into an ice cream maker and follow manufacturer's instructions. Spoon prepared ice cream into a plastic or other non-reactive container and chill until firm.

SERVES 12

PARIS

PARIS We always give each other a knowing grin when we talk about our February journey to Paris. Unpleasant weather and an uncomfortable hotel room (closet?) kept us in cafés and bistros sipping strong coffee and snacking as the rain drizzled outside.

>While our Casual Bistro menu (page 32) is relaxed and true to form, this menu reflects the Parisian flair we felt while dining there.

Fresh Oysters and Brown Bread

Poule au Pot

Soft Cheeses and Salad

Lemon Chocolate Tart

FRESH OYSTERS AND BROWN BREAD

We enjoyed fresh oysters at the "Au Chien Qui Fume" bistro in Paris' Les Halles area. The dog wasn't the only one smoking — everyone else was too!

48	48	fresh oysters, washed and scrubbed
4 cups	1 L	crushed ice
4	4	lemons, quartered
4 Tbsp	50 mL	freshly grated horseradish
16	16	slices dark brown or rye bread
½ cup	125 mL	unsalted butter at room temperature

Ensure that oysters have been cleaned of any grit by rinsing multiple times in cold water and scrubbing the shells. If you do this ahead of time, store in the fridge with the "cup," or bottom side, of the oyster side down (on a baking tray is best).

Place a wet towel on the counter so the oysters won't slide around. Place the tip of the oyster knife into the "hinge" of the oysters and, holding the oyster firmly in one hand, gently work the handle of your knife in a rocking fashion until you can wedge open the shell. Slide the oyster knife between the meat and the top shell to free the adductor muscle (the little tough bit that hangs onto the shell) from its grip. Carefully slide the knife under the meat to free the bottom shell without tipping out the juice that remains in the "cup." There shouldn't be any chips of shell or grit on the meat or in the oyster liquor.

Arrange the oysters on serving platters filled with crushed ice and the top parts of the shells. In one of the shell tops, place the grated horseradish and surround with lemon wedges.

Serve with a side plate of brown bread and butter. You may want to add a bottle of hot sauce for those who like it spicy.

SERVES 8

ANNA It seems you either love 'em or hate 'em. We absolutely love oysters. Make sure you get them from a reputable supplier and enjoy them for the special occasion they create.

MICHAEL A crisp Sancerre is perfect with fresh oysters, but in a relaxed atmosphere, ice-cold lager does well, too.

Shucking oysters as a novice may produce a few rough ones, but with a little practice you'll reach competition caliber in no time. And really, oysters aren't that pretty, so what's a little nick or two?

POULE AU POT

Hmm, chicken in a pot? Well, when we ordered this at the bistro of the same name, we were surprised to each get our own pot, with enough chicken and vegetables to feed a family. This wasn't an error: they were single servings.

2	2	large roasting chickens, each cut in 8 pieces
16 cups	4 L	water
2 cups	500 mL	dry white wine
4	4	cooking onions, quartered
4 ribs	4 ribs	celery, washed and diced
4	4	parsnips, peeled and diced
4	4	carrots, peeled and diced
8	8	small white turnips, peeled and quartered
2 cloves	2 cloves	garlic, peeled
8 sprigs	8 sprigs	fresh thyme
4	4	bay leaves
½ tsp	2 mL	ground nutmeg
8	8	new potatoes, quartered
½ cup	125 mL	chopped fresh parsley
		coarse salt and ground black pepper

Rinse chicken pieces, place in a large casserole or stewing pot and cover with water. Bring to a boil, skim off the froth that has collected at the surface and reduce heat to simmer.

After 15 minutes, skim again and add onions, celery, parsnips, carrots, turnips, garlic, thyme, bay leaves and nutmeg. Cook 10 minutes, add potatoes and simmer another 25 minutes until potatoes are tender and chicken is thoroughly cooked.

To finish, add chopped parsley, and season with salt and pepper to taste. Serve piping hot in soup bowls with plenty of broth.

SERVES 8

ANNA It may seem silly to buy a roasting chicken for poaching, but since you're not going to cook the chicken to death, you want to enjoy not stringy but tender, juicy meat. Sometimes I add a few Brussels sprouts near the end of cooking, just for some green.

MICHAEL This is my second favorite Sunday supper, my first being Perfect Lemon Roasted Chicken (page 15). It's perfect when winter colds are making their rounds. When Anna and I make this recipe for just the two of us (this recipe divided by 4), we usually reach first for the white turnips — so sweet in their rich broth.

SOFT CHEESES AND SALAD

At the same restaurant where we enjoyed the Poule au Pot, wo finished our meal with a simple salad and a gigantic piece of raw milk Brie. Hello, Mediterranean diet!

1 head	1 head	Boston or leaf lettuce
1 bunch	1 bunch	watercress
½ cup	125 mL	French vinaigrette (page 35)
		coarse salt
¼ cup	50 mL	sliced green onions
1	1	apple, cored and sliced
8 oz	250 g	Brie or Camembert cheese

Wash and tear lettuce into bite-sized pieces and drain or spin-dry. Trim the bottom off the watercress and leave the stems whole. In a mixing bowl, toss the lettuces with the vinaigrette, a pinch of salt and the green onions. Arrange on a plate and top with the apple slices.

Cut the Brie into 4 wedges and place alongside the salad greens. Serve with a grinding of pepper from the pepper mill.

SERVES 8

ANNA This is a great opportunity to try a new cheese. Canada produces some exceptional ones. Look for something new.

MICHAEL In winter, toss in a few bitter greens like radicchio or escarole to bulk up on your greens.

LEMON CHOCOLATE TART

This recipe combines the best of two of the finest French bistro desserts: Tarte au Citron and Tarte au Chocolat. Both are slender, intensely flavored desserts, and only a small slice is meant to be served. In this recipe, we add the refreshing taste of lemon to a chocolate tart. What a great combination!

FOR CRUST

½ cup	125 mL	unsalted butter at room temperature
3 Tbsp	45 mL	sugar
2	2	large egg yolks
¾ cup	175 mL	all-purpose flour
¼ cup	50 mL	cocoa powder
1 tsp	5 mL	freshly grated lemon zest
½ tsp	2 mL	fine salt

FOR FILLING

6 oz	175 g	bittersweet or semi-sweet chocolate, chopped
¾ cup	175 mL	whipping cream
2 Tbsp	25 mL	lemon juice
1 tsp	5 mL	vanilla
2 tsp	10 mL	freshly grated lemon zest
1	1	large egg
1	1	lemon

ANNA This is another occasion to tell you to use only the finest baking chocolate, also known as couverture chocolate. Since this dessert's ingredients are simple, quality makes a difference.

MICHAEL The elegant presentation of thin slices of a scalloped-edge tart is irresistible, even to the fullest of your guests.

To prepare crust, cream butter and sugar together. Stir in egg yolks, adding one at a time. Sift together flour, cocoa, lemon zest and salt and add to butter mixture. Mix until dough just comes together. Shape into a disk and chill until ready to roll. If preparing ahead of time, pull dough from fridge an hour before rolling.

On a lightly floured surface, roll out dough to just over ¼ inch (5 mm) thick. Line a 9-inch (23-cm) removable-bottom tart shell with dough, trim edges and chill for 20 minutes.

Preheat oven to 350°F (180°C). Dock pastry with a fork and bake for 18 to 20 minutes. Allow to cool.

Reduce oven temperature to 325°F (160°C). Place chopped chocolate in a large bowl. Heat cream to just below a simmer and pour over chocolate. Let it sit for a minute then stir slowly. Stir in lemon juice, vanilla and zest. Whisk egg in a small cup then stir into chocolate. Pour into tart shell and bake for 12 minutes. Let cool for 15 minutes, then chill for 2 hours before slicing.

To garnish, peel away the skin and outer membrane of a lemon with a sharp knife. With a paring knife, pull out segments of lemon and remove seeds. Garnish top of each tart slice with 2 sections of lemon. The tart kick is so refreshing against the chocolate.

MAKES ONE 9-INCH (23-CM) TART

BAVARIA

On a chefs' cooking trip to Germany, we made a welcome stop in Anger, a small town near the Austrian border. We spent lots of time working in the kitchens, looking out the window, expecting to see Julie Andrews, with the Alps as her backdrop, warbling, "The hills are alive …" >In the kitchens we got an inside look into contemporary German cuisine, which on the modest side uses the Canadian flavors of pork, potatoes and cabbage, and on the elegant side uses asparagus and foie gras. Even the humbler ingredients are now prepared in a lighter style than was traditional in Germany.

Chilled Asparagus Soup

Wiener Schnitzel with Lemon and Capers

Mustard Seed Spaetzle

Braised Red Cabbage

Frozen Rhubarb Parfait

CHILLED ASPARAGUS SOUP

Absolutely silky and sinful — you won't have a better asparagus soup.

4 Tbsp	50 mL	unsalted butter
2	2	medium cooking onions, diced
1 cup	250 mL	diced celery
pinch	pinch	salt
3 Tbsp	45 mL	all-purpose flour
1 cup	250 mL	dry white wine
6 cups	1.5 L	chicken stock
1¼ lb	625 g	fresh asparagus, trimmed and washed
⅓ cup	75 mL	whipping cream
		coarse salt and ground black pepper

Melt the butter in a heavy-bottomed saucepot and cook the onions and celery until they are transparent. Add a pinch of salt and the flour and stir until the flour and butter take on a "sandy" look. Add the wine and stir to a smooth paste. Add the chicken stock and bring to a simmer.

Trim the tips off the asparagus (just about the size of your soup spoon) and reserve. Chop up the rest of the asparagus, add to the soup and cook until tender. Meanwhile, blanch the asparagus tips in hot water just until they're tender. Chill in ice water and reserve.

Once the onions, celery and asparagus have cooked through, purée the soup using a food processor or immersion blender, and strain. Set aside to cool and then chill overnight in the fridge.

Add the cream to the soup and season to taste. If too thick, correct the consistency with milk or chicken stock until it coats the back of a spoon (about the thickness of heavy cream). Pour into chilled soup bowls and garnish with the asparagus tips.

SERVES 10

ANNA Adding the whipping cream just before you serve the soup accentuates the soup's freshness and ensures it's ice-cold.

MICHAEL A perfect wine match for this soup is a Sauvignon Blanc, which often has a cooked asparagus note, or a crisp Riesling.

WIENER SCHNITZEL WITH LEMON AND CAPERS

Start yodeling — this is a true taste of the Bavarian Alps.

10	10	5-oz (150-g) veal cutlets, cut thinly or pounded very thin
2/3 cup	150 mL	all-purpose flour
2	2	large eggs
1 cup	250 mL	2% milk
3 cups	750 mL	breadcrumbs
		coarse salt and ground black pepper
1/2 cup	125 mL	canola oil
1/4 cup	50 mL	capers
3	3	lemons, quartered

Have your butcher cut the cutlets as thinly as possible, or pound them gently with a meat mallet to the desired thickness.

Set up three dishes to make a "breading station." The first will contain the flour, the second the egg wash (the egg and milk mixed together) and the third the breadcrumbs.

Season the meat with a little salt and pepper and carefully dredge each piece, one at a time, in the flour, ensuring that you coat the entire surface evenly, then dip in the egg wash and, finally, coat evenly with breadcrumbs. Do so without leaving any holes in the filling as these will soak up unwanted oil during the cooking process.

Heat the oil in a pan until a drop of water sputters and cook one or two cutlets at a time until they are golden brown on both sides. This will take 2 to 3 minutes per side. Keep warm on a paper towel-lined plate while you cook the remaining cutlets.

Set on a large dinner plate, sprinkle with capers and serve a lemon wedge on the side.

SERVES 10

ANNA I couldn't get enough of this dish when we were in Germany. It has always been one of my favorites, and it's always a fun night when we make it at home.

MICHAEL If veal cutlets aren't available, pork cutlets or even pork tenderloin cut into medallions will do just fine.

MUSTARD SEED SPAETZLE

Spaetzle are tasty, slippery, easy-to-eat mini dumplings that are ideal for sopping up sauces.

3 cups	750 mL	all-purpose flour
2 Tbsp	25 mL	grainy mustard
½ tsp	2 mL	fine salt
4	4	large eggs
1¼ cups	300 mL	water
2 Tbsp	25 mL	butter
		coarse salt and ground black pepper

Stir the flour, mustard and salt together by hand. Add eggs and water and beat with a wooden spoon until dough is elastic, but still sticky.

Meanwhile, bring a large pot of salted water to a boil. Place a colander over the pot and pour in the batter. Stir vigorously with a whisk or rubber spatula to force the batter through the holes of the colander. You must do this quickly before the colander heats up and the holes are sealed shut by the batter. Cook the dumplings until they rise to the top, about 2 minutes. Drain and refresh under cold water to stop the cooking.

Melt butter in a frying pan until it's foaming but not browning. Reheat the spaetzle in hot butter and season with salt and pepper.

SERVES 10

ANNA We bought ourselves a spaetzle maker, which looks like a cheese grater that isn't sharp. However, the colander trick works very well. Just use one with big holes.

MICHAEL For added flair, toss the spaetzle in the foaming butter, season and then pop in a 400°F (200°C) oven for 5 minutes. The spaetzle get souffléd and turn fluffy.

BRAISED RED CABBAGE

Properly cooked red cabbage is a beautiful thing, and very affordable, too!

2 Tbsp	25 mL	unsalted butter
1 cup	250 mL	diced onion
½ head	½ head	red cabbage, cored and sliced
½ cup	125 mL	raisins
3 Tbsp	45 mL	red wine vinegar
3 Tbsp	45 mL	sugar
½ cup	125 mL	apple juice
		coarse salt
¼ tsp	1 mL	ground nutmeg

ANNA I love the raisins in this recipe. Their sweetness sets off the dish beautifully.

MICHAEL Sometimes I sneak a little caraway into this dish, for added zing. The red wine vinegar is a must for flavor and preserves the bright cabbage color.

Melt the butter in a heavy-bottomed saucepan and cook the onions until translucent. Add the cabbage, raisins, vinegar, sugar and apple juice and simmer, covered, for 15 minutes until the cabbage is tender. Season with salt and nutmeg to taste.

SERVES 10

FROZEN RHUBARB PARFAIT

In Italy, they call this frozen mousse a *semifreddo*.

FOR RHUBARB

2 cups	500 mL	chopped rhubarb, fresh or frozen
½ cup	125 mL	sugar
2 tsp	10 mL	vanilla

FOR PARFAIT

5	5	large egg yolks
⅔ cup	150 mL	sugar
6 Tbsp	90 mL	water
1¼ cups	300 mL	whipping cream
2	2	large egg whites
⅓ cup	75 mL	sugar

For rhubarb, simmer rhubarb, sugar and vanilla until soft. Purée and set aside to cool.

To prepare parfait, whip egg yolks in a stand mixer fitted with the whisk attachment, or with electric beaters, until thick and foamy. Bring ⅔ cup (150 mL) sugar and water up to a boil over high heat. Cook sugar to 270°F (140°C) (hard ball stage), about 7 to 9 minutes. It shouldn't color. Pouring the hot sugar down the side of the bowl, whisk sugar into whipped egg yolks. Increase speed to high and whip until mixture is thick, pale and doubled in volume, 3 to 4 minutes. Let cool completely.

Whip cream to soft peaks and chill. Whip egg whites until foamy and gradually add ⅓ cup (75 mL) sugar and whip until stiff peaks form. Fold whipped cream into egg yolk mixture, then fold in egg whites. Fold in cooled rhubarb and pour into a loaf pan lined with plastic wrap. Freeze overnight.

To serve, turn parfait out onto a plate and slice with a hot, dry knife to serve.

SERVES 10

ANNA I like it that Canada and Germany have similar climates, which means many parallel harvests, including rhubarb. German cuisine treats rhubarb as a treasure, not an underrated fruit.

MICHAEL We enjoyed this dessert at the restaurant of our friends Otto and Uli, on our very first night in Bavaria. What a way to set the standard!

FARMERS' MARKET

>We're lucky to live in a region that hosts a different farmers' market in a different town almost every day of the week. Even if you get to a farmers' market only once every few weeks, take advantage of it, to appreciate the source of your food. If the grocery store is your only option, then stick as much as possible to buying produce that's in season. You'll appreciate the quality.

SPRING
Green, green, green! We love the vivid verdure of spring's first picks: asparagus, snap peas, green onions. Then come the pinks and reds: rhubarb, radishes and strawberries. It's a party on a plate!

Riesling Braised Halibut with Tarragon and Chives

Creamy Orzo with Lemon

Warm Buttered Radishes

Strawberry Jellies with Black Pepper Shortbread

RIESLING BRAISED HALIBUT WITH TARRAGON AND CHIVES

This makes a nice entrée for entertaining, but it's easy enough to pull off during the week.

FOR POACHING LIQUID

1 cup	250 mL	water
1 cup	250 mL	Riesling
3/4 cup	175 mL	chopped onion
1/2 cup	125 mL	chopped celery
1	1	lemon, sliced

FOR HALIBUT

1 Tbsp	15 mL	unsalted butter
1/2	1/2	small onion, minced
6 pieces	6 pieces	halibut fillet, about 6 oz (180 g) each
		coarse salt
1 Tbsp	15 mL	chopped fresh tarragon
2 Tbsp	25 mL	thinly sliced chives
1	1	lemon, cut in 6

Bring water and wine to a simmer with onion, celery and lemon. Simmer 15 minutes, strain and keep warm.

For halibut, melt butter in large shallow pan over medium heat and sauté onions until translucent, about 5 minutes. Season fish with salt and add to pan. Add poaching liquid and tarragon and simmer gently 8 minutes, or until fish is firm to the touch and white in the center. Carefully remove with a slotted spoon and top with chives and a little of the poaching liquid. Serve with lemon wedges.

SERVES 6

ANNA In the absence of halibut, try haddock, salmon or any other firm-fleshed fish. For a rich chive sauce, reduce 1 cup (250 mL) of the poaching liquid with the juice of 1 lemon to a third of its volume and whisk in 2 Tbsp (25 mL) diced cold butter and 2 Tbsp (25 mL) chopped chives.

MICHAEL If it's spring and you're celebrating your first meal alfresco, prepare this in advance and serve it chilled with greens and an herbed mayonnaise.

CREAMY ORZO WITH LEMON

A simple little rice dish that isn't rice at all — it's pasta!

1 cup	250 mL	orzo pasta
2 Tbsp	25 mL	sour cream
1	1	lemon, zest and juice
		coarse salt and ground black pepper

Cook pasta in boiling, salted water until tender. Drain, reserving ½ cup (125 mL) cooking water. In a small pot or casserole, toss pasta with sour cream, lemon zest and juice and add a little of the pasta water to make a creamy consistency. Season and heat.

SERVES 6

ANNA Michael likes to get creative with his "soup pastas," as they're sometimes called — the little pasta pieces that float in your chicken or minestrone soup. He's used *acini di pepe* (pepper seed) and *pepe di melone* (melon seed) pasta, just to name two.

MICHAEL Stir in some baby spinach leaves or rainbow swiss chard for a complete starch and vegetable dish.

WARM BUTTERED RADISHES

These radishes, warmed to take off their edge, retain their crunch and follow this menu's springtime-on-a-plate theme.

2 Tbsp	25 mL	unsalted butter
2 bunches	2 bunches	fresh radishes, trimmed, washed and quartered
		coarse salt and ground black pepper

Melt butter in a sauté pan over medium heat and add radish quarters. Toss radishes in pan to warm, just for 3 minutes. Season lightly and serve.

SERVES 6

ANNA I love spring's first radishes that crack open with moisture when you bite into them.

MICHAEL When buying radishes with the leaves attached, remove them as soon as you get home: they get slimy quickly and make your radishes taste just a little off.

STRAWBERRY JELLIES WITH BLACK PEPPER SHORTBREAD

Black pepper heightens the flavor of strawberries. These easy cookies add a nice spice to a fresh strawberry gelatin dessert.

FOR STRAWBERRY JELLIES

4 cups	1 L	fresh strawberries, hulled
1 cup	250 mL	sugar
4 tsp	20 mL	gelatin powder
1 cup	250 mL	white wine

FOR BLACK PEPPER SHORTBREAD

3/4 cup	175 mL	unsalted butter at room temperature
1 cup	250 mL	icing sugar, sifted
2 Tbsp	25 mL	lemon zest
3 Tbsp	45 mL	fresh lemon juice
1 Tbsp	15 mL	vanilla
1 3/4 cups	425 mL	all-purpose flour
2 Tbsp	25 mL	cornstarch
1 tsp	5 mL	cracked black pepper
1/4 tsp	1 mL	fine salt

For strawberry jellies, purée strawberries with sugar and strain. Soften gelatin in white wine for 5 minutes. Heat wine on low heat, stirring until gelatin dissolves. Pour wine into strawberry purée and mix well. Pour into wine glasses or dessert cups and chill for at least four hours before serving.

For shortbread, cream together butter and icing sugar until smooth. Stir in lemon zest, juice and vanilla. In a separate bowl, sift together flour, cornstarch, black pepper and salt. Stir into butter mixture, shape into logs, wrap and chill for 1 hour.

Preheat oven to 325°F (160°C). Slice 1/4-inch (5-mm) rounds and place on a parchment-lined baking sheet. Bake for 12 to 15 minutes and allow to cool.

Serve shortbread alongside strawberry jellies.

SERVES 6

ANNA Of course, any berry makes a nice jelly, but I do like the orange-pink of the strawberries.

MICHAEL You can set these jellies in a ramekin or jelly mould and immerse them in hot water for a moment to loosen, and then tip them out onto a plate to serve.

SUMMER

The challenge in creating a summer menu is keeping it simple. With a plethora of tastes and textures available, it's easy to go overboard. We've tried to build a menu that holds together, but please feel free to add more courses.

Garden Greens with Bulb Onions and Pickled Apricots

Whole Grilled Chicken with Scorched Herbs

Corn Zucchini Griddle Cakes

Nectarine Blueberry Strudel

GARDEN GREENS WITH BULB ONIONS AND PICKLED APRICOTS

Serving apricots in a savory course is a great way to celebrate summer. When fresh picked, their lively, floral personality floats above the intense flavor of onion.

FOR PICKLED APRICOTS

6		6	fresh apricots
½ cup		125 mL	water
½ cup		125 mL	white vinegar
1 Tbsp		15 mL	sugar
½ tsp		2 mL	salt
1 tsp		5 mL	lime zest
1		1	bay leaf

FOR SALAD

1		1	bunch spring bulb onions
½		½	head leaf lettuce, green or red
½		½	head Boston lettuce
2 Tbsp		25 mL	extra virgin olive oil

Cut apricots in half, remove pit and cut each half into 4 wedges. Bring the water, vinegar, sugar, salt, lime zest and bay leaf to a boil, pour over the apricot wedges and allow to cool to room temperature.

For salad, wash and trim just the end from the bulb onions, split in half lengthwise and grill over medium heat, turning occasionally, until they are tender to the touch. Set aside.

Wash and prepare the salad greens, dress with olive oil then arrange on a plate. Top with grilled onions and apricots. Sprinkle a little (about 1 tsp (5 mL) per person) of the pickling juice over the salad greens.

SERVES 6

ANNA In summer, we get enthusiastic about making preserves. We set up an outdoor kitchen at the lake, hit the farmers' market and spend the day boiling jars and making pickles and jams.

MICHAEL To make a salad dressing or a glaze for vegetables, chicken or fish, purée the apricots in the pickling juice after removing the bay leaf. Add to it an equal amount of olive oil and season with salt and pepper.

WHOLE GRILLED CHICKEN WITH SCORCHED HERBS

Grilled chicken is as basic as a meal gets. Your key to success is to watch the cooking to ensure a golden-brown, crisp skin and tender, moist chicken. Yaahhhh, Colonel!

3	3	whole chickens, "fryers," about 2 lb (1 kg) each
6	6	bay leaves
½ bunch	½ bunch	fresh thyme
½ bunch	½ bunch	fresh rosemary
6 cloves	6 cloves	garlic, crushed
1 cup	250 mL	red wine
1 cup	250 mL	red wine vinegar
1 Tbsp	15 mL	cumin seeds
1 Tbsp	15 mL	coriander seeds
		coarse salt and ground black pepper

Rinse chicken under cold water and dry with paper towels. Remove the backbone and split in half lengthwise through the breastbone. You can also simply flatten the chicken by pressing down on the breastbone from the skin side until it "cracks," and cook it whole.

Blend the bay leaves, thyme, rosemary, garlic, wine, vinegar, cumin and coriander together and marinate the chicken 30 minutes, or up to 12 hours, refrigerated. Preheat the grill to medium and make sure the surface is scrubbed clean with a grill brush. Remove the bay leaves, thyme and rosemary from the marinade, and place them on the grill, then season the chicken with salt and pepper and place over the herbs. Cover the grill and allow to cook 8 to 10 minutes. Baste with half of the remaining marinade and cook 5 minutes, then turn over and brush with the last of the marinade. Finish cooking, about 15 minutes more, or until chicken reaches an internal temperature of 175°F (85°C). The juices of the chicken should run clear and the meat should have lost its "pink" look around the bone (check near the thigh bone). Serve hot from the grill and encourage your guests to use their fingers!

SERVES 6

ANNA I love Michael's marinades. Their tartness brings out the chicken's sweetness, and the built-in sugars caramelize and scorch to make a finger-licking treat!

MICHAEL This cooking technique uses the marinade herbs to provides a fragrant smoke. Grill this chicken with the lid on to keep those fragrances in contact with the chicken as long as possible.

CORN ZUCCHINI GRIDDLE CAKES

When the heat of summer forces you to keep it light, a side dish like this makes an easier accompaniment than potatoes.

2 cups	500 mL	shredded green zucchini
1/2 cup	125 mL	fresh or frozen corn kernels
1/3 cup	75 mL	all-purpose flour
1	1	large egg
1/4 tsp	1 mL	baking powder
1/2 tsp	2 mL	fine salt
2 Tbsp	25 mL	unsalted butter

Stir zucchini, corn, flour, egg, baking powder and salt in a large bowl. Allow batter to rest 10 minutes. Heat the butter until it foams in a large skillet. Drop spoonfuls of the batter into the butter and fry over medium heat for 4 minutes per side until golden brown.

SERVES 6

ANNA Make miniature versions of these griddle cakes to serve as canapés topped with cream and a little shrimp.

MICHAEL The cakes freeze well, so make lots when zucchini is in season and package them up for when you need a taste of summer.

NECTARINE BLUEBERRY STRUDEL

A strudel made with phyllo pastry is an easy way to get a baked dessert to the table without fussing with pastry doughs, especially if it's hot outside.

4	4	nectarines, diced (not peeled)
1½ cups	375 mL	fresh or frozen blueberries
¼ cup	50 mL	sugar
3 Tbsp	45 mL	all-purpose flour
½ tsp	2 mL	cinnamon
¼ tsp	1 mL	nutmeg
6 sheets	6	phyllo pastry
⅔ cup	150 mL	unsalted butter, melted
		turbinado sugar, for sprinkling

Preheat oven to 350°F (180°C). Toss diced nectarines with blueberrries, sugar, flour, cinnamon and nutmeg and set aside. Lay 1 sheet of phyllo pastry on work surface (keep unused phyllo under a moist towel to prevent drying). Brush sheet with butter and lay a second sheet of phyllo on top. Continue layering and brushing with butter until all 6 sheets have been used. Spoon nectarine filling along long end of pastry, leaving 2 inches (5 cm) at either end. Roll up phyllo, encompassing fruit. After first roll that covers fruit, fold over outside edges to seal in ends of strudel and continue rolling. Lift carefully and place seam side down onto a parchment-lined baking sheet.

Brush strudel with remaining butter and sprinkle top with turbinado sugar. Pierce top of strudel to allow steam to escape. Bake for 25 to 35 minutes, until a light golden brown. Enjoy warm or at room temperature.

Strudel will keep refrigerated for 2 to 3 days; just warm in oven or microwave to serve.

SERVES 6

ANNA I tend to blend together my summer fruits. The fruit seasons overlap in such a cavalcade that I usually have many fruits in my fridge.

MICHAEL Ice cream, anyone?

AUTUMN
Autumn is one of our favorite times of year — especially September when summer's produce still abounds but autumn's sugary squash and sweet root vegetables are fit to be roasted with heady herbs.

Caramelized Onion Risotto with Oven-Roasted Tomatoes

Potato Cheddar Stuffed Pork Loin with Cider Glaze

Turnip Carrot Bake

Warm Apple and Hazelnut Crêpes

CARAMELIZED ONION RISOTTO WITH OVEN-ROASTED TOMATOES

Now a familiar dish on North American tables, risotto was once limited to households with Northern Italian roots. It's a wonderful first course and can be modified to reflect seasonal ingredients in any number of ways. Bravo!

FOR OVEN-ROASTED TOMATOES

6	6	plum tomatoes
1½ tsp	7 mL	fine salt
1 Tbsp	15 mL	sugar
1 clove	1 clove	garlic, crushed

FOR RISOTTO

4 Tbsp	50 mL	vegetable oil
4	4	onions, diced
1½ cups	375 mL	arborio rice
½ cup	125 mL	white wine
5 cups	1.25 L	chicken stock
2 Tbsp	25 mL	chopped parsley
2 Tbsp	25 mL	unsalted butter
½ cup	125 mL	grated Parmesan cheese
		coarse salt and ground black pepper

ANNA I've admitted that rice is my nemesis, but I enjoy cooking risotto. Some swear that you should never leave the pot, but I reduce the heat a little and carry on making my salad or what-have-you, while the rice slowly absorbs the liquid.

MICHAEL To check the doneness of your rice, bite into a single grain and look at the middle. There will be a tiny "white" spot to show that you've reached the optimal doneness, not the "mushy" point of no return. Northern Italians will give you the evil eye if you overcook the risotto.

To roast the tomatoes, preheat oven to 250°F (120°C) and line a baking sheet with parchment paper. Core tomatoes and cut into 6 wedges. Toss in salt, sugar and garlic and lay, skin side down, on prepared pan. Roast for 1½ to 2 hours, until the tomatoes are shrivelled and about half their original size. Tomatoes will keep in the fridge for up to 1 week or frozen for 2 months.

For risotto, heat vegetable oil in a large, heavy-bottomed saucepot and sweat the onions over medium heat, stirring often, until they've caramelized and taken on a rich brown color. This will take about 25 minutes. Add the rice and stir to coat with oil, cooking for 3 minutes. Add white wine and stir until the rice has absorbed all liquid. Add stock, 1 cup (250 mL) at a time, stirring regularly until each portion of stock has been absorbed. Test the rice for doneness by tasting. The grains should be tender but still have a little resilience.

To finish, warm roasted tomatoes in a separate pan for 5 minutes over medium heat and reserve. Add parsley, butter and Parmesan to risotto and season to taste. There should be enough liquid to be a built-in sauce, but the dish shouldn't appear "soupy." Serve in shallow bowls and top with the warmed roasted tomatoes.

SERVES 6

POTATO CHEDDAR STUFFED PORK LOIN WITH CIDER GLAZE

Roasts are the perfect fall food. They fill the house with good, hearty aromas and take you back to your childhood.

FOR STUFFING

4 strips	4 strips	bacon, diced
1	1	medium onion, diced
1 clove	1 clove	garlic, crushed
2	2	large Yukon Gold potatoes, peeled and diced
1 cup	250 mL	grated cheddar cheese

FOR ROAST

1	1	3 lb (1.5 kg) boneless pork loin roast
2 Tbsp	25 mL	Dijon mustard
		coarse salt and ground black pepper

FOR CIDER GLAZE

1 cup	250 mL	apple cider
1 cup	250 mL	dark beer
2 Tbsp	25 mL	molasses
1 sprig	1 sprig	fresh rosemary
1 sprig	1 sprig	fresh sage

ANNA Carving a hole in a roast requires a very sharp knife and careful motions. Sometimes Michael switches to a long knife steel and moves it in circular motions to create an opening for the stuffing.

For stuffing, sauté bacon and onion in a skillet over medium heat until onions are translucent, about 6 minutes, and remove from heat. Drain excess fat and add garlic to pan, stir and set aside. Cook potatoes in boiling, salted water until tender and drain. Mash potatoes roughly with onion mixture and season to taste. Stir in grated cheddar and allow to cool completely.

For pork roast, preheat oven to 375°F (190°C). Make a tunnel in the pork loin, end-to-end through the center of the "eye" of the roast by using a sharp pointed knife to make the incision and then open up the cut with careful side-to-side movements. Do not break through the surface of the meat or the stuffing will leak out. Using a spoon (and your fingers), force the stuffing into the hole and try to keep it as evenly distributed as possible. A butter knife or the handle of a wooden spoon will help push in the mixture. Place pork in a roasting pan and season the outside with mustard, salt and pepper. Roast to an internal temperature of 145°F (65°C), about 45 to 55 minutes. Allow 5 to 10 minutes to rest the roast before you carve and serve.

For cider glaze, reduce the cider, beer, molasses, and herbs over medium heat until half its original volume. Strain and serve warm with the roast.

SERVES 6

MICHAEL For a restaurant-style presentation, roll the potato mixture in wax paper or plastic wrap and freeze. Then slide the cylinder into the roast cavity.

TURNIP CARROT BAKE

This is a delicious home flavor created with basic vegetables from your local produce stand and a no-fuss, quick soufflé method!

1½ cups	375 mL	carrots, peeled and diced
1½ cups	375 mL	yellow turnips, peeled and diced
1 Tbsp	15 mL	
+ 1 tsp	+ 5 mL	coarse salt
½ cup	125 mL	sour cream
¼ cup	50 mL	2% milk
2	2	large eggs
½ tsp	2 mL	ground black pepper
½ cup	125 mL	grated medium cheddar cheese
1 Tbsp	15 mL	unsalted butter
¼ cup	50 mL	breadcrumbs

In a medium saucepot, cover carrots and turnips with cold water, add 1 Tbsp (15 mL) salt, bring to a boil and simmer for about 15 minutes or until tender. Drain well and purée in a food processor to a smooth paste. Add sour cream, milk and eggs, remaining 1 tsp (5 mL) salt and pepper, and pulse. The consistency should be like a loose batter, but not too runny.

Preheat oven to 375°F (190°C). Grease a 6-cup (1.5-L) baking dish with the butter and line with breadcrumbs. Spoon in purée and bake for 30 minutes until puffed and golden brown.

SERVES 6

ANNA For a change of flavor, try adding 1 cup (250 mL) celery root or parsnip instead of 1 cup (250 mL) turnip. I sometimes add a teaspoon (5 mL) of chopped sage or rosemary to make the dish more fragrant.

MICHAEL My sister-in-law, Linda, makes a delicious "Turnip Puff" every time there's a turkey on the table. It's one of those familiar flavors you look forward to on special occasions.

WARM APPLE AND HAZELNUT CRÊPES

This is an autumn take on Crêpes Suzette.

FOR CRÊPES

½ cup + 2 Tbsp	125 mL + 25 mL	all-purpose flour
1 Tbsp	15 mL	sugar
2	2	large eggs
6 Tbsp	90 mL	water
½ cup + 2 Tbsp	125 mL + 25 mL	2% milk
½ cup	125 mL	unsalted butter, melted

FOR FILLING AND ASSEMBLY

2 Tbsp	25 mL	unsalted butter
¼ cup	50 mL	hazelnuts, roughly chopped
dash	dash	fine salt
2 Tbsp	25 mL	dark brown sugar, packed
2 Tbsp	25 mL	pure maple syrup
3 Tbsp	45 mL	hazelnut liqueur
dash	dash	cinnamon
4	4	sweet apples, such as Honey Crisp or Royal Gala, peeled and sliced vanilla ice cream, optional

ANNA This may be the first time in weeks that you're cooking indoors with the windows closed, so why not fill the house with the fragrance of apples, butter and hazelnuts?

MICHAEL Just like those summer Corn Zucchini Griddle Cakes (page 175), we make big batches of crêpes and freeze them for a later day.

For crêpes, blend all ingredients with a hand blender (or in a food processor) and let batter rest for 20 minutes. If you are whisking by hand, strain batter before resting.

To make crêpes, heat a large non-stick pan over medium heat. Spray with food release, or lightly coat with oil (repeat only as needed while you cook crêpes). Pour ¼ cup (50 mL) of batter into the center of the pan and lift the pan off the heat, swirling the batter around to coat the pan evenly. Return pan to heat and cook crêpes for 3 minutes, until edges turn light brown. Gently loosen edges of crêpe with a spatula and flip crêpe over in pan. If this presents a challenge, simply turn burner down to medium low heat and cook crêpe longer on one side, until crêpe is completely dry looking (crêpe will cook without flipping). Loosen edges of crêpe and slide onto a plate to cool. Repeat with remaining batter.

After crêpes have cooled, be sure to wrap well until ready to sauté. Don't store in the fridge. If not using right away, freeze and thaw when ready to fill.

For filling, fold crêpes into quarters and reserve. Melt butter in a large sauté pan over medium-high heat and add hazelnuts and salt. Stir until hazelnuts are lightly toasted. Stir in brown sugar and maple syrup and cook, stirring often until sauce is bubbling. Add folded crêpes (2 per person) and coat with sugar mixture. Turn off heat and remove pan from burner. Pour in hazelnut liqueur. Be cautious since even with the heat off, there's a small risk of flames. Return pan to heat and stir in cinnamon. Remove crêpes from pan and place onto serving plates or platter. Return pan to medium-high heat and stir in apples. Simmer, stirring often until apples are tender, about 4 minutes. Spoon apples over crêpes and serve with vanilla ice cream if you wish.

SERVES 6

WINTER

Even though the melon man won't be seen for months, and the strawberry lady is sunning herself in Florida, the winter farmers' market still has lots to offer. Grab a hot coffee and stop at the smoked meat stall, or try a new cheese from the cheese truck, or scope out some properly stored apples or pears.

Garlic Roasted Turkey Breast

Twice-Baked Potatoes with Bacon

Spaghetti Squash with Parmesan

Chocolate Pear Charlotte

GARLIC ROASTED TURKEY BREAST

A great alternative to chicken, turkey isn't just for the holidays. The smaller breasts are juicy, tender and sweet.

2 cups	500 mL	shallots, peeled
6 cloves	6 cloves	garlic
2 Tbsp	25 mL	extra virgin olive oil
3 sprigs	3 sprigs	fresh thyme
1	1	3 lb (1.5 kg) turkey breast
2 Tbsp	25 mL	unsalted butter
		coarse salt and ground black pepper
¼ cup	50 mL	balsamic vinegar

Preheat oven to 325°F (160°C). Toss shallots and garlic with olive oil and spread over the bottom of a roasting pan or baking dish. Arrange thyme over shallots and place turkey breast on top. Rub turkey with butter and season with salt and pepper. Roast turkey until juices run clear and an internal temperature of at least 175°F (80°C) is reached.

Remove turkey from pan and keep warm. Skim excess fat off shallots and place pan over medium heat. Add balsamic vinegar and cook, stirring shallots, until vinegar is absorbed. Serve turkey sliced with sauce spooned on top.

SERVES 6

ANNA The balsamic vinegar in this recipe brings out the turkey's sweetness. Don't use your good 25-year-old drizzling balsamic here. A regular grocery store variety does just fine.

MICHAEL A small turkey breast can take less time to cook than a whole roasted chicken, so it's an achievable mid-week meal. And the sandwiches — don't forget the sandwiches!!

TWICE-BAKED POTATOES WITH BACON

While the oven is on for roasting the turkey, you might as well do the potatoes too.

3	3	large baking potatoes, such as russet
¼ cup	50 mL	unsalted butter
¾ cup	175 mL	sour cream
1	1	large egg
½ cup	125 mL	chopped green onions
6 strips	6 strips	bacon, cooked, drained and crumbled
1 tsp	5 mL	coarse salt
¼ tsp	1 mL	ground black pepper

Preheat oven to 325°F (160°C). Wash and prick potatoes with a fork. Bake until tender, about an hour.

While still warm, cut potatoes in half lengthwise and scoop out flesh into a bowl. With a potato masher or electric beaters, beat in butter, sour cream and egg. Stir in green onions, half of the bacon, and salt and pepper. Spoon filling back into potatoes and place on a baking tray. Bake potatoes for 25 minutes and top with remaining bacon to serve.

SERVES 6

ANNA When I visited my friend Courtney in England, I was amazed at how popular "jacket potatoes" were. Pubs had entire menus of baked potatoes with various fillings and toppings.

MICHAEL Avoid buying baking potatoes already in foil: you want to see what you're buying. Bake a few extra potatoes for home fries the next day.

SPAGHETTI SQUASH WITH PARMESAN

Spaghetti squash seems to have a longer season than other squash varieties and stays nice and sweet throughout the winter.

3 lb	1.5 kg	spaghetti squash
3 Tbsp	45 mL	unsalted butter
2/3 cup	150 mL	grated Parmesan cheese
		coarse salt and ground black pepper

Preheat oven to 325°F (160°C). Cut squash in half lengthwise and scoop out seeds in center. Place face-down on a parchment-lined baking tray and dock skin with a fork. Bake until tender, about an hour.

Scrape out flesh of squash with a fork, to extract the "spaghetti." Stir squash with butter and Parmesan to melt and season to taste. Serve immediately.

SERVES 6

ANNA Pop a large egg into the mixture along with 1/2 cup (125 mL) of whipping cream and bake this squash for 20 minutes for a marvelous casserole.

MICHAEL This squash is best for eating just like this: it's a little stringy for soups and stews.

CHOCOLATE PEAR CHARLOTTE

The chocolate dessert Poire Belle Hélène is a poached pear filled with chocolate and served with a custard sauce. We've built these flavors into a toasted egg bread shell for a delicious warm treat when you break into it.

1 cup	250 mL	peeled and diced pear
¼ cup	50 mL	Poire Williams or brandy
3 Tbsp	45 mL	sugar
2–3 drops	2–3 drops	almond extract
½ cup	125 mL	whipping cream
3½ oz	100 g	bittersweet chocolate, chopped
¼ tsp	1 mL	fine salt
7 Tbsp	105 mL	unsalted butter at room temperature
1½	1½	fresh loaves challah or large brioche, about 1½ lb (750 g) total, sliced ½ inch (1 cm) thick

Bring pears, Poire Williams, or brandy, and sugar to a boil in a small saucepot, stirring occasionally. Remove from heat and let stand, covered, 15 minutes. Stir in almond extract.

Heat cream, chocolate and salt in another small heavy saucepot over low heat, stirring until chocolate is melted and smooth, about 3 minutes. Remove from heat and stir in 1 Tbsp (15 mL) butter until incorporated, then stir in cooked pears and their liquid.

Transfer filling to a metal bowl and freeze, stirring occasionally, until firm but not frozen solid, about 2½ hours.

Preheat oven to 350°F (180°C). Cut out 12 rounds from bread slices with cookie cutter, then cut forty-two 2-inch (5-cm) by 1½-inch (3.5-cm) rectangles from trimmings and remaining slices. Spread 1 side of each round and rectangle with some of remaining butter. Put 6 rounds, buttered sides down, in molds and line sides with rectangles (5 to 7 per mould), buttered sides against mould, arranging them vertically and slightly overlapping. Press slices gently to adhere. Trim any overhang flush with rims.

Divide filling among molds and top with 6 remaining bread rounds, buttered sides up, pressing gently to fit inside bread rim.

Bake charlottes on a baking sheet in middle of oven until bread is golden, about 25 minutes. Cool 5 minutes, then invert plates over charlottes and flip charlottes onto plates. Serve warm.

SERVES 6

ANNA When teaching cooking classes I've used this recipe as my ace card. I love to hear the oohs and aahs as guests break into their charlottes. I enjoy the silence that follows as they savor the melted chocolate pear interior.

MICHAEL Keep your eyes open for good ramekins. They're indispensable for individual portions of appetizers, entrées and desserts.

BEER

Beer as an adventure? Well beyond the days of Friday night frat parties, we now enjoy beer tastings as much as wine tastings.

>Here are a few tips to keep in mind when matching beer with food:

1 A lighter style of beer should pair with subtle flavors.

2 Beers with a pronounced hop flavor have a bitter, palate-cleansing taste that pairs well with rich dishes.

3 Use beer in the dishes you're cooking to create a link from the dish to the beverage.

BEER TASTING WITH THE BOYS

When we spend time with friends who have young kids, the girls go out to a movie adaptation of a Jane Austen novel while the boys stay home and let the kids run around, draw on the walls and bathe in the toilet. We also like to stand around the kitchen, tell jokes, cook and eat.

Guinness Onion Soup

Ribeye Steak a la Plancha

Fantastic Frites

Steamed English Pudding

GUINNESS ONION SOUP

This is the best French onion soup you'll ever make. Perhaps it's the Irish twist that makes it so good!

4 strips	4 strips	bacon, diced
8 cups	2 L	thinly sliced onions
3 cloves	3 cloves	garlic, minced
4 sprigs	4 sprigs	fresh thyme
4	4	bay leaves
4 cups	1 L	Guinness beer
5 cups	1.25 L	chicken stock
		coarse salt and ground black pepper
12 slices	12 slices	crusty bread
3 cups	750 mL	grated Gruyère cheese

In a large pot over medium heat, cook bacon until crisp and drain on a paper towel. Reduce heat to medium-low, add onions and cook slowly for about 30 minutes until they've completely broken down and caramelized to a light golden brown.

Add reserved bacon, garlic, thyme, bay leaves, beer and stock. Bring to a boil and simmer 15 minutes until onions are very tender. Season to taste.

Meanwhile, toast bread and preheat oven to broil. Pour soup into ovenproof crocks, top with bread, and sprinkle with cheese. Broil until the cheese is melted and golden brown. Serve piping hot.

SERVES 12

ANNA Michael is a beer aficionado, that's for certain, but he doesn't like the dark beers. I, on the other hand, enjoy the coffee and chocolate extracts of a dark or stout beer, but only in the winter: I'm a lager girl in the summer.

MICHAEL Even though Guinness is in the soup, try pairing this with a Belgian beer, like Hoegaarden, which is brewed with citrus peel and coriander seed. These flavors work well with the bitter in the beer and the creaminess of that stretchy cheese.

RIBEYE STEAK A LA PLANCHA

"A la plancha" refers to the method of cooking steaks that has become our favorite, beating out grilling. Try it once and you'll get hooked.

12	12	10-oz (250-g) ribeye steaks, the best quality you can afford
3 Tbsp	45 mL	fresh cracked black pepper
4 Tbsp	50 mL	coarse pickling salt

Let the steaks sit at room temperature for 30 minutes to take the chill out of the meat. Coat both sides of each steak with the black pepper.

Heat a cast iron skillet (or several) until very hot — until the pan literally starts to smoke. For each steak, sprinkle 1 tsp (5 mL) of coarse salt onto the skillet. Allow the salt to heat up and drop in the steaks. Open a window or turn on the fan!

Allow the steaks to cook for 3 minutes on high heat without touching them, then turn over. The salt transfers the heat and leaves a crisp, salty, golden crust. Cook the steak 3 minutes longer for rare doneness and remove to a plate. Wait at least 3 minutes before slicing and enjoy!

SERVES 12

ANNA We picked up this technique in Spain. It means cooking on a very hot, flat surface sprinkled generously with coarse salt that in turn gets very hot. This heat sears the meat, immediately holding in all juices and creating a caramelized exterior. A red wine like a Zinfandel or Rioja seems perfect, but it's beer night, so how about an earthy Guinness to stand up to the iron and salt?

MICHAEL This method isn't limited to steaks. Our first experience "a la plancha" was with whole shrimp seared on the salt with a scattering of thinly sliced garlic. The garlic roasted and stuck onto the shrimp with the salt. We found ourselves licking our fingers as we peeled and sucked back the shrimp.

FANTASTIC FRITES

Yukon Gold potatoes are the best for making gorgeous, crispy fries with golden creamy centers.

5 lb	2.2 kg	Yukon Gold potatoes
		canola oil for frying
		fine salt to taste

Peel and cut the potatoes into fries about ½ inch (1 cm) thick and rinse under cold water to remove excess starch. Drain in a colander and dry well with kitchen towels.

Heat 3 inches (8 cm) of oil in a deep pot to 325°F (160°C). For safety, use a thermometer. Cook the fries in 4 separate batches until tender. They'll crush easily when pinched, but don't worry about the fries getting any color. This is called "blanching." Drain fries on paper towel and allow to cool. This step can be done up to a day in advance.

Increase the temperature of the oil to 365°F (185°C) (use that thermometer!), drop in the blanched fries in batches and cook 2 to 3 minutes until the potatoes are golden brown and crisp. Remove from the oil with a strainer or slotted spoon and drain on paper towels. Season with salt immediately and serve.

SERVES 12

ANNA I was impressed with this double-fry, or blanching, technique, which makes fries that are tender and soft inside but have a crunchy, but not overly dark, exterior.

MICHAEL For a decadent fry experience, toss the fries in a bowl with 2 Tbsp (25 mL) caesar salad dressing, a trick that makes these fries addictive.

STEAMED ENGLISH PUDDING

A traditional English pudding is the only appropriate way to finish a meal such as this — unless you want to deep-fry Mars bars.

3½ cups	875 mL	pitted dates, about 20 oz (600 g)
2 cups	875 mL	stout beer
2 cups	875 mL	water
1 Tbsp	15 mL	baking soda
4 cups	1 L	all-purpose flour
1 tsp	5 mL	baking powder
1 tsp	5 mL	ground ginger
1 tsp	5 mL	fine salt
¾ cup	175 mL	unsalted butter at room temperature
1 cup	250 mL	sugar
1 cup	250 mL	light brown sugar, packed
4 tsp	20 mL	finely grated orange zest
6	6	large eggs

Preheat oven to 350°F (180°C) and grease and flour six 5-ounce (150-g) ramekins. Place ramekins in a baking dish with a 2-inch (5-cm) lip.

Roughly chop dates and simmer in beer and water, uncovered, for 5 minutes. Remove from heat and stir in baking soda. Let cool while preparing batter.

Sift flour, baking powder, ginger and salt. In a separate bowl, cream butter and sugars together until light and fluffy. Stir in orange zest and add eggs one at a time, stirring well after each addition. Add flour mixture alternately with date mixture, stirring well after each addition, starting and ending with flour. Spoon batter evenly among prepared ramekins, pour hot water around ramekins — coming up ½ inch (1 cm) — and bake for 20 to 25 minutes, until a tester inserted in the center of a pudding comes out clean. Remove from water bath and allow to cool at least 15 minutes before unmolding.

SERVES 12

ANNA Dates are the key dried fruit in this pudding, but there are many natural variations — figs for figgy pudding, prunes for plum pudding. Does anyone hear a Christmas carol?

MICHAEL To stay in the beer-tasting spirit, serve a Lambic beer with desserts. Its cherry notes make a perfect finish to a great meal.

SUMMER BARBECUE

SUMMER BARBECUE Sometimes it's too hot even for wine! Crack open an ice-cold lager, squirt in a hint of lime and relax on the deck for hours before the sun sets. Make-ahead, low-maintenance food is key here, and paper plates are definitely permitted.

Chilled Corn, Peach and Basil Buttermilk Soup

Dry Rub Pork Ribs

Spicy Boiled Potatoes

Radish and Beet Salad

Corn on the Cob with Onion Butter

Peaches Foster

CHILLED CORN, PEACH AND BASIL BUTTERMILK SOUP

We've been making this soup for years. Making it the night before allows the flavors to marry.

2 Tbsp	25 mL	extra virgin olive oil
½ cup	125 mL	finely diced onion
2 cups	500 mL	corn, freshly cut from the cob
1 cup	250 mL	peeled and sliced fresh peaches
1 cup	250 mL	fresh basil leaves
4 cups	1 L	buttermilk
1 Tbsp	15 mL	honey
		coarse salt and ground black pepper

In a sauté pan over medium heat, add oil and onion. Sauté onion for 5 minutes until translucent, then add corn. Sauté until corn is tender and yellow, about 3 minutes. Remove from heat and cool.

In a blender or food processor, blend two-thirds of the corn mixture with peaches and basil leaves. Pour in buttermilk while blending and add honey. Pour soup into a bowl and stir in remaining corn mixture (for texture). Season to taste and chill completely before serving, at least 4 hours.

Taste after chilling, to see if seasoning needs to be adjusted. If you wish, you can garnish soup with a peach slice and a basil leaf.

SERVES 8

ANNA This soup makes perfect picnic fare. I pack the soup in a thermos or large mason jar and pour it into glasses or cups to serve.

MICHAEL Yes, this does make a great picnic soup, except for one thing: when we go on a picnic, we pull out our basket and start snacking before we hit the end of the driveway!

DRY RUB PORK RIBS

The secret is in the spice! You'll love this blend of spices that works well for just about any grilled meat. Then finish 'em off with a juicy "mop."

FOR RIBS

2 racks	2 racks	fresh pork back ribs, 2 to 2½ lb (1 to 1.25 kg) each
2 Tbsp	25 mL	ground cumin seed
2 Tbsp	25 mL	ground coriander seed
1 tsp	5 mL	whole celery seed
4 Tbsp	50 mL	Hungarian paprika
1 Tbsp	15 mL	ground black pepper
4 Tbsp	50 mL	fine salt

FOR MOP

½ cup	125 mL	white vinegar
½ cup	125 mL	store-bought barbecue sauce

Peel away the thin membrane of the pork ribs from the interior of the rib cage. You can use the tine of a fork to start and then simply pull away with your finger (although thin, this membrane is tough when cooked).

Blend all the spices together and rub evenly onto both sides of the ribs. Set on a tray and refrigerate to allow the spice rub to "set" into the meat, at least 45 minutes.

Preheat the grill and reduce the heat to low. Set the ribs across the grill and cook, covered, for 45 minutes. Turn and repeat the slow cooking for another 45 minutes.

For mop, stir vinegar and barbecue sauce together. After 1 hour of slow cooking, begin basting the ribs with the mop by applying with a brush or spoon every 15 minutes over the course of 45 minutes to 1 hour, until the ribs are tender and the meat pulls away from the bone easily.

SERVES 8

ANNA Michael used to agonize over creating his own "best" barbecue sauce. But with so many choices on the market, you can take a good one and tweak it to suit your style.

MICHAEL Side ribs, generally cheaper (though with a little more bone and a little less meat), can be cooked in the same way with equal success.

SPICY BOILED POTATOES

We first made these potatoes using a Maryland spice blend meant for boiling blue crabs, but then we dissected the flavors to create this recipe. The heat of the jalapeño peppers brings out the sweetness in the potatoes.

3 lb	1.5 kg	red or white skinned mini potatoes
3	3	jalapeño or cayenne peppers
2 Tbsp	25 mL	coarse salt
3	3	bay leaves
2 Tbsp	25 mL	white vinegar
3 Tbsp	45 mL	unsalted butter
1 tsp	5 mL	coarse salt
1 tsp	5 mL	celery salt
1 tsp	5 mL	ground black pepper

Wash potatoes and cover with cold water in a large saucepot. Split peppers in half and add to water along with 2 Tbsp (25 mL) coarse salt, bay leaves and white vinegar. Bring potatoes up to a simmer, uncovered, and cook until fork-tender. Drain thoroughly and remove peppers and bay leaves. Toss warm potatoes with butter and dress with remaining coarse salt, celery salt and black pepper. Serve immediately.

SERVES 8

ANNA When you hit the farmers' market in mid-summer, look for creamer potatoes. They're potatoes that are 1/2 inch (1 cm) across or less. Some are as small as peas. They're the sweetest-tasting little things and yummy when cooked in a spicy liquid — but also perfect tossed with just a little butter and salt.

MICHAEL Every visit to my nephew's in-laws, the Borges, we get a gigantic jar of John's homemade Portuguese hot pepper sauce. This fermented pepper sauce is very salty, and you think, "Oh, I'll just have a little." Then you want a little more and then a little more … until you need a new jar. Time to visit the Borges again!

RADISH AND BEET SALAD

Color, color, color! This is the perfect punch to a barbecue buffet.

2 lb	1 kg	fresh beets
2 Tbsp	25 mL	white vinegar
2 Tbsp	25 mL	extra virgin olive oil
1 bunch	1 bunch	fresh radishes (about 10)
3 Tbsp	45 mL	chopped fresh chives
2 Tbsp	25 mL	chopped fresh mint
1 Tbsp	15 mL	fresh lime juice
		salt and pepper

Cover unpeeled beets with cold water and add vinegar. Bring beets up to a simmer and cook, uncovered, until fork-tender, about 50 minutes. Drain and let cool. Trim stem ends from beets and peel by rubbing gently with your hands or a paper towel. Cut beets into wedges and toss with olive oil. Chill until ready to serve.

Wash radishes and cut into wedges. Toss radishes with chives, mint and lime juice. When ready to serve salad, combine beets with radishes and season to taste.

SERVES 8

ANNA We're assuming that you understand this meal is buffet-style. We wouldn't dare explain how to arrange a plate that includes all these foods. Just pile it up!

MICHAEL Roasting beets is an effortless way to cook them, especially if the grill is already hot. Just peel the beets and cut them into wedges. Toss them with a little oil and salt and wrap in foil. Place the packets on the grill and cook until tender, usually about 45 minutes.

CORN ON THE COB WITH ONION BUTTER

Get the kids to help you shuck the corn on the back deck so that the corn silk doesn't end up all over the kitchen floor.

8 ears	8 ears	fresh corn on the cob
2/3 cup	150 mL	unsalted butter at room temperature
3 Tbsp	45 mL	finely minced red onion
3 Tbsp	45 mL	finely chopped green onion
2 tsp	10 mL	Dijon mustard
1 tsp	5 mL	onion powder
		coarse salt and ground black pepper
dash	dash	cayenne pepper

Peel off outer corn husks, leaving a single layer surrounding kernels. Remove silk and soak corn in water for at least an hour before grilling.

For onion butter, beat softened butter with red onion, green onion, mustard and onion powder and season to taste with salt and pepper, and cayenne pepper. Remove corn from water and gently peel away husk but don't remove it. Rub corn with butter and fold husk back over. Chill until ready to grill.

Preheat grill on medium-high and grill corn for 10 minutes, turning often, until outer husk chars and kernels are dark yellow. Serve hot from the grill with remaining onion butter.

SERVES 8

ANNA Shucking corn was one of the first kitchen jobs I had as a kid, and I remember sitting on the back porch with my grandma, peeling off the husks. I can still hear the screen door slam and ice cubes clinking in my iced tea. Aahhh, summer!

MICHAEL My childhood summers were spent at "the lake" — Fishing Lake, Saskatchewan — running along the beach, staring at the Northern lights on cool, clear nights.

PEACHES FOSTER

At a summer barbecue, most people are so relaxed that you'll have spare time in between batches.

6	6	fresh peaches
½ cup	125 mL	unsalted butter, cut into pieces
1 cup	250 mL	light brown sugar, packed
1	1	orange, cut in half
1	1	lemon, cut in half
¼ cup	50 mL	rum (any kind)
1 tsp	5 mL	ground cinnamon
		vanilla ice cream

Peel and slice peaches. In a sauté pan over high heat, melt butter and brown sugar together until bubbling. Squeeze in orange and lemon juices and stir. Add rum, watching out for flames. Sprinkle in cinnamon and wait until sauce bubbles again. Add peaches, stir for 1 minute and remove from heat. Spoon over ice cream and enjoy!

SERVES 8

ANNA To add rum to a hot pan without creating a flame, remove the pan from the heat and let the sugar stop bubbling. Stir in the rum and return to a low heat setting, cooking out the alcohol slowly to avoid unwanted flames.

MICHAEL To achieve maximum flame, cook the peaches foster outside for safety. Pour your rum into a separate glass (never hold the bottle over the pan). Pour in the rum all at once and stand back!

WINE

>This is where we shine! Having spent almost two decades between us at Inn on the Twenty, a winery restaurant in Niagara, in addition to our personal explorations, we've come to appreciate food and wine pairing, though we'd never suggest we're wine professionals.
>We take you through our two wine-focused menus and propose wine matches. But we also want you to experiment or to use your own tried-and-true matches. After all, you know what you like best.

WINEMAKER'S MENU

WINEMAKER'S MENU This menu is seasonless, which adds flexibility in finding wine matches. These recipes are for a large group. If the wine tasting is as much a focus for your event as the food, a large group of people means opening and trying more wine without overindulging. Ask each couple to bring a bottle, so that everyone can try a little bit of a number of wines, even side by side, to see which wine suits a dish best.

Lobster Mango Salad with Lime and Coriander

Grilled Lamb Loin with Sundried Tomato Vinaigrette

Chèvre Potatoes

Summer Berry Pudding

LOBSTER MANGO SALAD WITH LIME AND CORIANDER

Everyone gets excited when lobster is brought to the table. An appetizer course is a great way to offer your guests a decadent treat without first having to get a bank loan.

6	6	1½-lb (750-g) live lobsters
2 Tbsp	25 mL	coarse salt
3	3	ripe mangoes
4	4	limes, quartered
1 cup	250 mL	mayonnaise
1 cup	250 mL	green onions, thinly sliced
⅓ cup	75 mL	chopped fresh coriander
		coarse salt and ground black pepper
12 cups	3 L	washed and torn Boston lettuce
		extra virgin olive oil for drizzling

Bring a large pot of water to a boil and add 2 Tbsp (25 mL) of salt. Dunk 2 lobsters completely into the water, turn off heat, cover and let stand 10 minutes; remove the lobsters and allow to cool completely. Return pot to the boil and repeat with remaining lobsters, 2 at a time. To shell lobsters, work over a tray or large bowl and remove the tail and claws. Press the underside of the tail to crack the shell and remove the meat. On a cutting board, strike the claw with the back of a large knife to break the shell. Crack the knuckle part of the leg and remove all the meat. Cut all the meat into bite-sized pieces and refrigerate.

Peel, slice and dice the mangoes. Squeeze around the pit to remove any extra pulp. Mix the mango pulp with the mayonnaise, the juice of 2 limes, green onion and coriander. Toss dressing with lobster and season to taste.

To plate, arrange lettuce on plates and drizzle with olive oil. Spoon lobster onto salad greens and serve with wedges of remaining lime.

SERVES 12

ANNA This salad is a wonderful shock of color. If lobster is too rich for you, use a few shrimp instead. A Gewürztraminer would make the perfect pairing.

MICHAEL For much of this book, we present dishes served family-style, or on a buffet, or in the simplest, most efficient way. This lobster salad is a good reason to take the time to plate. The result is that everyone will get to enjoy the same amount of lobster.

GRILLED LAMB LOIN WITH SUNDRIED TOMATO VINAIGRETTE

A delicate portion of lamb grills up beautifully. The tang of a sundried tomato vinaigrette keeps it summery and lively.

FOR VINAIGRETTE

2/3 cup	150 mL	diced sundried tomatoes
2/3 cup	150 mL	chopped Italian flat leaf parsley
1/4 cup	50 mL	extra virgin olive oil
1/4 cup	50 mL	balsamic vinegar
1/4 cup	50 mL	water
		coarse salt and ground black pepper

FOR LAMB

12	12	boneless lamb loins, 6 to 7 oz (175 to 200 g) each
6 cloves	6 cloves	garlic, crushed
1 Tbsp	15 mL	chopped fresh thyme
2 tsp	10 mL	cracked black pepper
1/4 cup	50 mL	extra virgin olive oil
2 tsp	10 mL	coarse salt

For vinaigrette, purée all ingredients in a food processor and season to taste. Chill until ready to serve.

For lamb, preheat grill to highest setting. Marinate the lamb in the garlic, thyme, pepper and oil at room temperature for 20 minutes. Add salt and place on grill. After 4 minutes, turn lamb over and reduce heat to medium. Cook 5 minutes for medium doneness.

To serve, slice the lamb loin into 5 pieces diagonally across the grain of the meat. Fan out the meat, overlapping the slices on the plate or platter, and top with the vinaigrette.

SERVES 12

ANNA I love lamb served with a tangy finish — be it this dressing, an olive sauce or even crumbled goat cheese — that brings out the lamb's full character.

MICHAEL This is a nice way to cook and enjoy a piece of lean, boneless lamb. Try it with a fruity but not too intense red, like a Pinot Noir or even a Gamay Noir.

CHÈVRE POTATOES

This is an easy summer version of roasted potatoes.

3 lb	1.5 kg	new potatoes, washed and quartered
1/4 cup	50 mL	extra virgin olive oil
2 Tbsp	25 mL	chopped fresh rosemary
1 Tbsp	15 mL	coarse salt
2 tsp	10 mL	cracked black pepper
4 oz	125 g	goat cheese, crumbled

Toss potatoes in oil with rosemary, salt and pepper. Place on a large sheet of aluminum foil and fold into a tightly sealed package. Cook on the cooler side of a hot grill 40 to 50 minutes or until soft to the touch (you can check this by pressing on the foil). Turn potatoes into a bowl and toss with goat cheese.

SERVES 12

ANNA See, I told you I like lamb with goat cheese. Now I get to have my lamb and eat it too!

MICHAEL While the grill is fired up, you might as well cook a few things on it. I think my foil packet potatoes should be patented. Not a grill day goes by without that foil packet on the barbecue.

SUMMER BERRY PUDDING

This elegant English dessert finishes this menu as it started — with a splash of vibrant color.

2 cups	500 mL	fresh red or black currants
3 cups	750 mL	fresh raspberries
2 cups	500 mL	fresh blueberries
3 cups	750 mL	fresh blackberries
2 cups	500 mL	hulled and sliced fresh strawberries
1½ cups	375 mL	sugar
3 Tbsp	45 mL	fresh lemon juice
40 slices	40 slices	white sandwich bread (2 loaves)

Combine berries, water, sugar and lemon juice in heavy large saucepan. Bring to simmer, stirring occasionally. Strain berry mixture, reserving juices.

Line twelve 5-oz (150-g) ramekins with plastic wrap, so it hangs over the sides. Using a 2½-inch (6-cm) round cookie cutter, cut out 24 rounds from bread slices. Trim crusts from 16 remaining bread slices and cut each slice into 4 equal squares.

To build a pudding, dip a round slice into fruit juices and place in bottom of ramekin. Dip 5 bread squares, one at a time, into juices and place around sides of ramekin. Spoon ½ cup (125 mL) berries into ramekin. Dip 1 more bread round into juices, place atop berries and wrap. Repeat with bread rounds and squares, juices and berries. Combine remaining berries and juices in bowl; cover and chill. Place puddings on baking sheet. Top with another baking sheet. Place heavy object on sheet. This extracts more juices and pectins to set the puddings. Chill overnight.

To serve, unwrap puddings. Turn out onto plates and remove plastic.

SERVES 12

ANNA This recipe lets nature do its thing. The natural pectin in fresh berries, currants in particular, set this pudding. Serve this summer-colored dessert with a generous dollop of whipped cream and any extra berry mixture.

MICHAEL You can also make this dessert in a large bowl or mold, by cutting the slices of bread larger. To avoid leakage when you unmold this spectacular dessert, just make sure the bread overlaps completely. Try serving this with a chilled glass of Prosecco, a sweet Italian sparkling wine.

FEDERWEISSER (a.k.a. Riesling-o-Rama)

>Every September our friends Tom and Anne invite us to this traditional German dinner, during which we indulge in still-fermenting Riesling drawn right from the tank. Its sweet, grapefruit effervescence is magical. Just bear in mind the "cleansing" effect of actively fermenting grape juice.

Alsatian Bacon Sour Cream Tart

Roasted Rack of Pork with Apricot Mustard Glaze

Pumpernickel Bread Pudding

Braised Leeks

Apfelkuchen with Almond Cream

ALSATIAN BACON SOUR CREAM TART

A more relaxed appetizer than the Sherry Onion Tarts (page 33), this tart should be enjoyed outside in the fading September daylight or around the kitchen while the rest of dinner is being prepared.

1	1	14-oz (397-g) package frozen puff pastry, thawed
4 strips	4 strips	double-smoked or thick bacon, diced
4	4	medium onions, sliced
1 tsp	5 mL	chopped fresh thyme
2 tsp	10 mL	chopped fresh tarragon
2 Tbsp	25 mL	sherry
		coarse salt and ground pepper
8 Tbsp	115 mL	crème fraîche or sour cream

On a lightly floured surface, roll out pastry to ¼-inch (5 mm) thickness and cut into eight 6-inch (15-cm) disks (or desired shapes). Place on a plate and chill until ready to build tarts.

In a heavy-bottomed saucepot, cook bacon until crisp and remove. Add onions and cook over medium-low heat, stirring often until they caramelize (this will take about 40 minutes). Add thyme, tarragon and sherry and season to taste. Cook until sherry is absorbed, then cool. Stir in cooked bacon.

Preheat oven to 375°F (190°C). Arrange pastry disks on a parchment-lined baking sheet and dock with a fork. Spread 1 Tbsp (15 mL) of sour cream over each disk. Top with cooled onions and bake for 15 to 18 minutes, until edges of pastry turn rich brown.

Slice into wedges and serve warm.

SERVES 8

ANNA A traditional dish to serve with Riesling (partially or fully fermented), this tart is also great with a Pinot Gris or Gewurtztraminer.

MICHAEL We get our double-smoked bacon at a European deli, but many grocery stores now carry it as demand increases.

ROAST RACK OF PORK WITH APRICOT MUSTARD GLAZE

This is a showpiece, a roast to put on your grandest platter and parade around the room before you carve it up.

FOR ROAST

1	1	8-bone rack of pork, frenched
3 Tbsp	45 mL	chopped fresh thyme
		coarse salt and ground black pepper

FOR GLAZE

1 cup	250 mL	chopped onion
1 clove	1 clove	garlic, minced
½ cup	125 mL	apricot jam
½ cup	125 mL	coarse grain mustard
		coarse salt and ground black pepper

Preheat oven to 375°F (190°C). Place pork rack in a roasting pan and sprinkle with thyme, salt and pepper. Roast for 20 minutes at 375°F (190°C), then reduce heat to 325°F (160°C) and continue roasting until meat reaches at least 155°F (75°C) measured at the center of the roast, a total cooking time of about 75 minutes.

While the rack is cooking, prepare glaze. Purée all ingredients in a food processor and season to taste. Halfway through cooking, spoon the glaze over the pork and baste as needed until done.

Let rack of pork rest at least 10 minutes before slicing.

SERVES 8

ANNA "Frenched" roasts are racks that have had the tops of the bones completely cleaned. If you have a large roast that may spend a long time in the oven, you can cover the bones with foil to prevent them from burning.

MICHAEL In this easier version of one of my favorite sauces, apricot onion soubise, the combination of apricots and onions is a delight, a perfect bridge to a fruity Riesling.

PUMPERNICKEL BREAD PUDDING

Earthy rye characteristics come through in this deeply flavored, but fluffy, savory bread pudding.

5 Tbsp	75 mL	unsalted butter, melted
1 clove	1 clove	garlic, chopped
1/2 cup	125 mL	diced onion
1/2 cup	125 mL	diced celery
1 Tbsp	15 mL	chopped fresh lovage (or 2 Tbsp (25 mL) chopped celery leaves)
2 tsp	10 mL	chopped fresh thyme
5 cups	1.25 L	cubed pumpernickel bread
2	2	large egg yolks
2	2	large whole eggs
2 tsp	10 mL	Dijon mustard
2 1/4 cups	550 mL	2% milk
2 tsp	10 mL	salt
3/4 tsp	4 mL	ground black pepper
1/3 cup	75 mL	shelled unsalted pumpkin seeds
1 1/2 cups	375 mL	grated smoked cheddar cheese

Preheat oven to 350°F (180°C). Butter the sides of a 9-inch (23-cm) square baking dish and rub with a piece of the garlic. In a sauté pan over medium heat melt remaining butter. Add onion and celery and cook, stirring often, until translucent, about 5 minutes. Stir in lovage, thyme and chopped garlic. Remove from heat and allow to cool while preparing other ingredients.

Place pumpernickel into prepared dish. Whisk together egg yolks, whole eggs and Dijon mustard. Whisk in milk, salt and pepper. Stir in pumpkin seeds and cheese and pour over bread cubes. Press down gently on bread to help liquid soak in. Let stand for about 15 minutes.

Place baking dish into a larger pan and pour boiling water around pudding dish, halfway up sides. Cover dish with aluminum foil. Bake for 50 to 60 minutes, removing foil during the last 20 minutes of cooking, until the center of the pudding springs back when pressed. Remove baking dish from water bath.

SERVES 8 TO 10

ANNA The pumpkin seeds in this recipe add an unexpected crunch and depth to this side dish. If smoked cheddar isn't your choice, regular medium cheddar works well.

MICHAEL If you omit 1 cup (250 mL) of the milk, this recipe makes a great turkey stuffing.

BRAISED LEEKS

Our friend Anne, who first introduced us to the Federweisser tradition, also introduced us to this simple but incredibly succulent vegetable course.

2	2	large bunches of leeks (green *and* white parts)
2 Tbsp	25 mL	unsalted butter
		coarse salt and ground black pepper
½ cup	125 mL	Riesling
3	3	bay leaves
3 Tbsp	45 mL	whipping cream

Preheat oven to 350°F (180°C). Trim ends of leeks and cut into ½-inch (1-cm) pieces and wash well.

Heat butter in a large saucepot over medium heat and add leeks. Season lightly and sweat for 10 minutes, reducing heat to medium to prevent browning. Add Riesling and bay leaves and cover. Let leeks simmer gently for an hour, stirring often and adding a little more wine if needed. When leeks are soft and ready to serve, stir in whipping cream and adjust seasoning if necessary.

SERVES 8

ANNA We braise meats here in North America, but braising vegetables is mostly European. Some day we'll appreciate a slowly stewed vegetable for its wonderfully concentrated richness.

MICHAEL A humble vegetable is elevated to elegant heights when prepared with respect.

ALMOND CREAM
(FOR APFELKUCHEN, OPPOSITE PAGE)

4 oz	125 g	cream cheese at room temperature
⅓ cup	75 mL	icing sugar, sifted
1 cup	250 mL	whipping cream
½ tsp	2 mL	vanilla
½ tsp	2 mL	almond extract

Beat cream cheese until smooth. Add icing sugar and continue beating. Switching to a whisk, slowly add whipping cream, whisking constantly until incorporated. Stir in vanilla and almond extract, and chill until ready to serve.

For a pourable sauce, follow the above instructions. For a spoonable cream, use electric beaters and whip cream as you pour it in, just until cream holds a soft peak.

APFELKUCHEN WITH ALMOND CREAM

Hearty and fragrant, this apple cake makes a perfect finish to autumn's
first celebration.

FOR CAKE

3 cups	750 mL	all-purpose flour
2 tsp	10 mL	cinnamon
1 tsp	5 mL	baking soda
1 tsp	5 mL	fine salt
3 cups	750 mL	peeled and diced Mutsu (Crispin) apples
1 cup	250 mL	light brown sugar, packed
1½ cups	375 mL	vegetable oil
1 cup	250 mL	sugar
3	3	large eggs
1 Tbsp	15 mL	vanilla
½ tsp	2 mL	almond extract
½ cup	125 mL	slivered almonds, lightly toasted

FOR GLAZE

½ cup	125 mL	unsalted butter
¼ cup	50 mL	2% milk
1 cup	250 mL	light brown sugar, packed
1 tsp	5 mL	vanilla

Preheat oven to 350°F (180°C), grease a 12-cup (3-L) Bundt or Kugelhopf pan and dust with flour, shaking out excess. Sift flour, cinnamon, baking soda and salt and set aside. Toss apples with 2 Tbsp (25 mL) of flour mixture and reserve. In a large bowl, beat brown sugar, oil, eggs, vanilla and almond extract with electric beaters until smooth, about 4 minutes. Beat in flour on low speed just until incorporated. Stir in apples and almonds and pour into prepared pan. Bake for about 1 hour, until a tester inserted in the center of the cake comes out clean. Let cake cool while preparing glaze.

Bring butter, milk and brown sugar up to a simmer in a pot over medium-high heat. Stir until mixture is smooth and bubbling, about 5 minutes. Remove from heat and stir in vanilla. Spoon ¼ cup (50 mL) of glaze over bottom of warm cake while still in the pan and let absorb, about 15 minutes. Turn cake onto a platter, pour remaining topping over and let cool completely.

SERVES 16 TO 20

ANNA The new silicone Bundt pans are great because you won't leave pieces of cake stuck in the crevices as happened with your metal pans.

MICHAEL I'd try to suggest another fruit for this cake but, you know, apples suit it perfectly.

OCCASIONS

>Celebrations usually mean sharing the joy of an occasion over a meal. Life's markers — weddings, birthdays, holidays and even funerals — bring out our best as we share together.

>HOLIDAYS focus on traditions honored and created. We're happy to share with you many family recipes that have made holiday mealtimes special for us. But let's not ignore treasured time alone — let ROMANCE reign over a meal. And who could forget our noisy PARTIES? Big music, big food and big fun are the norm at our house. If only we could plan the clean-up as enthusiastically as the party itself!

HOLIDAYS

>Whether or not they involve religious celebrations, holidays are really about traditions — respecting established ones and introducing new ones.

>These menus probably mean the most to us out of any in this book. Our memories are sparked as we prepare our parents', aunts' and grandparents' recipes, and we look forward to marking future occasions with our own special traditions.

ANNA'S CHRISTMAS EVE SUPPER It may seem

a small number for a holiday dinner, but I come from a small family. This is a traditional Slovak Christmas Eve supper with just a few evolutions.

Poppy Seed and Honey Bobalky

Sauerkraut Mushroom Soup

Perogies in Brown Butter

Sole Mousse with Chives

Wine Butter Sauce with Peas

Chocolate Crinkle Cookies

Cherry Walnut Cookies

Pineapple Squares

POPPY SEED AND HONEY BOBALKY

If you've never had a Slovak holiday supper, then you probably don't recognize this recipe. These are just like little bagel bites, rolled in honey and poppy seeds.

FOR BOBALKY

2 tsp	10 mL	instant yeast
½ cup	125 mL	2% milk, just above room temperature
½ cup	125 mL	warm water
¾ cup	175 mL	evaporated milk, just above room temperature
1 tsp	5 mL	sugar
1 Tbsp	15 mL	unsalted butter, melted
1	1	large egg yolk
3 cups	750 mL	all-purpose flour
½ tsp	2 mL	fine salt

FOR TOPPING

¾ cup	175 mL	poppy seeds
1 cup	250 mL	2% milk
½ cup	125 mL	honey
½ cup	125 mL	sugar

Stir yeast into milk, water and evaporated milk. Whisk in sugar, melted butter and egg yolk. Add 2 cups (500 mL) flour and salt and stir until dough becomes too hard to work with a spoon; switch to working in remaining flour by hand. Turn out dough onto a clean work surface and knead by hand for 5 minutes. Return dough to mixing bowl and cover bowl with plastic wrap. Let dough rise in a warm, draft-free place for 2 hours.

While dough is rising, prepare topping. Simmer poppy seeds in milk with honey and sugar for 15 minutes and set aside.

Preheat oven to 375°F (190°C) and line a baking tray with parchment paper. On a lightly floured surface, cut dough in half and roll out each portion into a long rope. Cut each length into 12 pieces and shape into balls. Place balls on baking sheet, at least 1 inch (2.5 cm) apart and let rise for 10 minutes. Bake for 15 minutes, until they're a light golden brown. While still warm, tip bobalky into a colander in the sink and pour 4 cups (1L) of boiling water over it, turning the balls while pouring. Drain bobalky and toss with poppy seed topping, coating well. Spread on a baking sheet to dry and set.

Bobalky can be made a day in advance and stored in an airtight container.

MAKES ABOUT 24 BOBALKY

ANNA The ritual of Christmas Eve supper starts with eating a piece of raw garlic for good health. Then we have the bobalky; the honey symbolizes prosperity.

MICHAEL Having grown up in the Prairies, I am no stranger to the food customs of Eastern Europeans. It's certainly rewarding to enjoy it now from inside the "garlic curtain."

SAUERKRAUT MUSHROOM SOUP

By this time of year in days gone by, autumn's cabbages would have been fermented and brined as sauerkraut, and late mushrooms would have been dried. This soup really celebrates what the past year has reaped.

FOR SOUP

1 cup	250 mL	peeled potatoes, cut into ½-inch (1-cm) dice
1	1	14-oz (398-mL) can sauerkraut
2 Tbsp	25 mL	vegetable shortening
2 Tbsp	25 mL	unsalted butter
¼ cup	50 mL	all-purpose flour
1 lb	500 g	white mushrooms, sliced
		coarse salt and ground black pepper

FOR DUMPLINGS

¾ cup	175 mL	all-purpose flour
¼ tsp	1 mL	fine salt
½ cup	125 mL	water

For soup, boil diced potatoes in salted water until tender. Drain potatoes, reserving ½ cup (125 mL) of water for the soup. Open sauerkraut and drain, reserving ½ cup (125 mL) of juice for the soup. Rinse sauerkraut lightly and set aside.

In a heavy-bottomed pot, melt shortening and butter over medium heat. Add flour and stir constantly, cooking into a deep golden brown color, about 8 minutes. Add sliced mushrooms and cook about 2 minutes — the moisture of the mushrooms will turn the flour paste to the texture of peanut butter.

Add 4 cups (1L) of water to mushroom mixture, a little at a time, stirring well to prevent lumps. Add sauerkraut and bring up to a simmer. Simmer, covered, for 15 minutes. Add reserved potato water and sauerkraut juice and season to taste.

For dumplings, mix flour, salt and water to make a soft dough. Drop teaspoonfuls of dough into a pot of vigorously boiling salted water and cook until they float to the surface, about 2 minutes. Remove dumplings with a slotted spoon and allow to cool. Dumplings can be made a day in advance and chilled until ready to serve.

To serve, add cooked potatoes and dumplings to soup and return soup to a simmer.

SERVES 6

ANNA I could eat this soup any time of year — it's a real mood-lifter, but it truly does represent Christmas Eve for me.

MICHAEL Take the time to brown the roux to achieve the proper consistency, color and flavor of this soup.

PEROGIES IN BROWN BUTTER

This is the best perogy dough you'll ever make. It rolls easily, the perogies stay closed when pinched together and they cook up tenderly.

FOR FILLING

3 cups	750 mL	peeled and diced Yukon Gold potatoes
1/3 cup	75 mL	unsalted butter
		coarse salt and ground black pepper
dash	dash	ground nutmeg
1 cup	250 mL	finely grated cheddar cheese (optional)

FOR DOUGH

5 cups	1.25 L	all-purpose flour
2 tsp	10 mL	fine salt
4	4	large eggs
1 cup	250 mL	2% milk
3/4 cup	175 mL	water

FOR SERVING

1/4 cup	50 mL	unsalted butter
3/4 cup	175 mL	finely diced onion
		coarse salt and ground black pepper
1/2 cup	125 mL	small or medium pitted prunes (optional)

ANNA When I was rewording and testing my grandma's recipe, I noticed that it stated that the recipe makes 2 to 3 servings. Since when do 30 perogies feed 2 people? Michael and I can usually down 16 at most. I guess my grandpa and Uncle Dennis (and mom) could eat a ton of perogies.

MICHAEL I find it interesting that almost every culture has a dumpling — China has giozai, Japan has gyoza, Italy has ravioli, and most of Eastern Europe shares the perogy.

For filling, cook potatoes in boiling salted water until tender, and drain. If you have a ricer, rice potatoes and stir in butter while hot, otherwise mash with electric beaters. Season to taste and add nutmeg. If adding cheese, allow potatoes to cool, then stir in grated cheese. Chill potato filling before using.

For dough, combine flour and salt. In a separate bowl, whisk eggs, milk and water. Add liquid to flour and stir until blended. The dough should be soft enough that it sticks to the bottom of the bowl, but not so soft that it doesn't hold its shape. ("You can always add a little more liquid or flour if you need to," said Grandma.) Cover dough and let rest 1 hour.

On a lightly floured surface, roll out dough as thinly as possible without tearing. Use a round cutter 3 inches (8 cm) in diameter and cut out circles of dough. Place 1 Tbsp (15 mL) of potato filling into the center of each perogy and pinch the perogy edges closed. Perogies can be frozen on a baking sheet or kept chilled until ready to cook.

To serve, melt butter in a sauté pan over medium-high heat. Add onions, stirring constantly until onions are richly browned. Reduce heat to medium-low. In a pot of boiling salted water, cook about half of the perogies until they float, about 5 minutes. Remove from water with a slotted spoon, add to browned butter and cook remaining perogies. Stir in prunes to warm them, if you like, then transfer to a bowl to serve.

MAKES 24 TO 30 PEROGIES

SOLE MOUSSE WITH CHIVES

A fish course isn't a traditional part of a Slovak Christmas Eve supper (although it's a Polish and Italian tradition), but we decided to add a fish component over the past few years to lighten the density of so many starches.

8 oz	225 g	sole fillets
2	2	large egg whites
½ tsp	2 mL	fine salt
1 tsp	5 mL	Dijon mustard
½ cup	125 mL	whipping cream
1 bunch	1 bunch	chives, finely sliced (not chopped)
1 Tbsp	15 mL	unsalted butter
4 cups	1 L	boiling water

In a food processor, purée the sole with the egg whites, salt and Dijon mustard. With the food processor running, slowly add the cream, starting a drop at a time. Once all the cream has been added, the mousse will have the consistency of toothpaste — not runny, but not too solid. Mix in the sliced chives in pulses of the processor, but don't purée.

Preheat the oven to 325°F (160°C). Butter a 9-inch (23-cm) square pan and, with two tablespoons (or an ice cream scoop), shape the sole mousse into little egg-shaped dumplings (these are called quenelles) and place in the pan. Pour the hot water gently over the quenelles, just enough to cover, and place in the oven for 12 minutes, until mousse springs back when touched. Serve with Wine Butter Sauce with Peas (page 225).

SERVES 6

ANNA Michael became a champion in my mother's eyes when he created this dish, and now he has made a vital contribution to our family's tradition.

MICHAEL Any lean white fish will do in this recipe, saltwater or freshwater. It's a great way to use pike after you've shredded it, picking out all those little bones.

WINE BUTTER SAUCE WITH PEAS

A big bowl of plain peas is a traditional dish to serve at this supper, but once again Michael found a great way to dress them up (another present for Michael!).

3 Tbsp	45 mL	minced shallots
1 cup	250 mL	dry white wine
½ cup	125 mL	frozen peas
4 Tbsp	50 mL	unsalted butter, diced and kept cool
		fine salt and ground black pepper

In a saucepot, reduce shallots and wine to ¼ cup (50 mL). Add peas, return to the boil, then remove pan from heat and whisk in butter, a piece at a time, until it's a creamy sauce. Season to taste and spoon over sole mousse.

CHOCOLATE CRINKLE COOKIES

You might have your own variation of this recipe. It's such a widely recognized cookie staple. Rolled in icing sugar before they're baked, the cookies crack and crinkle as they spread in the oven.

1/2 cup	125 mL	unsalted butter at room temperature
10 oz	300 g	bittersweet or semi-sweet chocolate, chopped
4	4	large eggs at room temperature
1 1/2 cups	375 mL	sugar
2 tsp	10 mL	vanilla
1 tsp	5 mL	instant espresso or coffee powder
1/2 cup	125 mL	all-purpose flour
1/2 tsp	2 mL	baking powder
1/4 tsp	1 mL	fine salt
6 oz	175 g	white chocolate, chopped
2/3 cup	150 mL	icing sugar, sifted

Over a pot filled with 2 inches (5 cm) of simmering water, place a metal or glass bowl and add butter. Stir until melted halfway and add chopped bittersweet chocolate. Stir until just melted and remove from heat. Set aside.

Whip eggs with sugar, vanilla and espresso powder with electric beaters or in a mixer fitted with the whisk attachment, until pale and thick, about 5 minutes. In a separate bowl, combine flour, baking powder and salt.

Whisk melted chocolate into egg mixture until incorporated. Whisk in flour mixture and stir in white chocolate chunks. Cover batter with plastic and chill for at least 4 hours before baking.

Preheat oven to 325°F (160°C). Spoon cookie dough by tablespoonfuls, or teaspoonfuls for dainty cookies, and roll gently to shape into a ball. Roll cookie in icing sugar and place on a parchment-lined or greased cookie sheet, leaving 2 inches (5 cm) between cookies.

Bake for 18 to 20 minutes. To test doneness, lift a cookie off the tray — if it comes off cleanly, then cookies are done.

Cool cookies before storing. Cookies will keep up to a week at room temperature in an airtight container. Batter also freezes well.

MAKES ABOUT 3 DOZEN LARGE,
OR 5 DOZEN SMALL, COOKIES

ANNA These have been a staple in our family cookie tin for years. I like this version in particular because it stays nice and chewy in the center.

MICHAEL This is one of Santa's favorites at the Olson house, so we always stay on his "nice" list and not his "naughty" list.

CHERRY WALNUT COOKIES

A traditional ice box cookie, these show off two holiday staple ingredients: candied fruit and walnuts.

1 cup	250 mL	unsalted butter at room temperature
1 cup	250 mL	icing sugar, sifted
1	1	large egg
1 tsp	5 mL	vanilla
2¼ cups	550 mL	all-purpose flour
¼ tsp	1 mL	fine salt
2 cups	500 mL	candied red cherries, cut in half
1 cup	250 mL	walnut halves

Cream butter and icing sugar until smooth. Beat in egg and vanilla. Sift flour and salt over butter mixture and stir until well blended. Stir in halved candied cherries and walnuts. Divide dough into 3 equal pieces and shape into logs, 10 inches (25 cm) in length, about an inch (2.5 cm) in diameter. Wrap and chill until firm, at least 3 hours.

Preheat oven to 325°F (160°C) and line a baking tray with parchment paper. Cut rounds of cookie dough as thinly as possible, about ⅛ inch (3 mm) thick and place on baking tray 1 inch (2.5 cm) apart. Bake 8 to 10 minutes, just until the outside edge of the cookie begins to color. Remove and cool completely.

Cookies can be made and stored in an airtight container for up to 2 weeks. Baked cookies or wrapped dough can be frozen.

MAKES ABOUT 4 DOZEN

ANNA Grandma used to get upset when her cookies would brown too much on the bottom. If you have the same trouble, bake your cookies on the center rack of the oven, keep the convection fan off and rotate the cookies halfway through cooking. And remember to set the timer!

MICHAEL "No, no, really I couldn't. Well, okay, maybe just three more."

PINEAPPLE SQUARES

These squares freeze well, so they're great for making in advance.

FOR SHORTBREAD BASE

1¼ cups	300 mL	all-purpose flour
¼ cup	50 mL	sugar
½ cup	125 mL	unsalted butter

FOR PINEAPPLE FILLING

2	2	large eggs
1 cup	250 mL	light brown sugar, packed
½ cup	125 mL	crushed pineapple, drained
1 cup	250 mL	unsweetened coconut
¼ cup	50 mL	candied pineapple, diced
1 tsp	5 mL	vanilla
2 Tbsp	25 mL	all-purpose flour
½ tsp	2 mL	baking powder

FOR ICING

3 Tbsp	45 mL	unsalted butter at room temperature
1½ cups	375 mL	icing sugar, sifted
1½ Tbsp	22 mL	orange juice or pineapple juice
½ tsp	2 mL	vanilla

For shortbread base, preheat oven to 350°F (180°) and line an 8-inch (20-cm) square pan with enough parchment paper so that it hangs over the sides of the pan. Combine flour and sugar and cut in butter until it's a rough, crumbly texture. Press crumble into prepared pan and bake for 15 minutes or until golden brown around the edges. Cool completely.

For filling, beat eggs by hand with brown sugar. Stir in pineapple, coconut, candied pineapple, vanilla, flour and baking powder and spread over cooled base. Bake for about 25 minutes, until it's an even golden brown color. Cool.

For icing, beat all ingredients together until smooth and spread over cooled pineapple layer. Let set before slicing into squares or bars.

MAKES 16 LARGE, OR 25 MEDIUM, SQUARES

ANNA My dad is the pineapple-lover in our family and he's the first to reach for these. If pineapple isn't your favorite, try an apricot or orange marmalade and omit the brown sugar in the filling.

MICHAEL Make these in mini-muffin tins for little pineapple tarts. They stack and store well in airtight containers, so they're good to take on the road if you're the one doing the traveling over the holidays.

CHRISTMAS DINNER

We'll be honest — we're not turkey people, so a prime rib dinner is what you're most likely to see on our Christmas dinner table. For us, this is a meal that should be prepared at a relaxed pace, making sure to leave time for multiple naps in between games of euchre or croquinole, or a holiday movie.

Rulapylsa

Spicy Shrimp Cocktail

Winter Greens with Apple Vinaigrette and Cheddar

Perfect Prime Rib Roast and Mushroom Gravy

Popovers

Boulangère Potatoes

Orange Honey Carrots

Eggnog Trifle

RULAPYLSA

Rulapylsa is a spiced meat roll served cold on buttered brown bread with salt. It's a familiar taste to those of Icelandic heritage. In some cases, it's one of the few reminders of a heritage that was quickly assimilated into mainstream North American life.

1		1	3 to 4 lb (1.5 to 1.8 kg) beef flank, trimmed of fat and butterflied
1 Tbsp		15 mL	ground cloves
1 Tbsp		15 mL	ground allspice
3 Tbsp		45 mL	fresh cracked black pepper
2 Tbsp		25 mL	pickling salt
1		1	large white onion, minced

Lay out flank on an old clean tea towel or large piece of cheesecloth. Blend cloves, allspice, pepper and salt together, sprinkle over the surface of the meat and cover with minced onion. Roll up the flank into a tight cylinder with the grain of the meat running along the length. Tie the meat roll with butcher's twine at 2-inch (5-cm) intervals and wrap in the tea towel or cheesecloth. Place the roll in a non-reactive dish and allow to "cure" in the refrigerator for 3 to 4 days, turning over each day.

Poach the roll in barely simmering water for 90 minutes, covered with a loose-fitting lid. Allow to cool to room temperature in the liquid. Drain and press overnight under a heavy plate in the refrigerator.

To serve, remove string and slice thinly. Serve on buttered brown bread with a salt shaker and pepper mill close at hand.

SERVES 16

ANNA I love to see Michael's face when he takes his seasonal first bite of Rulapylsa — a smile of pure ecstasy as he reaches for another bite.

MICHAEL It's important to celebrate your background in language, culture and, of course, food. The smell and taste of rulapylsa speak volumes of wonderful family gatherings, good laughs and love. This dish was originally made with mutton, but we've had great results with beef flank; have your friendly neighborhood butcher butterfly the flank or do it yourself with a very sharp filleting knife.

SPICY SHRIMP COCKTAIL

This is the typical shrimp cocktail that used to be on every menu. Did we really get tired of it? Use tall martini glasses for a fun presentation.

FOR SHRIMP

2	2	small onions
4 cloves	4 cloves	garlic, crushed
2	2	jalapeño peppers, cut in half
48	48	large raw shrimp, peeled and deveined

FOR COCKTAIL SAUCE

1 cup	250 mL	ketchup
4 Tbsp	50 mL	horseradish
3 Tbsp	45 mL	fresh lime juice
2 squirts	2 squirts	Tabasco sauce
2 squirts	2 squirts	Worcestershire sauce

FOR ASSEMBLY

8 cups	2 L	shredded iceberg lettuce
4	4	lemons, quartered

In a saucepot, bring 4 cups (1 L) water to a boil with the onions, garlic and jalapeño. Add shrimp, turn off heat and let sit 6 minutes. Remove shrimp and cool in ice water. Drain and chill completely.

To make sauce, blend ketchup with horseradish, lime, Tabasco and Worcestershire. This sauce can be made several days ahead of time and held in the refrigerator.

To plate, place shredded lettuce in a martini glass, top with sauce and hang 3 shrimp on the rim. Garnish with a wedge of lemon.

SERVES 16

ANNA The first year Michael and I hosted my family for Christmas dinner, Michael wanted to really impress my mom, knowing she loves shrimp cocktail. He started the spicy boil mixture, which was unexpectedly hot, and soon the kitchen and family room were filled with spicy hot smells, strong enough to have us gasping and opening windows! Michael diluted the spices a bit and Mom really liked her shrimp.

MICHAEL Always cook to please your mother-in-law.

WINTER GREENS WITH APPLE VINAIGRETTE AND CHEDDAR

This simple salad is a nice offset to some of those richer flavors going on, and that's not including the eggnog.

FOR VINAIGRETTE

1/3 cup	75 mL	cider vinegar
1 cup	250 mL	olive oil
1/2 cup	125 mL	chopped green onion
3	3	green apples, cored and shredded
		fine salt and ground black pepper

FOR SALAD

2 heads	2 heads	radicchio, shredded
2 bunches	2 bunches	watercress, trimmed, washed and drained
4 heads	4 heads	Belgian endive, cut into leaves
2/3 cup	150 mL	grated aged cheddar

For vinaigrette, whisk vinegar, oil and green onion. Stir in shredded apple and season to taste. Chill until ready to serve.

Arrange lettuce on a plate, dress with apple vinaigrette and top with cheddar.

SERVES 16

ANNA A salad course is nice for a holiday dinner, because we're more inclined to overindulge on the other courses. A few toasted sunflower seeds would finish this salad off nicely.

MICHAEL Keep in mind that the recipes for this menu are for 16 people. Should you have a smaller group, just cut the recipe in half, and if it's a huge party (time to pull out the card tables), then double it up. Most of our recipes batch up and down quite easily.

PERFECT PRIME RIB ROAST AND MUSHROOM GRAVY

Prime rib roast is the finest of beef roasts. It's best if it cooks slowly, and it's a real showpiece when brought to the table. Pull out that carving set!

1	1	whole prime rib roast, about 15 lbs (6.5 kg)
1/2 cup	125 mL	Dijon mustard
3 Tbsp	45 mL	chopped fresh rosemary
3 Tbsp	45 mL	salt
2 Tbsp	25 mL	ground black pepper

Preheat oven to 275°F (140°C) and place roast upright in a roasting pan. Stir mustard, rosemary, salt and pepper and rub over surface of roast. Place uncovered in center rack of oven and cook for 2 hours to an internal temperature of 125°F (55°C). Remove roast from pan to a cutting board and rest, tented with foil, for at least 10 minutes before carving.

To carve, use a sharp knife to carefully slice down the bones to remove. Carve thin or thick slices of beef, as desired.

SERVES 16

ANNA You've probably invested a bit of money in buying this prime rib roast, so spend a few bucks more on a good probe thermometer. This tool will save tons of stress. The probe portion is inserted into the center of the roast and attaches to the digital unit that sits outside the oven. Simply program your required temperature (I always set mine about 10 to 20 degrees less so I know when to start cooking my vegetables) and let the beeper alert you when the roast is ready. It's great for turkey, too.

MICHAEL The standard temperatures for beef doneness are as follows:

Rare: 125°F (55°C)
Medium-Rare: 135°F (60°C)
Medium: 145°F (65°C)
Medium-Well: 150°F (68°C)
Well-Done: 160°F (75°C)

Do remember that your roast continues to cook out of the oven. You can expect the beef to cook at least another 10°F and the larger the roast, the greater the carry-over cooking.

MUSHROOM GRAVY

3 Tbsp	45 mL	drippings from roast
8 cups	2 L	sliced button mushrooms
3 Tbsp	45 mL	all-purpose flour
1 cup	250 mL	red wine
2 cups	500 mL	water or beef broth
		coarse salt and ground black pepper

Use the roasting pan from the prime rib roast and drain all but 3 Tbsp (45 mL) drippings. Over medium heat, sauté mushrooms in the drippings until soft, about 8 minutes. Add flour and cook over medium heat 3 minutes until flour is worked into a paste. Add red wine gradually, whisking in slowly to avoid lumps. Add water or broth and bring to a boil, stirring often. Simmer 5 minutes, season to taste and serve with sliced roast beef.

MAKES 4 CUPS (1 L)

POPOVERS

These are great gravy sponges!

2²/₃ cups	650 mL	2% milk
8	8	large eggs
4¼ cups	1.05 L	all-purpose flour
1 tsp	5 mL	fine salt
dash	dash	black pepper
dash	dash	nutmeg

Whisk milk and eggs together. Sift flour over mixture and whisk in. Stir in salt, pepper and nutmeg and let batter rest for at least 30 minutes.

Preheat oven to 400°F (200°C) and grease two muffin tins. Pour 2 Tbsp (25 mL) of batter into each cup and immediately return pan to oven. Bake puddings for 15 to 18 minutes, without opening the oven door for the first 12 minutes, until puffy and a light golden brown. Serve warm.

MAKES 24 POPOVERS

ANNA The difference between a popover and a Yorkshire pudding is in the fat. The batter is exactly the same, but a Yorkshire pudding requires you to preheat your muffin tins with a spoonful of roast drippings, and then the batter is quickly poured into the hot tins. We find that making popovers is a simpler process at home.

MICHAEL Most large hotel restaurants that serve buffet dinner make Yorkshire puddings, and the key to their success is well-seasoned pans that are only used for baking these puddings. Heavy-gauge muffins pans hold the heat and, like a well-seasoned cast iron skillet, the puddings come out perfectly every time.

BOULANGÈRE POTATOES

Scalloped potatoes may be a holiday tradition, but these are a lighter style made with chicken stock, and are just as tasty. For 16 people, you may have to make this in 2 pans.

5 lb	2.5 kg	Yukon Gold potatoes
1 clove	1 clove	garlic
4 Tbsp	50 mL	unsalted butter
6 cups	1.5 L	sliced onions
1 Tbsp	15 mL	chopped fresh thyme
6 cups	1.5 L	chicken stock

Preheat oven to 350°F (180°C). Peel and slice potatoes as thinly as possible. Rub one large or 2 smaller casserole dishes with the garlic clove. In a sauté pan over medium heat, melt butter. Sauté the onion until soft, about 10 minutes, and remove from heat. Stir in thyme.

Layer one-third of the sliced potatoes in prepared dish, top with half the onions and season lightly. Repeat with remaining potatoes and onion. Pour chicken stock over potatoes, cover dish with parchment paper and then with foil. Bake for 45 minutes then remove foil and paper and bake 10 to 15 minutes longer until golden brown.

SERVES 16

ANNA This potato dish translates to "Baker's Potatoes," not because the potatoes are baked, but because it was the tradition for the town baker to make this as his dinner in the wood-fired ovens that still held lots of heat after the breads were baked.

MICHAEL It's amazing how the potatoes release their starches and absorb flavors as this dish cooks. You'll have a moist potato dish that spoons easily into portions, and it really holds that heat, which is important when preparing such a large meal.

ORANGE HONEY CARROTS

4 lb	2 kg	carrots, peeled and cut into strips
2 cups	500 mL	orange juice
1/3 cup	75 mL	honey
1/3 cup	75 mL	minced shallot
		coarse salt and ground black pepper

Add carrots, orange juice, honey and shallots to saucepot, cover and bring up to a simmer. Cook 10 minutes, then uncover and simmer until orange juice is reduced to a glaze and carrots are tender. Season to taste and serve.

SERVES 16

EGGNOG TRIFLE

Trifle is an appropriate holiday dessert as it presents well, and people can enjoy just a spoonful if they're full, or a bowlful if they've saved room.

FOR CRANBERRIES

6 cups	1.5 L	fresh or frozen cranberries
2½ cups	625 mL	sugar
1 cup	250 mL	water
4	4	cinnamon sticks

FOR FILLING

10	10	large egg yolks
1 cup	250 mL	sugar
½ cup	125 mL	rum (any kind)
3 Tbsp	45 mL	fresh lemon juice
1½ tsp	7 mL	nutmeg
2 cups	500 mL	whipping cream
1 Tbsp	15 mL	vanilla
32 oz	900 g	(2 tubs) mascarpone cheese

FOR WHIPPED CREAM

2 cups	500 mL	whipping cream
4 tsp	20 mL	sugar
¼ cup	50 mL	brandy

FOR SOAKING LIQUID

1½ cups	375 mL	sugar
1½ cups	375 mL	water
½ cup	125 mL	rum (any kind)
1 Tbsp	15 mL	vanilla
3	3	packages ladyfinger biscuits
		chocolate shavings for garnish (optional)

ANNA I think trifle was invented for large, grand occasions (and buffet tables on cruises) because it has a little something for everyone — a little cake, a little fruit, a little cream, a lot of booze … something for everyone.

MICHAEL Christmas is probably the one time out of the entire year that we use rum at home, except for those hot toddies Anna makes for me when I catch that post-Christmas cold.

For cranberries, simmer fruit with sugar, water and cinnamon sticks over medium heat, stirring occasionally, for 20 minutes, until most berries "pop." Remove cinnamon sticks and set aside.

For filling, whisk egg yolks with sugar, rum, lemon juice and nutmeg over a pot of simmering water until doubled in volume. Remove from heat. In a separate bowl, whip cream with vanilla. Whisk mascarpone into egg mixture and fold in whipped cream. Chill until ready to assemble.

For whipped cream, whip cream to soft peaks, add sugar and brandy and chill.

For soaking liquid, heat sugar, water, rum and vanilla until a simmer is reached. Cool to room temperature.

To assemble in a trifle dish or individual cups, dip ladyfinger biscuits in soaking liquid and line bottom of dish. Cover with one-third of mascarpone filling and spoon in one-third of cranberries. Repeat process twice. Top with whipped cream and garnish with chocolate shavings, if you wish. Chill until ready to serve.

SERVES 16

NEW YEAR'S EVE
We've spent years working New Year's Eve in the restaurant business, so the first year we were able to spend it at home was such a treat. Many people have Chinese takeout on New Year's (why, we have no idea), but we love to do Japanese food.
>This menu is a very sociable way to dine and also makes for great post-midnight leftovers.

Make-Your-Own Sushi Buffet

Beef Sukiyaki

Green Tea Ice Cream with Jasmine Shortbread

MAKE-YOUR-OWN SUSHI BUFFET

We've made this a meal itself when entertaining friends. Now that ingredients for sushi are more widely available, you can try your hand at the art of making sushi. Even if it looks messy, it'll still taste great.

FOR RICE

2 cups	500 mL	Japanese short grain rice
4 cups	1 L	water
¼ cup	50 mL	rice vinegar
2 tsp	10 mL	fine salt
1 Tbsp	15 mL	sugar

Rinse rice in a mesh strainer until water runs clear. Cook rice in water, covered, until all liquid is absorbed. Spoon into a bowl, and while still warm, mix in vinegar, salt and sugar. Cover and keep warm until ready to use.

FOR BUFFET

12 sheets	12 sheets	nori sushi wraps, cut in half
1 cup	250 mL	cooked small shrimp
½ cup	125 mL	diced ripe avocado
¼ cup	50 mL	mayonnaise
½ cup	125 mL	canned tuna
3	3	cooked sausages, sliced lengthwise in quarters
½	½	English cucumber, sliced into thin strips
½ cup	125 mL	crabmeat, frozen or tinned
2 Tbsp	25 mL	wasabi powder, mixed with water to a smooth paste
¼ cup	50 mL	pickled ginger
½ cup	125 mL	Japanese soy sauce

Set up a buffet and have your guests fill a nori wrap with rice, wasabi and the fillings of their choice. Set out cups of soy for dipping.

SERVES 6

ANNA Making sushi in a situation like this can be educational and fun. If you want to follow technique and use sushi mats, spread a thin layer of rice over nori, fill with a little filling of your choice and roll up, using the mat to keep the roll tight. Slice into little pieces and enjoy. My first roll is always a little sloppy and leaky, but that's just part of the fun.

MICHAEL You can also go for the super-casual approach and make hand rolls. Take a square of nori, put in a spoonful of rice, add a few fillings and roll up in the shape of an ice cream cone. Sometimes, toward the end of the buffet, we just spoon the combinations onto our plates and eat them with chopsticks.

BEEF SUKIYAKI

Sukiyaki is a classic taste of the Japanese kitchen and uses a one-pot cooking style that encourages conversation and sharing.

1 lb	500 g	beef tenderloin
1/4	1/4	10-oz (400-g) package rice vermicelli noodles
1 bunch	1 bunch	green onions, trimmed and cut into 2-inch (5-cm) pieces
1 cup	250 mL	button mushrooms, quartered
4 cups	1 L	Napa cabbage, cut into 1-inch (2.5-cm) pieces
1 lb	500 g	firm tofu, cubed
1 recipe	1 recipe	brown rice (page 64)
1 Tbsp	15 mL	extra virgin olive oil
1/3 cup	75 mL	sugar
1/3 cup	75 mL	sake rice wine
1/3 cup	75 mL	Japanese soy sauce (available at most grocery stores)

Freeze beef tenderloin for 20 minutes. Remove, slice as thinly as possible with a sharp knife, and chill until ready to cook.

Bring a pot of water to a boil, add vermicelli noodles and turn off heat. Let pot sit for 3 minutes, then drain and cool noodles under running water. Drain well and reserve.

Arrange green onions, mushrooms, Napa cabbage and tofu on a platter and chill until ready to serve. Everything up to this point can be prepared in advance and chilled.

Prepare one recipe of brown rice (page 64) and hold warm while preparing sukiyaki.

Heat a large, shallow skillet over medium heat and add oil. Add one-third each of the green onions and mushrooms and sauté 2 minutes. Add sugar, sake and soy sauce and bring up to a simmer. Place one-third each of the cabbage and tofu into the broth and cook 3 minutes. Drop one-third of the cooked vermicelli and some of the beef into the broth to poach — try to keep each ingredient separate, no excessive stirring. As the beef cooks, have each guest pluck out the beef as it cooks to their liking, and then draw out the vegetables and tofu over bowls of warm brown rice.

While enjoying eating the first round of cooked items, get the second round going, in the same order as above. As the meat and vegetables cook, the broth may reduce in volume and thin out as the vegetables release their juices. Add more sugar, sake and soy sauce in equal measures to the broth, as needed.

SERVES 6

ANNA This is the Japanese version of fondue. If you can, serve this main course on a low coffee table over a propane burner, for a spirited, communal welcome to the New Year.

MICHAEL For an extra rich flavor, serve a whisked raw egg to each guest in a separate bowl. Dip the beef or vegetables into the egg and then eat it over the rice — Oishii!

Keep in mind that any leftovers can be reheated and served over rice for a delicious hangover-helper lunch the next day!

GREEN TEA ICE CREAM WITH JASMINE SHORTBREAD

A make-ahead dessert like this is good planning for a late-night meal. Japanese gunpowder green tea powder is a finely ground tea found in most Japanese food stores. It gives the ice cream its beautiful green hue, but the recipe will still be as delicious without it.

2 cups	500 mL	2% milk
1 Tbsp	15 mL	loose green tea
6	6	large egg yolks
½ cup	125 mL	sugar
2 cups	500 mL	whipping cream
1½ Tbsp	22 mL	Japanese gunpowder green tea powder

Heat milk with tea for 5 minutes just below a simmer. Whisk together egg yolks and sugar. Gradually whisk hot milk into egg mixture until all milk has been added. Return to pot and cook over medium-low heat, stirring until mixture coats the back of a wooden spoon. Strain and chill completely. Stir in cream and green tea powder and churn in an ice cream maker according to manufacturer's instructions. Spoon into a container and freeze until firm.

MAKES ABOUT 6 CUPS (1.5 L)

ANNA Any tea flavor infuses beautifully into the ice cream and the cookies. Try Earl Grey, a fruit tea or Rooibos, a South African red bush plant that is often blended with vanilla or Provencal flavors.

MICHAEL The bitter nature of green tea is a favorite finish at Japanese restaurants for cleansing the palate. Sweets are not typically part of a Japanese kitchen, and they tend to be straightforward and simple.

JASMINE SHORTBREAD

3¼ cups	800 mL	all-purpose flour
2 tsp	10 mL	baking powder
¼ tsp	1 mL	fine salt
2 Tbsp	25 mL	jasmine green tea
1 cup	250 mL	unsalted butter at room temperature
1½ cups	375 mL	sugar
2 Tbsp	25 mL	lemon zest
1 Tbsp	15 mL	grated fresh ginger
1	1	large egg
2 Tbsp	25 mL	fresh lemon juice
		milk for brushing

Sift together flour, baking powder and salt. Stir in jasmine tea. Cream butter, sugar, zest and ginger until fluffy. Stir in egg and lemon juice. Add dry ingredients and blend until dough comes together. Divide dough in half and shape into logs. Wrap and chill for at least 2 hours (or freeze).

Preheat oven to 325°F (160°C). Unwrap dough, slice into thin wafers and place on a greased or parchment-lined baking sheet. Brush cookies with milk and bake for 12 to 15 minutes, just until edges turn golden.

MAKES ABOUT 4 DOZEN COOKIES

PARTIES

>We love to throw parties — the bigger, the better. We start talking about having a few friends over and somehow it evolves into a blowout for thirty people just for the fun of it. We feel lucky because we have equal doses of fun planning, shopping, cooking and then actually hosting the event.

THE OLSON OPEN HOUSE

Time to pull out every pot, pan and serving dish we can find — it all gets used. Fortunately, we have a spacious house and guests can spread out, but we keep in mind that the idea of an open house is to have guests drop by, have a drink, a snack and a visit and then move on. While the food preparation may seem daunting, if you schedule your open house for mid-to-late afternoon or later in the evening, a full meal won't be expected by your guests.

Winter Crudités

Pea Salad

Tourtière

Mini Beef on Wecks

Sausage Choucroute

Cheese Potatoes

Pumpkin Chocolate Tiramisù

Almond Cherry Tart

Angel Food Cake

WINTER CRUDITÉS

A vegetable platter doesn't have to be made up of predictable carrots, celery, broccoli and cauliflower. Try interesting and inexpensive winter vegetables with a hearty white bean dip.

FOR WHITE BEAN DIP

1		1	14-oz (398-mL) can navy beans, drained and rinsed
2 cloves		2 cloves	garlic, roughly chopped
1		1	lime, zest and juice
½ cup		125 mL	extra virgin olive oil
			water, as needed
3 Tbsp		45 mL	fresh coriander, chopped
			fine salt and ground black pepper
2–3 drops		2–3 drops	truffle oil (optional)
½ head		½ head	cabbage, center cored
2 Tbsp		25 mL	chopped green onion

FOR CRUDITÉS

1 head		1 head	fennel, trimmed into pieces
½ head		½ head	cauliflower, trimmed into florettes
½ lb		250 g	green beans, trimmed
½ lb		250 g	beets, cooked and peeled
1 lb		500 g	baby or small carrots, tops on but trimmed
¼ head		¼ head	cabbage, cut into pieces

For dip, purée beans, garlic, lime zest and juice, olive oil and enough water to achieve desired consistency. Stir in coriander and season to taste. Immediately before serving, stir in truffle oil, if using, and spoon into hollowed-out cabbage. Top with green onion.

For crudités, blanch each vegetable except beets and cabbage in salted boiling water just for 1 minute (to soften only a little and to set color) and shock immediately in ice water. Drain and keep chilled until ready to serve.

To serve, arrange crudités around dip.

SERVES 24
MULTIPLY BY 2 FOR 60 PEOPLE

ANNA The art of blanching is a well-used tool in a restaurant kitchen. Hours ahead of dinner service, we parcook the vegetables and shock them in ice water, to be heated, seasoned and served to you perfectly cooked in no time at all.

MICHAEL I have to brag just a little — I am a master of setting up a buffet table. Balance in color and texture is very important — get creative with your crudité platter and serve it on a mirror. It looks splashy and cleans up easily.

PEA SALAD

We really weren't going for the typical red and green salad for Christmas, it just happened that way. This pea salad does add a nice splash of color to the buffet table, though.

¼ cup	50 mL	mayonnaise
¼ cup	50 mL	sour cream
1 Tbsp	15 mL	Dijon mustard
2 Tbsp	25 mL	white wine vinegar
¼ cup	50 mL	chopped green onion
2 tsp	10 mL	chopped fresh tarragon
2 tsp	10 mL	chopped fresh mint
		fine salt and ground black pepper
5 cups	1.25 L	frozen baby peas, thawed
1 cup	250 mL	sliced radishes

Whisk mayonnaise, sour cream, mustard and white wine vinegar together. Stir in chopped green onion and herbs and season to taste. Toss peas and radishes together and dress. Adjust seasoning if necessary and chill until ready to serve.

Dressing can be prepared a day in advance and salad can be tossed up to 4 hours ahead of serving.

SERVES 10 AS A SIDE DISH, 20 ON A BUFFET TABLE

ANNA Actually, the truth about this salad is that we realized hours before our guests were about to arrive that we needed another vegetable on our buffet table. Scouring the freezer produced two open bags of peas and the rest is history.

MICHAEL Frozen peas are an excellent nutritional source, easy to work with and a convenient raw ingredient, especially to wake up bland winter foods.

TOURTIÈRE

This French Canadian specialty is a favorite for many around the holidays. The mustard and horseradish are already on the table for the Mini Beef on Wecks (page 249), and they make great condiments for this meat pie as well.

FOR PASTRY

2½ cups	625 mL	all-purpose flour
½ tsp	2 mL	fine salt
½ cup	125 mL	unsalted butter
½ cup	125 mL	vegetable shortening
2 Tbsp	25 mL	lemon juice
6–10 Tbsp	90–150 mL	cold water as needed
1 egg mixed with 2 Tbsp (25 mL) water for egg wash		

FOR FILLING

1½ cups	325 mL	diced, peeled potatoes
1½ lb	750 g	ground pork, veal or combination
2	2	onions, diced
2 cloves	2 cloves	garlic, minced
¾ tsp	4 mL	fine salt
¼ tsp	1 mL	ground black pepper
¼ tsp	1 mL	crushed celery seed
dash	dash	allspice
dash	dash	cloves

ANNA We make these a week or two ahead of time and freeze them. Then, when it's party time, we put them in the fridge the day before to thaw, and slowly warm through in the oven.

MICHAEL Tourtière may be delicious served hot, but I like slicing thin wedges of it cold the next day and eating it slathered with Dijon mustard.

For pastry, combine flour with salt. Cut in butter and shortening until mixture is a roughly even crumbly texture. Add lemon juice and water and blend just until dough comes together. Shape into a disk, wrap and chill for 30 minutes.

While pastry is chilling, prepare filling. Cook potatoes in an uncovered pot of salted water until tender, and drain, reserving liquid. Roughly mash potatoes and set aside to cool.

In a large sauté pan or skillet, sauté pork or veal over medium heat until no longer pink. Drain off excess fat, add onions, garlic and seasonings, and sauté until tender, about 10 minutes. Add 1½ cups (375 mL) of reserved potato liquid (or use water if short of liquid) and bring up to a simmer. Let mixture simmer for about 15 minutes, until most of liquid is absorbed. Remove from heat, stir in potatoes and cool to room temperature (or prepare a day in advance).

Preheat oven to 375°F (190°C). On a lightly floured surface, cut dough in half, roll out to just less than ¼-inch (5-mm) thickness and line an 8-inch (20-cm) springform pan. Fill with tourtière filling. Roll out remaining dough and place on top of filling. Pinch edges of crust together and brush with egg wash. Bake for 40 to 45 minutes, until pastry is a rich golden brown. Let cool 5 minutes, then remove from pan and serve.

Tourtière can be made up to 2 days in advance and reheated in a 275°F (140°C) oven.

MAKES ONE 8-INCH (20-CM) TOURTIÈRE
MAKE 4 FOR A PARTY OF 60

MINI BEEF ON WECKS

This is the short name for the Beef on Kummelweck, a staple of Buffalo, New York, second only to the chicken wing. "Kummel" means caraway in German. Rare roast beef is sliced thinly and placed on a Kaiser-style roll that has been topped with coarse salt and caraway seeds.

FOR BUNS

1 1/2 lb	750 g	store-bought pizza dough
1	1	large egg white
2 Tbsp	25 mL	Kosher or coarse salt
2 Tbsp	25 mL	caraway seed
		hot prepared horseradish
		Dijon mustard

FOR BEEF

1	1	2-lb (1-kg) top sirloin or inside round beef roast
		coarse salt and ground black pepper

For buns, preheat oven to 375°F (190°C) and line a baking tray with parchment paper. Divide pizza dough into pieces of about 1 oz (2 Tbsp). Shape into balls by rolling and place 1 inch (2.5 cm) apart on baking sheet. Brush tops with egg white and sprinkle generously with salt and caraway seeds. Bake for 15 minutes until rich golden brown. Allow to cool.

For beef, lower oven temperature to 325°F (160°C). Season beef and roast, uncovered, until it reaches an internal temperature of 125°F (55°C) and let rest for 10 minutes.

To assemble, slice mini buns open. Slice beef as thinly as possible and top with horseradish and Dijon mustard. Serve immediately.

MAKES ABOUT 20 SMALL SANDWICHES
MULTIPLY RECIPE BY 3 TO SERVE 60 PEOPLE

ANNA Whenever we crossed the border, we used to make a stop at a Buffalo grocery to pick up a dozen "weck" buns and a pound of slow-roasted beef. Now some grocery stores in Niagara sell the buns ready to enjoy.

MICHAEL Remember to season your meat generously before roasting. Keep in mind that a medium tender cut is a little more economical, but also has a beefier flavor.

SAUSAGE CHOUCROUTE

Big casseroles of sauerkraut loaded with sausages and smoked pork are
real crowd pleasers — everyone can find a bite of something they like, and
the casseroles are effortless to assemble.

2 Tbsp	25 mL	unsalted butter
2½ lb	1.25 kg	mixed smoked pork chops and sausages, cut into pieces
2	2	onions, diced
2	2	pears, diced
2 lb	1 kg	sauerkraut, rinsed and drained
1 cup	250 mL	white wine
1 cup	250 mL	apple cider
¼ tsp	1 mL	ground allspice
½ tsp	2 mL	caraway seed (optional)
		coarse salt and ground black pepper

Preheat oven to 350°F (180°C). Melt butter in a pan over medium heat and sauté meats until
brown. Remove meats, add onion and cook until translucent, about 5 minutes. Add pears and
cook 2 minutes more. Add remaining ingredients and bring up to a simmer. Transfer sauerkraut
to a baking dish and arrange meats on top.

Choucroute can be chilled until ready to serve at this point, and then baked for 40 to 45 minutes,
until bubbling. To hold while entertaining, reduce oven temperature to 200°F (95°C) and cover
loosely with aluminum foil.

SERVES 8
MULTIPLY BY 6 TO SERVE 60

ANNA I grew up eating the Slovak version of
choucroute called haloushki — a combination of
browned onion, cabbage and dumplings, often
with a little sausage thrown in.

MICHAEL Try this dish with a glass of chilled
Riesling — it really stands up to the acidity of the
sauerkraut and the fruitiness is great with the pork.

CHEESE POTATOES

The cheese sauce that envelopes these potatoes is the one that works on cauliflower, broccoli and, yes, even macaroni.

3 Tbsp	45 mL	unsalted butter
3 Tbsp	45 mL	all-purpose flour
3 cups	750 mL	2% milk
dash	dash	ground nutmeg
1 tsp	5 mL	Dijon mustard
2 cups	500 mL	grated medium cheddar cheese
1 cup	250 mL	grated Asiago cheese
1 cup	250 mL	grated Parmesan cheese
		coarse salt and ground black pepper
4 lb	2 kg	mini potatoes, red or white, washed and halved

For cheese sauce, melt butter in a saucepot over medium heat. Stir in flour and cook, stirring constantly, until mixture turns a light almond color and smells nutty, about 4 minutes. Switching to a whisk, gradually pour in milk and whisk until smooth. Add nutmeg and mustard and let sauce come up to a simmer and thicken. Strain if necessary and return to pan. Reduce heat to low and stir in three cheeses to melt. Season to taste.

Preheat oven to 350°F (180°C). Cook potatoes in boiling salted water and drain well. Pour potatoes into a baking dish and pour cheese sauce over. Bake for 20 minutes and serve.

Cheese potatoes can be prepared a day in advance and warmed covered in a 275°F (140°C) oven for an hour before serving. Remove cover for the last half hour of heating.

SERVES 10
MULTIPLY BY 4 TO SERVE 60

ANNA The combination of cheeses you choose can really vary the flavor and intensity of this dish. The cheddar, Parmesan and Asiago combination is balanced between their differing saltiness and creaminess, but toss in a blue cheese or a fresh goat cheese and you can tip the scale in either direction.

MICHAEL You may notice that to serve this dish to 60 people, you multiply this recipe by 4, not 6. We have found that starch dishes seem to grow exponentially larger as you increase the batch size, and on a buffet table, guests are more inclined to reach for the proteins than the starches.

PUMPKIN CHOCOLATE TIRAMISÙ

Pumpkin pie spices are divine when blended with chocolate and the color contrast is very festive.

FOR PUMPKIN FILLING

1½ cups	375 mL	whipping cream
1 Tbsp	15 mL	pure vanilla
8 oz	250 g	cream cheese at room temperature
¾ cup	175 ml	sugar
2 Tbsp	25 mL	brandy
2 cups	500 mL	pumpkin purée
1 tsp	5 mL	ground cinnamon
½ tsp	2 mL	ground ginger
¼ tsp	1 mL	ground cloves

FOR ASSEMBLY

1 cup	250 mL	sugar
1 cup	250 mL	water
2 tsp	10 mL	vanilla
2	2	packages chocolate wafer cookies
½ cup	125 mL	whipping cream
2 tsp	10 mL	sugar
		cocoa powder for dusting

ANNA Our open houses have been growing steadily in number every year, and last year there was a crisis when I ran out of serving bowls. Digging around in my cupboards, I came across a clear flower vase with a wide top. I built my tiramisù tall in the vase and it stood towering over the rest of the buffet, and garnered a few compliments as well.

MICHAEL The traditional tiramisù really exploded in popularity in the '80s, and I'm pleased to see a classic reinvented.

For pumpkin filling, whip cream to medium peaks, stir in vanilla and chill. Beat cream cheese with sugar until smooth. Stir in brandy then add pumpkin purée and spices and beat until smooth. Fold in whipped cream and chill until ready to assemble.

To assemble, heat 1 cup (250 mL) sugar and water until sugar dissolves. Stir in 1 tsp (5 mL) vanilla and remove from heat. Dip wafer cookies in syrup briefly and line the bottom of an 8-cup (2-L) trifle dish or serving dish. Spoon one-quarter of the pumpkin filling over cookies and place another layer of soaked cookies over mousse. Repeat layering with mousse and cookies, finishing with the mousse. Chill for at least 4 hours before serving.

To serve, whip cream with 2 tsp (10 mL) sugar and 1 tsp (5 mL) vanilla and dollop on top of tiramisù. Dust lightly with cocoa powder and serve.

MAKES ONE 8-CUP (2-L) TIRAMISÙ, SERVES 20 PEOPLE
MULTIPLY BY 3 TO SERVE 60 PEOPLE

ALMOND CHERRY TART

When good seasonal (and affordable) fresh fruits are hard to come by, delectable preserves, perhaps your own, can allow you to present a great fruit dessert option on the buffet table.

FOR CRUST

½ cup	125 mL	unsalted butter at room temperature
¼ cup	50 mL	icing sugar, sifted
½ tsp	2 mL	vanilla
dash	dash	almond extract
1¼ cups	300 mL	all-purpose flour
2 Tbsp	25 mL	ground almonds
¼ tsp	1 mL	fine salt

FOR FILLING

1 cup	250 mL	cherry jam
½ tsp	2 mL	ground cinnamon
2 Tbsp	25 mL	sugar
1 Tbsp	15 mL	2% milk
1 cup	250 mL	sliced almonds

For crust, preheat oven to 350°F (180°C) and lightly grease and line the bottom of an 8-inch (20-cm) round pan with parchment paper. Cream together butter and sugar until smooth. Add vanilla and almond extract and blend. In a separate bowl, blend flour, ground almonds and salt. Add to butter mixture and blend (it will be crumbly). Press crust into pan with your fingers. Bake for 18 to 20 minutes, until just brown around the edge of the pan. Allow to cool.

For filling, stir together cherry jam and cinnamon and spread over surface of cooled crust.

Heat together sugar and milk until sugar is dissolved. Pour over sliced almonds and toss to coat. Spread almonds over cherry filling. Bake for 18 to 20 minutes, until almonds turn golden brown. Cool completely before slicing.

MAKES ONE 8-INCH (20-CM) ROUND TART
MULTIPLY BY 3 TO SERVE 60

ANNA Not everyone indulges in dessert, so you don't have to factor one piece per person. What you should consider, though, is a balanced selection of whole desserts, cookies, candies and dessert that can vary in portion size.

MICHAEL We put the dessert buffet on a separate table from our savory items. In fact, we put it in a different room altogether. This keeps things visually appealing and also shifts people to the next room, giving you a chance to clean up where the last feeding frenzy was.

ANGEL FOOD CAKE

Desserts with height look impressive at the table, and angel food cake still looks great even after guests start slicing into it. It also stays moist after it has been sitting out for a while.

1 1/3 cups	325 mL	pastry flour
1 2/3 cups	400 mL	icing sugar
2 cups	500 mL	egg whites (about 16) at room temperature
1 tsp	5 mL	cream of tartar
1/4 tsp	1 mL	fine salt
1 1/3 cups	325 mL	sugar
1 1/2 tsp	7 mL	vanilla
4 cups	1 L	fresh strawberries
1/4 cup	50 mL	sugar
1	1	lime, zest and juice
1	1	lemon, zest and juice
1	1	orange, zest and juice

For angel food cake, preheat oven to 350°F (180°C). Sift together flour and icing sugar 3 times. Whip egg whites with cream of tartar and salt until foamy. Gradually pour in sugar while whipping and continue to beat until stiff peaks form. Add vanilla. Fold in flour mixture in 3 additions, folding well after each addition. Spoon into an ungreased angel food pan and level top. Bake for 40 to 50 minutes (wait at least 30 minutes before opening oven door), until cake springs back when touched. Remove from oven, invert and let cool in pan upside down. Use a palette knife to loosen edges of cake and tap to remove cake from pan.

Wash, hull and cut strawberries into quarters. Toss with sugar and citrus zests and juices. Spoon into center of angel food cake to serve. Dust with icing sugar.

SERVES 16 TO 20
MAKE 2 FOR A PARTY OF 60

ANNA As an alternative, serve this cake with a bowl of fruit compote and sweetened whipped cream on the side.

MICHAEL For an easy sauce, stir a little sugar and a liqueur of your choice into sour cream.

THE SUMMER EXTRAVAGANZA

Six months or more have passed since our holiday open house, and we're getting the urge to have another party. Summer parties are the simplest because the food is fresh and in season and best served straightforwardly. The barbecue outside keeps the guests and the mess outdoors, and you don't need a room to pile coats on the bed!

Finger Vegetables with Vinaigrette

BBQ Pulled Pork

Grill-Roasted Salmon in Foil "Canoe"

Peppered Cornbread

Caesar Potato Salad

Lime Meringue Pie

FINGER VEGETABLES WITH VINAIGRETTE

We've given you Winter Crudités (page 246), and this is our summer take on fresh and crunchy. A light dressing to swirl with a colorful mix of vegetables looks nice on a patio table next to a pitcher of sangria.

FOR VINAIGRETTE

¼ cup	50 mL	white wine vinegar
1 Tbsp	15 mL	Dijon mustard
1 clove	1 clove	garlic, minced
¾ cup	175 mL	extra virgin olive oil
¾ cup	175 mL	chopped green onion
½ tsp	2 mL	ground cumin
4 Tbsp	50 mL	chopped fresh basil
		fine salt and ground black pepper

FOR VEGETABLES

1½ lb	750 g	fingerling potatoes, cut in half lengthwise
1 lb	500 g	candystripe or golden beets
1 lb	500 g	pattypan or zucchini squash, raw
2 cups	500 mL	cherry or grape tomatoes
2 cups	500 mL	radishes

For vinaigrette, whisk together vinegar, mustard and garlic. Slowly add olive oil while whisking to incorporate. Stir in green onion, cumin and basil and season to taste. Chill until ready to serve.

For vegetables, cook potatoes in boiling, salted water until tender and drain. Cook beets in boiling water with a splash of white vinegar until tender, about 40 minutes, and drain. Peel and cut into wedges. Wash remaining vegetables and trim accordingly. Arrange vegetables on a platter and place a bowl of vinaigrette beside it for dipping.

SERVES 12
MULTIPLY BY 2 FOR 24 PEOPLE

ANNA Thick dips can be too filling sometimes, and if you're having a relaxed visit before dinner, you don't want to fill up — there's still lots of eating to do.

MICHAEL Precut and store your vegetables in resealable bags with a damp paper towel in them — they stay crunchy and fresh-looking for hours.

BBQ PULLED PORK

This style of barbecue is surprisingly done in a pot in a slow oven. Typical of North Carolina, this big pot o' food slowly stews in vinegary juices.

1 cup	250 mL	light brown sugar
2 Tbsp	25 mL	Dijon mustard
2 Tbsp	25 mL	chili powder
1 Tbsp	15 mL	coarse salt
1 Tbsp	15 mL	ground black pepper
1 Tbsp	15 mL	garlic powder
1	1	5-lb (2.2-kg) boneless pork shoulder
1	1	12-ounce (375-mL) bottle lager beer
1 cup	250 mL	white vinegar
1/2 cup	125 mL	fancy molasses
1/2 cup	125 mL	barbecue sauce

Preheat oven to 325°F (160°C). Combine brown sugar, mustard, chili powder, salt, pepper and garlic powder and rub over pork shoulder. Stir beer, vinegar, molasses and barbecue sauce in a Dutch oven or roaster and add seasoned pork shoulder. Cover and cook, basting often, for 3 to 4 hours, until meat pulls away easily with a fork.

Allow pork to cool slightly and skim off fat resting on top of juices. Use two forks to "pull" the pork into shreds and mix it into the juices. Return to oven to warm.

Pulled pork can be spooned onto plates or served on a bun.

SERVES 12
MULTIPLY BY 2 FOR 24 PEOPLE

ANNA This is a great party recipe because it can be completely prepared ahead of time. Like a good pot of soup, it always tastes better the next day.

MICHAEL After you get the hang of this slow-cooking technique that produces rich, intense flavors, you'll develop your own style in seasoning the final product. Perhaps a dash of hot sauce, extra molasses or even a splash of balsamic vinegar could become your signature twist.

GRILL-ROASTED SALMON IN FOIL "CANOE"

Salmon is always available at your local fish counter and it's ideal for the smoky intense heat of the barbecue.

1	1	4-lb (1.85-kg) fresh salmon
1 cup	250 mL	breadcrumbs
1 cup	250 mL	chopped fresh dill
½ cup	125 mL	vodka
4 Tbsp	50 mL	unsalted butter, melted
2	2	lemons, zest and juice
2 tsp	10 mL	fine salt
		dill sprigs and lemon wedges for garnish

Preheat grill to medium. Lay out 2 sheets of heavy aluminum foil, each a little longer than the length of the salmon fillet, and join the foil lengthwise with a simple fold. Place the salmon on the foil.

Stir together breadcrumbs, dill, vodka, melted butter, lemon zest and juice and salt. Pack the bread mixture over the salmon in an even layer.

Crimp the foil edges just over the salmon to make a ridge that will prevent juices from escaping. The salmon package will resemble a little canoe. Place the salmon on the grill and close the lid. Cook for 8 minutes for medium doneness and about 11 minutes for well-done.

Remove the salmon using 2 spatulas and place on a serving tray or platter. Decorate around the foil with dill sprigs and lemon wedges, and let everyone help themselves.

SERVES 12
MULTIPLY BY 2 FOR 24 PEOPLE

ANNA Leftover salmon can be used the next day on greens with dressing or as an excellent salmon salad sandwich.

MICHAEL We use Atlantic salmon or steelhead trout for this dish, but if you can get wild B.C. salmon, you're in for a treat. We like our salmon very lightly cooked, barely medium-rare, but if you like it medium or more, go for it!

PEPPERED CORNBREAD

A summer classic and great for swishing up those barbecue sauces left on your plate.

1 Tbsp	15 mL	extra virgin olive oil
½ cup	125 mL	diced onion
¾ cup	175 mL	diced red bell pepper
1 tsp	5 mL	chopped fresh thyme
1⅓ cups	325 mL	buttermilk
⅓ cup	75 mL	vegetable oil
2	2	large eggs
3 Tbsp	45 mL	sugar
1 Tbsp	15 mL	fresh lemon juice
1 cup	250 mL	cornmeal
1 cup	250 mL	all-purpose flour
2 tsp	10 mL	finely grated lemon zest
1 tsp	5 mL	baking soda
1 tsp	5 mL	fine salt
1 tsp	5 mL	ground cumin
dash	dash	cayenne pepper

In a sauté pan over medium heat, add oil and onion and sauté 4 minutes. Add red bell pepper and thyme and sauté until tender, about 5 minutes more. Set aside to cool.

Preheat oven to 375°F (190°C) and grease an 8-inch (20-cm) square pan. Whisk buttermilk, vegetable oil, eggs, sugar and lemon juice to combine. In a separate bowl, stir together cornmeal, flour, lemon zest, baking soda, salt, cumin and cayenne pepper. Add to buttermilk mixture and whisk until smooth (batter will be very liquid). Stir in cooled pepper mixture and pour batter into prepared pan. Bake for 15 to 18 minutes, until top is a light golden brown and cornbread springs back when touched.

Peppered cornbread is best served warm, but this will keep well for a day in an airtight container.

SERVES 12
MULTIPLY BY 2 FOR 24 PEOPLE

ANNA I rarely make cornbread in winter — it seems to suit summer just so perfectly. Leftover cornbread is ideal for grilling the next day.

MICHAEL Our friend Toshi would never decline an invitation to one of our barbecues. He would eat so enthusiastically that barbecue sauce would get everywhere, and he'd lift his wine glass by the stem with the sides of his hands. Now that's livin'!

CAESAR POTATO SALAD

We can't seem to have a barbecue at the cottage without making this salad. The same rule applies to this dish as to a regular Caesar salad — everyone must eat it so all share garlic breath.

6 lb	2.7 kg	red or white mini potatoes, washed and cut into quarters
3/4 cup	175 mL	mayonnaise
1 1/4 cups	300 mL	2% milk
2 Tbsp	25 mL	Dijon mustard
2 cloves	2 cloves	garlic, finely minced
1/3 cup	75 mL	fresh lemon juice
3/4 cup	175 mL	grated Parmesan cheese
		coarse salt and ground black pepper
4 strips	4 strips	bacon, cooked and crumbled

Cook potatoes in boiling, salted water until fork tender. Drain.

While potatoes are cooking, prepare dressing. Whisk mayonnaise, milk, mustard and garlic until smooth. Whisk in lemon juice and set aside 5 minutes to thicken. While drained potatoes are still warm, toss half of the dressing into the potatoes and chill completely. When ready to serve, toss potatoes with remaining dressing and Parmesan cheese, and season to taste. Spoon into serving dish and top with crumbled bacon.

SERVES 12
MULTIPLY BY 2 FOR 24 PEOPLE

ANNA While Michael owns the best Caesar salad dressing recipe, I'm the one in charge of this dish. Feel free to change it a bit — add some olives, diced tomato and feta to give it a Greek twist.

MICHAEL I love the casual feel of dinner at the lake. Mismatched plates, cutlery and a mish-mash of serving bowls keep it authentic.

LIME MERINGUE PIE

Break the rules. Use lime instead of lemon in this classic.

FOR CRUST

1½ cups	375 mL	all purpose flour
1 Tbsp	15 mL	sugar
½ tsp	2 mL	fine salt
⅔ cup	150 mL	unsalted butter, diced and chilled
1	1	large egg
1 Tbsp	15 mL	fresh lime juice

FOR FILLING

1¼ cups	300 mL	sugar
1½ cups	375 mL	water
5 Tbsp	70 mL	cornstarch
5	5	large egg yolks
dash	dash	fine salt
1 Tbsp	15 mL	finely grated lime zest
½ cup	125 mL	fresh lime juice
2 Tbsp	25 mL	unsalted butter

FOR MERINGUE

5	5	large egg whites
½ tsp	2 mL	cream of tartar
⅓ cup	75 mL	sugar
1 Tbsp	15 mL	cornstarch

ANNA Don't you love it that limes rarely, if ever, have seeds? There's reason right there to use lime in place of lemon.

MICHAEL Serve this pie with a fresh blueberry sauce or puréed berries, accented with a hint of lime.

For crust, combine flour, sugar and salt. Cut in chilled butter until it's a rough crumbly texture and little bits of butter are still visible. In a small bowl, whisk egg and lime juice. Pour all at once into flour mixture and combine just until dough comes together. Shape dough into a disk and chill for at least one hour.

Preheat oven to 400°F (200°C). On a lightly floured surface, roll out dough to just less than ¼ inch (5 mm) thick. Sprinkle a 9-inch (23-cm) pie plate with flour and line with dough. Tuck in rough edges and crimp with your fingers. Put pie plate in freezer just for 10 minutes to rest and firm up. Once chilled, line pastry with aluminum foil (and have foil hang over crust edges to protect it) and weigh down with pie weights, dried beans or raw rice. Bake for 10 minutes, then reduce oven temperature to 375°F (190°C) and bake 15 minutes more. Remove aluminum foil and weights and bake 10 minutes more, to dry out center of the shell. Cool completely before filling.

For filling, whisk sugar, water and cornstarch in a heavy-bottomed saucepot. Whisk in egg yolks and salt and cook over low heat for 5 minutes, whisking constantly. Increase heat to medium and, still whisking, cook until filling becomes glossy and thick, about 5 more minutes. Remove from heat and strain. Stir in lime zest, lime juice and butter until butter dissolves. Pour immediately into cooled pie shell and let cool 15 minutes. Chill completely before finishing with meringue, about 4 hours.

For meringue, preheat oven to 350°F (180°C). Whip egg whites with cream of tartar until foamy. While whipping, gradually pour in sugar and whip on one speed less than highest until whites hold a stiff peak (the meringue stands upright when whisk is lifted). Whisk in cornstarch and dollop over chilled lime filling. Use sweeping motions with your spatula to create swirls and peaks that look so enticing once browned. Bake pie for 10 minutes, just until meringue browns lightly (or use a propane blow torch carefully to brown the outside). Let pie cool or chill until ready to slice.

MAKES ONE 9-INCH (23-CM) PIE
MAKE 3 PIES FOR 24 PEOPLE

SEE PHOTO ON PAGE 264

A SIGNIFICANT BIRTHDAY Aaah — the markers of

time passing. While we might wish to forget them ourselves, our friends and family seem inclined to remind us of them. >A birthday meal can often include guests of all ages, so a menu that considers all generations is important.

Mushroom Asiago Tarts

Chicken Cordon Bleu

Chive Mashed Potatoes

Pepper Fennel Sauté

German Chocolate Cake

<LIME MERINGUE PIE, PAGE 263

MUSHROOM ASIAGO TARTS

A hot hors d'oeuvre is a great way to get everyone in the party spirit. Assemble these ahead of time and bake them when you're ready to serve.

2 lb	1 kg	button mushrooms
1 Tbsp	15 mL	unsalted butter
½ cup	125 mL	minced onion
2 cloves	2 cloves	garlic, minced
2 tsp	10 mL	chopped fresh thyme
		coarse salt and ground black pepper
1½ cups	375 mL	whipping cream
2	2	large eggs
1 cup	250 mL	grated Asiago cheese
48	48	mini pastry tart shells

Pulse mushrooms in a food processor until finely minced. In a large sauté pan over medium-high heat, melt butter and add mushrooms and onion. Cook, stirring often, until mushrooms are soft and all liquid has evaporated. Stir in garlic and thyme and cook 1 minute more. Remove from heat and season to taste. Allow to cool.

Preheat oven to 375°F (190°C). Whisk whipping cream and eggs until evenly blended. Stir in cooled mushroom mixture. Spoon mushroom filling into tart shells and top with Asiago cheese. Bake for 12 to 15 minutes, until pastry crust is browned and filling puffs up a little. Serve tarts warm.

Tarts can be baked in advance, chilled and reheated in a 325°F (160°C) oven for 12 minutes.

MAKES 48 MINI TARTS

ANNA These tarts were always a top pick of brides and grooms when we did weddings at Inn on the Twenty. They seem to be a timeless favorite, so why mess with them?

MICHAEL To heighten the sophistication of this tart, stir a few drops of truffle oil into the mushroom mixture before filling your tarts. The scent as they bake will drive everyone crazy!

CHICKEN CORDON BLEU

You may chuckle at such an old-school recipe, but we do get a craving for it and, admit it, when you're serving a group, chicken can always be counted on as a crowd pleaser.

16	16	8-oz (250-g) boneless chicken breasts
1½ lb	750 g	Emmenthal Swiss cheese, cut into 1½-oz (40-g) sticks
16 slices	16 slices	Black Forest ham
2 Tbsp	25 mL	unsalted butter at room temperature
		coarse salt and ground black pepper
2 Tbsp	25 mL	minced shallots
1 cup	250 mL	dry white wine
4 Tbsp	50 mL	unsalted cold butter

Preheat oven to 350°F (180°C). Place 4 chicken breasts on a cutting board with the skin side down and make a lengthwise cut into the center of the breast, just halfway through. Work the knife gently toward each side to create a pocket. Wrap 4 cheese sticks each with a slice of ham, place inside the chicken breast and close the pocket by simply folding the "flaps" back to their original position. If necessary, fix together with a toothpick, which can be removed later. Try to seal the package neatly in order to prevent the cheese from oozing out. Repeat with remaining 12 chicken breasts, 4 at a time.

Place the chicken breasts on two rimmed baking sheets or shallow roasting pans, leaving a few inches (about 7 cm) between breasts for even cooking. Rub the breasts with soft butter and season lightly. Roast 25 to 30 minutes to an internal temperature of 165°F (80°C) and remove to a warm platter.

For sauce, pour off all but 1 Tbsp (15 mL) fat and fry shallots 2 minutes in the pan over medium heat to soften. Add wine and scrape the bottom of the roasting pan with a wooden spoon to deglaze any brown bits that have caramelized. Increase heat and reduce the juices by half. Reduce heat to low and whisk in the cold butter to thicken and enrich the pan juices.

SERVES 16

ANNA These chicken breasts can be prepared a day in advance. Be sure to wrap them well and store them on the bottom shelf of the refrigerator in a dish or on a tray to avoid any stray juices.

MICHAEL An alternative to finishing the sauce with butter is to whisk in 1 tsp (5 mL) cornstarch dissolved in ¼ cup (50 mL) cold water, bring to a boil and strain.

CHIVE MASHED POTATOES

Mashed potatoes can be dressed up or customized to your own taste with the addition of one or two simple, but exceptionally fresh, ingredients. Chives lend a sweet, mellow onion flavor and add wonderful little bits of color to these creamy rich mashed potatoes.

8 lb	3.5 kg	Yukon Gold potatoes, peeled and cut into medium dice
1 Tbsp	15 mL	fine salt
½ cup	125 mL	unsalted butter
½ cup	125 mL	buttermilk
2 cloves	2 cloves	garlic, cut in half
1 sprig	1 sprig	fresh thyme
½ cup	125 mL	chives, cut thinly
		coarse salt and ground black pepper

Cover potatoes with cold water and bring to a boil with 1 Tbsp (15 mL) fine salt. Reduce to a simmer; cook gently until potatoes are tender. While potatoes are simmering, heat butter, buttermilk, garlic and thyme. Drain potatoes well, return to pot and, over low heat, cook for a few minutes to remove excess moisture (this will result in a lighter texture). Mash the potatoes with a hand masher, potato ricer or food mill. Remove garlic and thyme from butter mixture and pour over the potatoes, stirring to incorporate.

Fold in the fresh cut chives and season to taste.

SERVES 16

ANNA Nothing beats wonderfully made mashed potatoes. The investment in a food mill really makes the difference between good mashed potatoes, and potatoes that are fluffily out of this world!

MICHAEL Fifteen years ago, you wouldn't have dared put mashed potatoes on a restaurant menu, but now there are few menus of any caliber that don't show mashed potatoes in some form.

PEPPER FENNEL SAUTÉ

This dish will add beautiful color and a sweet fruit character to the meal without any complicated technique or long cooking.

¼ cup	50 mL	extra virgin olive oil
4	4	red bell peppers, seeded and thinly sliced
2 bulbs	2 bulbs	fresh fennel, trimmed, halved, cored and thinly sliced
2	2	medium red onions, thinly sliced
¼ cup	50 mL	chopped fresh mint leaves
		juice of 1 lime
		coarse salt and ground black pepper

In a large skillet over medium-high heat, add oil — pan is ready when a slice of vegetable sizzles when added. Add the peppers, fennel and onion and season lightly. Sauté for 6 minutes, until the vegetables are soft to the bite but not stringy. Stir in mint and lime juice. Adjust seasoning and serve.

SERVES 16

ANNA I'm not a big fan of fennel, personally, but with the sweetness of the red pepper, I could enjoy a full portion.

MICHAEL This is one of my top picks as a side dish to pair with salmon.

GERMAN CHOCOLATE CAKE

This chocolate cake isn't actually a recipe from Germany. It's named after a type of Baker's brand chocolate used to develop this recipe. Any good quality chocolate will work here.

FOR CAKE

½ cup	125 mL	unsalted butter at room temperature
1½ cups	375 mL	sugar
½ cup	125 mL	light brown sugar, packed
2	2	large eggs
2 tsp	10 mL	vanilla
½ cup	125 mL	water
4 oz	125 g	unsweetened chocolate, chopped
2 tsp	10 mL	instant coffee powder
2 cups	500 mL	pastry flour
1 tsp	5 mL	baking soda
¼ tsp	1 mL	fine salt
1 cup	250 mL	sour cream

FOR GOOPY TOPPING

1 Tbsp + 1 tsp	15 mL + 5 mL	cornstarch
1 cup	250 mL	whipping cream
1½ Tbsp	22 mL	corn syrup
½ cup	125 mL	sugar
½ cup	125 mL	light brown sugar, packed
6	6	large egg yolks
¼ cup	50 mL	unsalted butter
½ tsp	2 mL	vanilla
dash	dash	fine salt
1 cup	250 mL	pecans, chopped and lightly toasted
1 cup	250 mL	unsweetened shredded coconut

FOR FROSTING

8 oz	225 g	semi-sweet chocolate, chopped
6	6	large egg whites
½ tsp	2 mL	cream of tartar
¾ cup	175 mL	water
1½ cups	375 mL	sugar
3 cups	750 mL	unsalted butter at room temperature
1 tsp	5 mL	vanilla
¾ cup	175 mL	cocoa powder
dash	dash	fine salt
½ cup	125 mL	toasted pecan halves for garnish (optional)

ANNA This cake is a wonderful place to practice your piping techniques. You can always scrape off what you're not happy with and start again.

MICHAEL I think the sole reason Anna likes to make this cake is for the goopy topping. She even makes the topping by itself and fills chocolate tart shells for a fun caramel pecan tart.

Preheat oven to 350°F (180°C). Butter and flour two 9-inch (23-cm) round cake pans. Cream butter and sugars together until fluffy (by hand or with electric beaters). Beat in eggs and vanilla. In a small pan, stir water, chocolate and coffee powder over low heat until melted. Allow to cool slightly and then beat into butter mixture. Sift together flour, baking soda and salt, and stir into batter alternately with sour cream. Divide batter evenly between the pans and bake for 20 to 25 minutes, until a tester inserted in the center of the cake comes out clean. Allow to cool 15 minutes in the pans, then turn cakes out onto a plate to cool completely.

For topping, in a medium pot, whisk together cornstarch, cream, corn syrup, sugars and egg yolks. Cut butter into small pieces and add to pot. Over medium heat, whisk ingredients constantly until bubbly and shiny, 4 to 5 minutes. Remove from heat and immediately scrape out topping into a bowl, to halt the cooking process. Stir in vanilla, salt, pecans and coconut. Cover and chill completely.

For frosting, melt chocolate in a bowl over a pot of simmering water or in the microwave at medium power, stirring every 20 seconds. Set aside. Beat egg whites with cream of tartar until stiff peaks form. Bring water and sugar to a boil and cook over high heat until temperature reaches 240°F (115°C), the softball stage. You can use a candy thermometer, or test by spooning a little of the hot sugar syrup into a glass of ice water. If you can roll it between your fingers into a soft ball, then it's ready. While beating whites at medium speed, slowly add sugar syrup (be careful — it's hot!) until all the syrup has been added. Continue to beat whites until cool, 3 to 4 minutes. Start adding butter to egg whites, a little at a time, while mixing constantly and scraping the sides of the bowl often, until all the butter has been incorporated. If the frosting looks like it's separating (looks curdled) don't worry — just keep mixing and it will come together. Mix in melted chocolate, vanilla, cocoa powder and salt. Keep at room temperature to ice cake. If making a day ahead, chill frosting but bring to room temperature and beat well before using.

To assemble, level cakes if necessary, using a serrated knife. Spread a dollop of chocolate frosting on one layer of cake. Spoon one-third of the goopy topping over frosting and spread to 1 inch (2.5 cm) from the edge of the cake. Place second cake on top of first and dollop a generous amount of chocolate frosting on top. Spread to edges of cake, working from the middle and turning the cake as you work around. Ice the sides of the cake, but save about ½ cup (125 mL) of frosting for piping, if desired. Spread remaining goopy topping on top of cake, leaving ½ inch (1 cm) around the outside edge. If you do not wish to pipe outside edge with chocolate frosting, simply garnish the cake with toasted pecan halves to create a finished look.

To pipe an edge, place frosting in a piping bag fitted with a star tip or leaf tip. Pipe frosting as desired. Remember — it's just frosting! If you're not pleased with how it looks, just scrape it off and start again.

Cake can be chilled until ready to serve. Frosting will firm up once chilled.

SERVES 16

ROMANCE

>Time alone is to be treasured at any point in a relationship. A romantic meal doesn't have to focus on the stereotypical food aphrodisiacs to incite passion — oysters and chocolate are lovely, but humble ingredients layered with luxurious flavors can have a similar effect.

A SATURDAY ALONE Ever have one of those rare occasions where an evening's engagement has been cancelled, but the kids are already at your parents? Overnight? Need we say more?

Linguini with Clams

Pork Tenderloin Medallions with Madeira Pan Juices

Butternut Squash Purée

Slow-Roasted Vanilla Pineapple

LINGUINI WITH CLAMS

Well, it's not oysters, but it's still a romantic dish. Simplicity, once again, is key.

1 lb	500 g	small clams (Manilla or butter clams)
¼ cup	50 mL	extra virgin olive oil
½ cup	125 mL	diced onion
1	1	small red bell pepper, cut into strips
1 rib	1 rib	celery, cut into strips
1 clove	1 clove	garlic, minced
½ cup	125 mL	dry white wine
1 tsp	5 mL	chopped fresh thyme
2 Tbsp	25 mL	chopped Italian flat leaf parsley
		coarse salt and cracked black pepper
½ lb	250 g	dry linguini

Rinse clams in cold running water to get rid of sand; discard any broken or open clams.

In large sauté pan over medium heat, add oil, onion, pepper and celery and sauté 2 minutes to soften. Add garlic and clams and toss to coat. Add wine and thyme, cover and steam 8 to 10 minutes. Once clams have opened, add parsley and season to taste.

While clams are cooking, bring a large pot of water to the boil and salt generously. Add linguini and cook until tender. Drain and toss in some of the clam cooking juice, arrange in bowls and top with clams and remainder of sauce.

SERVES 2

ANNA A few clams go a long way when you make this dish. Just be sure to soak and rinse the clams for about 20 minutes in the sink, to get all the grit out. Grit is definitely not romantic.

MICHAEL If you regularly cook mussels but not clams, bear in mind that clams take a fair bit longer to open up — it's those tough shells.

PORK TENDERLOIN MEDALLIONS WITH MADEIRA PAN JUICES

Ah, yes, a romantic restaurant recreated in your own dining room, and a fine sauce to finish a pan-seared dish — so classy.

1	1	10-oz (350-g) pork tenderloin
1 Tbsp	15 mL	extra virgin olive oil
		coarse salt and ground black pepper
2 Tbsp	25 mL	all-purpose flour
1	1	shallot, minced
1 tsp	5 mL	Dijon mustard
½ cup	125 mL	Madeira wine
1 tsp	5 mL	cold unsalted butter

Trim pork tenderloin of excess fat and silver skin (the thin elastin layer on the outside). Cut into 6 medallions.

Heat a sauté pan over medium heat and add olive oil. Season pork lightly and dredge in flour. Shake off excess and fry in oil over medium heat 3 to 4 minutes per side until golden brown and firm. Remove to a plate, add shallots to pan and sauté 2 minutes. Add mustard and Madeira and reduce by half. Whisk in butter and return pork medallions to pan to warm. The sauce should coat the back of a spoon; you can add a bit more Madeira or water if the sauce reduces too much. Adjust seasoning and serve.

SERVES 2

ANNA A wine sauce of this style is perfect with many pan-roasted meats — chicken breasts, beef tenderloin or even fish. Try this technique, even using a different wine for your next pan-made meal.

MICHAEL The oxidized character of Madeira makes it very food friendly and leaves a lot of wine-pairing options open. Try an oaky Chardonnay, a Pinot Noir or a Gamay Noir.

BUTTERNUT SQUASH PURÉE

Naturally sweet and creamy, a purée of butternut squash complements the pork tenderloin.

1 cup	250 mL	peeled and diced butternut squash
1	1	bay leaf
pinch	pinch	ground nutmeg
1 Tbsp	15 mL	unsalted butter
1 Tbsp	15 mL	chopped Italian parsley
		coarse salt and ground black pepper

Cook squash in salted water with bay leaf and nutmeg until tender. Drain well, remove bay leaf and place squash in food processor with butter and parsley. Purée and season to taste. To serve, spoon onto plate into little egg shapes, known as quenelles.

SERVES 2

ANNA Check out your gourmet kitchen stores — I have an ice cream scoop in the shape of an egg, so I can do perfect quenelles every time.

MICHAEL I love the squash selection at the farmers' market, and I always seem to come home with more squash than we could possibly eat. It makes for a lovely harvest display, though.

SLOW-ROASTED VANILLA PINEAPPLE

They say that the scent of vanilla is more of an aphrodisiac that any other food aroma. This dessert should be ecstatic torture as it slowly roasts.

½	½	medium golden pineapple
		OR 2 baby pineapples
2	2	vanilla beans
2 Tbsp	25 mL	unsalted butter at room temperature
½ cup	125 mL	sugar

Preheat oven to 300°F (150°C). Peel pineapple and remove eyes. Slice lengthwise and place halves, flat side down, in a shallow baking dish. Slice vanilla beans in half and slice each half lengthwise. Extract vanilla seeds and stir them into butter. Rub surface of pineapple with vanilla butter. Insert vanilla pods into flesh of pineapple (make slits in fruit with a paring knife) and bake, uncovered, for 1 hour, basting often with the buttery juices. After the first hour, sprinkle pineapple with sugar and continue roasting for another hour, basting often.

If a lot of juices remain in the bottom of the baking dish after roasting, pour them into a small saucepot and reduce them to a glaze. Serve pineapple warm with glazed juices poured over fruit.

SERVES 2

ANNA The sight of those tiny vanilla bean seeds is immediately food-sexy. It reminds me of a vanilla pot de crème I enjoyed in Paris (with Michael, of course), that had so many vanilla seeds at the bottom that I could crunch on them.

MICHAEL This is a study in simplicity, keying in on the quality of the ingredients. A scoop of ice cream might be tempting, but that would push it over the top.

A REASON TO CELEBRATE A promotion, a raise, an accomplishment — there are many reasons to plan a private, special meal. Hold off on the bubbly, though, if it's an announcement of a baby on the way (please refer to "A Saturday Alone").

Sea Scallops with Lemon Risotto
Alaskan King Crab with Grand Marnier Butter
Pastry Baked Asparagus
Classic Chocolate Soufflé

SEA SCALLOPS WITH LEMON RISOTTO, PAGE 280>

SEA SCALLOPS WITH LEMON RISOTTO

We've been making this appetizer for years. The delicate flavors are beautifully balanced — fit to impress anyone, but most importantly, you.

FOR SWEET LEMON GARNISH

2 Tbsp	25 mL	lemon marmalade
1 Tbsp	15 mL	white wine
2 Tbsp	25 mL	finely diced red bell pepper

FOR LEMON RISOTTO

1 Tbsp	15 mL	extra virgin olive oil
2 Tbsp	25 mL	minced onion
1/4 cup	50 mL	arborio or carnaroli rice
2 Tbsp	25 mL	white wine
1 1/2 tsp	7 mL	finely grated lemon zest
pinch	pinch	Spanish saffron
1 1/2 cups	375 mL	water
1 Tbsp	15 mL	fresh lemon juice
2 Tbsp	25 mL	unsalted butter
1 tsp	5 mL	honey
		coarse salt

FOR SCALLOPS

6	6	fresh sea scallops
		coarse salt and ground black pepper
1 Tbsp	15 mL	extra virgin olive oil

ANNA When searing sea scallops, it's better to sear just a few at a time, leaving space between them. Overcrowding the pan just cools it down and the scallops will sweat out all their juices.

MICHAEL Choose a light-bodied white wine like Pinot Gris and, although you may be tempted by such a delicious dish, don't serve too generous a portion as an appetizer — there's more to come.

For lemon garnish, heat marmalade over medium-low heat with white wine and diced red pepper until pepper softens. Remove from heat and chill until ready to serve, but allow to come up to room temperature for serving.

For lemon risotto, heat olive oil in a heavy-bottomed saucepot over medium heat and add onion, stirring until translucent, about 5 minutes, reducing heat if any browning occurs. Add rice and stir for another 3 minutes to coat rice with oil. Add white wine all at once and stir until absorbed. Stir in lemon zest and saffron and add water, about 1/2 cup (125 mL) at a time, stirring after each addition and then stirring frequently (but no need to stir constantly), adding next addition of water only after the previous one has been fully absorbed. Check doneness of rice by tasting (remember that it will continue cooking once removed from heat). The cooking process should take only about 18 to 20 minutes, as it is such a small amount of rice. Set aside while preparing scallops.

For scallops, remove them from fridge when starting risotto, to come up to room temperature. Heat a large, non-stick sauté pan over high heat and add oil. Season both sides of scallops and place in pan, leaving a 1-inch (2.5-cm) space between them. Jiggle scallops slightly with a pair of tongs to loosen and cook 3 minutes on each side.

To serve, finish risotto by adding lemon juice, butter, honey and salt and pepper to taste and heat for a minute. Spoon risotto onto 2 plates and arrange 3 scallops on top of risotto. Top with a spoonful of the lemon marmalade and serve immediately.

SERVES 2

SEE PHOTO ON PAGE 279

ALASKAN KING CRAB WITH GRAND MARNIER BUTTER

How decadent! A feast like this must really mean you have a reason to celebrate.

2 lb	1 kg	king crab legs
1	1	lemon, quartered
1	1	shallot, minced
½ cup	125 mL	dry white wine
2 Tbsp	25 mL	Grand Marnier
¼ cup	50 mL	unsalted butter, diced and chilled
		coarse salt and ground black pepper

Warm crab legs and lemon in a roasting pan covered with foil for 20 minutes at 325°F (160°C).

Meanwhile, place shallots and wine in a saucepot and reduce to ¼ cup (50 mL). Add Grand Marnier and return to a simmer. Remove from heat and whisk in butter until a thick creamy consistency is achieved. Season to taste.

Serve crab with sauce on the side in ramekins for dipping.

SERVES 2

ANNA Frozen Alaskan king crab legs come already cooked, so all you have to do is heat and dig in!

MICHAEL One time at the grocery store, I noticed a whole stash of Alaskan crab legs marked at a ridiculously low price. Whether that was an error or not, I don't know, but I still find myself, after all these years, checking out the crab legs in the grocery hoping for another deal.

PASTRY BAKED ASPARAGUS

No vegetable speaks to a special, romantic occasion better than asparagus. Brussels sprouts just don't have the same appeal.

½ lb	250 g	asparagus
½	½	red bell pepper, julienned
1	1	small square frozen puff pastry
2 Tbsp	25 mL	sour cream
1	1	large egg yolk
2 Tbsp	25 mL	2% milk

Wash, trim and blanch asparagus for 1 minute in boiling, salted water. Drain and refresh in cold water and drain again.

Preheat oven to 400°F (200°C). Cut puff pastry in half and roll into 2 rectangles, long and wide enough to hold the asparagus and about ¼ inch (5 mm) thick. Add blanched asparagus, peppers and sour cream and season with salt and pepper. Whisk egg yolk and milk together. Seal pastry edges with egg wash and brush it over top of pastry. Bake for 12 to 15 minutes until packages are golden brown. Cut each in half and set on plate.

SERVES 2

CLASSIC CHOCOLATE SOUFFLÉ

The key to a successful soufflé is to relax: a soufflé can read your emotions and will fall if you're stressed about it, and even if it does fall, it still tastes great.

		unsalted butter and sugar for preparing soufflé dish
5 oz	150 g	bittersweet chocolate, chopped
3	3	large egg yolks at room temperature
6	6	large egg whites at room temperature
1/3 cup	75 mL	sugar

Preheat oven to 375°F (190°C). Butter a 6-cup (1.5-L) soufflé dish and sprinkle thoroughly with sugar, tapping out excess. Over a pot of barely simmering water, melt chocolate in a metal or glass bowl, stirring constantly. Remove from heat and stir in egg yolks, one at a time (chocolate will turn thick and glossy). Whip egg whites and add sugar when eggs become frothy. Continue whipping whites until stiff peaks form. Fold one-third of the whites into the chocolate and then fold in remaining two-thirds. Scrape soufflé mix into prepared dish and run your finger along the inside lip of the dish (this will help the soufflé rise evenly). Bake for 25 minutes, without opening the oven door.

Serve soufflé hot from the oven. It should have a crust on the top, but be soft inside with a small, almost fluid, center.

SERVES 2

ANNA At cooking school in the Rocky Mountains, we spent our pastry classes adjusting to baking at high altitude. Our professors just scrapped the notion of soufflé at 10,000 feet above sea level, so I had to learn after graduation — in New Orleans, which is below sea level. How ironic!

MICHAEL If you master a technique like soufflé, you have thousands of possibilities, both savory and sweet. It just takes understanding the principle of starting with a heavy base and folding in egg whites.

INDEX

Bold numbers indicate photographs.